UNDERSTANDING UNEMPLOYMENT

By the late 1980s a policy and public consensus appeared to have emerged that a level of unemployment around 1.6 million was satisfactory. This consensus was not shared by many academics who, throughout the 1980s, continued to argue that the British economy was, at a fundamental level, 'an economy of unemployment', with all the human and economic waste and inefficiency such an economy entails. In view of the rapid rise in unemployment that has occurred in 1990 and 1991, such pessimism has proven well-founded. The British economy remains an 'economy of unemployment', vulnerable to cyclical recession and large scale job loss. Why this should be so, and what was wrong with policy towards unemployment and the labour market, are the twin foci of this book. Its emphasis is on the analysis of the structure of unemployment and through that identification of responsible policies which could address unemployment.

The book includes contributions from economics, sociology, social policy, law, psychology and geography. It addresses such crucial issues as the nature of labour supply and demand, employer recruitment practices, the effect of unemployment on individuals and families and the potential impact of European harmonization. Taken together, the contributions to the book offer new and positive perspectives on unemployment and on the nature of effective, active labour market policies.

UNDERSTANDING UNEMPLOYMENT

New perspectives on active labour market policies

Edited by
Eithne McLaughlin

London and New York

First published 1992
by Routledge
11 New Fetter Lane, London EC4P 4EE

Simultaneously published in the USA and Canada
by Routledge
a division of Routledge, Chapman and Hall, Inc.
29 West 35th Street, New York, NY 10001

© 1992 Eithne McLaughlin

Phototypeset in Baskerville by Intype, London
Printed and bound in Great Britain by
Mackays of Chatham PLC, Chatham, Kent

British Library Cataloguing in Publication Data
A catalogue record for this book is available from the British Library

0–415–07805–9 Hb
0–415–07806–7 Pb

Library of Congress Cataloging in Publication Data

Has been applied for

CONTENTS

FIGURES

TABLES

NOTES ON CONTRIBUTORS

Eithne McLaughlin is a Lecturer in Social Policy and Women's Studies at the Queen's University of Belfast and was formerly Research Fellow at the Social Policy Research Unit, University of York. Her research fields include equal opportunities policies; social security, unemployment and labour supply; informal care and community care. She is the co-author of *Work and Welfare Benefits* (1989) and *All Stitched Up: sex-segregation in the Northern Ireland Clothing Industry* (1991); author of *Social Security and Community Care: the case of the invalid care allowance* (1991); and joint editor of *Women, Employment and Social Policy in Northern Ireland: a problem postponed?* (1991).

Simon Deakin is an Assistant Lecturer in the Faculty of Law, University of Cambridge. He has published a number of papers on the subjects of labour and social security law, with special reference to the economics of labour standards and to European developments.

Andrew Dilnot is the Director of the Institute for Fiscal Studies. He is a co-author of the *Reform of Social Security* (1984) and joint editor of *The Economics of Social Security* (1989).

David Fryer is a Senior Lecturer in Psychology at the University of Stirling where he is engaged in research into the links between unemployment, poverty and mental health. He is the joint editor (with P. Ullah) of *Unemployed People* (1987), and Guest Editor of a Special Edition of the *Journal of Occupational Psychology* (1992), which is devoted to psychological consequences of unemployment.

Catherine Hakim was formerly Professor of Sociology at the University of Essex, after many years as Principal Research Officer in the Department of Employment. She is the author of books on Research Design and Secondary Analysis, cross-national studies of labour market issues, and studies of labour market sub-groups.

Richard Jackman is a Reader in Economics to the London School of Economics. He has been involved in research on a number of labour market topics, including the causes of growth in unemployment, wage rigidities, long-term unemployment and structural imbalance, and with the impact of policies such as inflation taxes, profit-sharing and special employment measures. He is the co-author of *Unemployment: Macroeconomic Performance and the Labour Market* (1991) and is a Director of the Human Resources Programme at the Centre for Economic Performance at the LSE.

Malcolm Maguire is Co-director of the Centre for Labour Market Studies at Leicester University. He has published widely on issues relating to employment, unemployment, the transition from school to work and training, and is the co-author of *Restructuring the Labour Market: the implications for youth*.

Hilary Metacalf is a Senior Research Fellow at the Policy Studies Institute. She is a labour economist who has specialized in discrimination and disadvantage in employment, particularly amongst women and older people, and the role of employers' practices and attitudes on employment opportunities. She is the author of numerous studies on aspects of employment for, amongst others, the Department of Employment, the Training Agency, the Equal Opportunities Commission and the National Economic Development Office.

Christopher Pissarides is a Professor of Economics at the London School of Economics and Director of the National Economic Performance programme at the Centre for Economic Performance. He has published widely in the field of labour economics and is the author of two books on the economics of search theory.

Alan Townsend is a Reader in Geography at the University of Durham and co-Director of the National Online Manpower Information System. After working in the civil service on regional development, he qualified as a Member of the Royal Town Planning Institute and was Director of the North-East Area Study of the University of Durham. He is the author of *The Impact of Recession* (1983), joint editor of *The North–South Divide* (1989) and co-author of *Contemporary Britain* (1990).

Jonathan Wadsworth is a Research Officer at the Centre for Economic Performance at the London School of Economics.

Michael White is Senior Fellow and Head of Employment Studies at the Policy Studies Institute, which he joined in 1979. His main areas of research have been unemployment and employers' policies, but he has also done work on training and innovation. He is the author of *Long-term Unemployment and Labour Markets* (1983) and *Against Unemployment* (1991) and co-author of *Young Adults in Long-term Unemployment* (1989).

Frank Wilkinson is a Senior Research Officer at the Department of Applied Economics, University of Cambridge. He has written widely in the areas of labour market regulation, business structure, inflation and low pay, and is the co-author of *Do Trade Unions Cause Inflation?* and *Labour Market Structure, Industrial Organisation and Low Pay*.

PREFACE AND ACKNOWLEDGEMENTS

> There would be the certainty of disaster if a Conservative pro-market sector government came to power and just sat back, balanced the budget, and let unemployment mount, waiting for the market to resolve its problems.

So wrote two economists (Bacon and Eltis) in 1978 just before the election of the first Thatcher government. We now have the disaster they so prophetically spoke of. Yet in 1989, when the plans for this book were first laid, the British economic 'success story' of the late 1980s was being widely applauded. A policy and public consensus had emerged which appeared satisfied with levels of unemployment around 1.6 million. This consensus was not shared by many academics who, throughout the 1980s, continued to argue that the British economy was, at a fundamental level, 'an economy of unemployment', with all the human and economic waste and inefficiency such as economy entails. In view of the rapid rise in unemployment that has occurred in 1990 and 1991, such pessimism has proven well-founded.

That all people are equal but some people are more equal than others is nowhere more true than in the experience of unemployment. Unemployment is not a price 'we' all have to pay to restructure the economy and hold down inflation. Presented in this way, the real story of unemployment is hidden – that it is the same people who are always at risk of unemployment in an inefficient labour market founded on structured inequalities of locality, sex, race, disability, and age. This book aims to show that it is possible to alter that story, that the storyline does not unfold unbidden and uncontrolled, that it is both possible and wise to rework the plot on terms beneficial to all people and parts of Britain and Northern Ireland. The book is explicitly multi-disciplinary, though it will be obvious that behind the different styles and language of each of the disciplines represented, there lies a consensus about the value of intervening in the labour market in an active rather than reactive way.

The contributors to this book originally prepared papers for the 'Understanding Unemployment: lessons from the 80s, prospects for the 90s'

Conference, organized by the Social Policy Research Unit, University of York, held in York in May 1990. All the papers have since been revised and updated and, as editor, I would like to thank the contributors for the diligent reworking of their original papers. And similarly to thank Mr Alan Jarvis, Social Sciences Editor of Routledge, who took on publication of this book despite the well-known publishing maxim that 'books on unemployment don't sell'. I would also like to record a personal debt to Professor Sally Baldwin of the Social Policy Research Unit at York for the intellectual support and encouragement she has given to me and for her friendship.

Eithne McLaughlin
The Queen's University of Belfast
November 1991

1

TOWARDS ACTIVE LABOUR MARKET POLICIES: AN OVERVIEW

Eithne McLaughlin

A CRISIS OF UNEMPLOYMENT?

By the late 1980s, unemployment was becoming a forgotten policy issue in Britain. This was not because there was little unemployment, but because unemployment had been redefined as a residual and individualized problem, for which the enterprising free-market Thatcher administration had no direct responsibility. There was, then, no crisis. This book aims to provide a well-informed, easily understandable and up-to-date explanation of why unemployment has been a continuing crisis for the British and Northern Irish economies, as well as for the many people, adults and children, who have had to experience the effects of unemployment. In this and subsequent chapters the emphasis is on an analysis of the structure of unemployment, and through that the identification of a responsible set of policies which could address this long-running crisis. The purpose of this first chapter is to provide an overview of the analyses in the context of a critique of approaches to unemployment in the 1980s and early 1990s.

Unemployment levels

Is unemployment still the most serious economic problem facing the UK? One way of answering this question is to compare unemployment levels over time and between countries. Unlike the United States, though in common with many European countries, Britain had found it possible to achieve low unemployment rates for long periods of time since 1945. For most of the period unemployment was substantially below 5 per cent, reaching a low of just over 1 per cent in the mid-1950s. In the 1960s and the 1970s unemployment did tend to rise but it was a slow process. As Jackman (Chapter 3) asks, if in the twenty-five years after the Second World War, the unemployment rate in Britain was generally less than 2 per cent, why is it 8.5 per cent and rising in 1991? Why, too, did unemployment rise faster in the UK than in other European countries? In the early 1990s, for example, unemployment in the UK rose by 31 per cent, compared with an increase of 4 per cent for France and a drop of 13 per cent in (West) Germany (*Eurostat*, July 1991).

Why too has UK unemployment tended to stick, that is, not to fall back once a new peak has been reached? Both White (Chapter 2) and Jackman (Chapter 3) discuss the reasons for the 'sticky' nature of British unemployment. White points to a higher level of wage rigidity in Britain combined with a reliance on a more unqualified and low qualified work-force compared with our European counterparts. Jackman, too, points to the inflexibility of structural skill imbalances and the minimal influence of unemployment levels on wage determination. This perspective is very different to the one espoused by the Conservative administrations of 1979 onwards, a point which will be taken up further in the next section.

What of unemployment levels in the future? Table 1.1 shows registered unemployment levels in the UK between 1979 and 1991 together with a projection for 1992. Even the decrease in registered unemployment in 1988–90 only brought unemployment levels down to 1980/1 levels, themselves historically high. There is little evidence to sustain a belief that unemployment will fall below 2 million by the mid-1990s (National Westminster Bank forecast, May 1991) and some forecasters argue that it will be considerably higher. The National Institute of Economic and Social Research's quarterly review in May 1991 predicted that registered unemployment would rise to 2.75 million by mid-1992 and remain at 2.5 million or above for the rest of the century. In comparative terms, across the EC, by 1992, only Spain, Ireland and the former East Germany are expected to have higher unemployment than the UK.

As Table 1.1 also shows, vacancy levels fell sharply in 1990 and this fall is likely to continue. Although inflation fell to around 4 per cent by the end of 1991/beginning of 1992, this has been accompanied by falls in manufacturing investment of 15 per cent in 1991 and an anticipated 7 per cent in 1992. For the first time since records began, manufacturing firms employ fewer than 5 million people (4,945,000 in Jan. 1991, Dept of Employment *Gazette*).

Measuring unemployment

In fact, the full extent of both current and future unemployment is not well measured by the data in Table 1.1. The definition and measurement of unemployment has been a contentious issue throughout the 1979–91 period. Registered unemployment as shown in Table 1.1 includes only those receiving social security benefits by virtue of their unemployed status. Therefore this method of measuring unemployment is more dependent on social security regulations and entitlements than on unemployment *per se*.

Throughout the 1980s, new restrictions on social security benefits for unemployed people were introduced at various points (see Chapter 11,

Table 1.1 Unemployment and vacancy levels, 1979–91 UK

	Annual average registered unemployment (seasonally adjusted[a])	Annual average vacancies Jobcentres[b] Est. total (seasonally adjusted)	
1979	1,227,300	241,300	723,900
1980	1,560,800	143,000	429,000
1981	2,419,800	97,000	291,000
1982	2,793,400	111,300	333,900
1983[c]	3,104,700	145,100	435,300
1984	3,159,800	150,200	450,600
1985	3,271,200	162,100	486,300
1986[d]	3,289,100	188,800	566,400
1987	2,806,500	235,400	706,200
1988	2,274,900	248,600	745,800
1989	1,784,400	219,500	658,500
1990	1,661,700	173,500	520,500
1991 (Sept.)	2,460,600		
1992 (projection[e])	2,750,000		

Source: Dept of Employment Gazettes
Notes:
[a] Figures prior to 1982 are estimates of seasonally adjusted unemployment.
[b] Excluding Community Programme vacancies in GB.
[c] Figures after April 1983 no longer include some men aged 60 or over who choose not to sign on for work (between April 1983 and August 1983 this reduced the unemployment count by an estimated 161,800).
[d] Change in compilation of unemployment statistics from February 1986 means that later figures are not directly comparable with pre-1986 figures (this change reduced the total UK count by an estimated 50,000 on average).
[e] NIESR projection, May 1991.

and next section). In addition, the claimant count has excluded all those on government-supported training schemes, such as Employment Training and Youth Training. In early 1991, the numbers of people excluded from the claimant count because of participation on training schemes totalled around 610,000.

The cumulative result has been an increasing disparity between the claimant count and more direct measurements of unemployment. So, for example, as Pissarides and Wadsworth (Chapter 4) show, the claimant count and the Labour Force Survey rates of unemployment were very similar in 1979, but by 1989 the two rates had moved apart, with only 68 per cent of unemployed people in the LFS also being claimants. This systematic undercounting has made unemployment among certain population groups particularly invisible. Only 40 per cent of unemployed women in the 1986 LFS were also claimants and hence included in the claimant count. The biggest single factor accounting for this under-representation is the lack of independent entitlement to means-tested benefits of unemployed married or cohabiting women. In addition to unregistered unemployment,

3

captured by definitions based on those seeking work rather than those receiving benefits, Metcalf (Chapter 9) points out that there may by a considerable level of what she calls 'hidden unemployment'. This is caused by the acceptance as legitimate of some, but not other, barriers to employment. These barriers include the constraints of caring for children and disabled adults, low pay and discouragement from job search – the latter two being caused by labour market segmentation and discrimination against women (particularly mothers), ethnic minority groups, older people and people with disabilities.

By the early 1990s, the number of people in either registered or unregistered unemployment in Britain and Northern Ireland probably approached nearly 4 million, after people on government training schemes and married and cohabiting women with no social security entitlements are added to the claimant count. Such a figure clearly demonstrates a continuing crisis of unemployment in Britain and Northern Ireland (see also Gordon 1988). Were the hidden unemployed to be added to this count, the figure could well rise to nearly 10 million, assuming half of those now classified as non-participants but still of working age (see Chapter 9) represent hidden unemployed rather than 'true' non-participants.

The cost of unemployment

The cost of this systematic underutilization of the labour force is considerable, resulting in a national output lower than would otherwise be the case, poor returns on public investments in education and training, and of course, income and opportunity inequities between population groups. Registered unemployment alone carries a massive cash price tag. For example, the cost in total public expenditure of 1991 levels of registered unemployment was nearly £21 billion. Interestingly, this figure was arrived at from two very different sources with different perspectives on both the causes of, and the solutions to, unemployment (the Unemployment Unit, September 1991, and the Adam Smith Institute, November 1991). In terms of public expenditure planning, each 100,000 increase in the registered unemployment figure above the 1.75 million forecast in spending plans for 1991 onwards, means the Treasury will have to find an extra £320 million.

It is argued by all the contributors to this book that, without a renewal of government commitment to active labour market intervention, there is little hope of even registered unemployment levels dropping to pre-1979 levels. The implications of continued high levels of unemployment for public expenditure on other areas of concern (such as the health service) are very serious, as are the equality of opportunity and economic welfare implications for women, ethnic minority people, older people and people living in high unemployment areas (an issue discussed later in this chapter). Interpreting these levels of unemployment, and their associated costs, as anything other than a crisis, is only possible by a massive abdication of state responsibility in economic affairs.

MONETARISM AND UNEMPLOYMENT POLICY IN THE 1980s

The 1980s have been characterized by just such an abdication of state responsibility. Twenty years ago, when unemployment rose to approximately one million for the first time since the end of the Second World War, the shock-waves prompted a policy U-turn by the Heath government. In current times, however, government has succeeded in distancing itself politically from responsibility for high unemployment levels. By 1985, unemployment was treble that of 1979, and by 1991, it was double 1979 levels. Manufacturing output was experiencing its second slump and was almost back to its levels of 1979, and the prospects of the UK ever being in the black seemed remote. Yet remarkably, at a fundamental level, the Government has remained unchallenged. A new orthodoxy has gripped what little macro-economic debate remains:

> the great traditional goals of economic policy, with the important exception of price stability, are disappearing from view. In particular, growth and unemployment are ceasing to be seen as objectives of policy, but rather as natural events, like hurricanes or snow, which are news, certainly, but which the government can neither predict nor control.
>
> (Professor Wynne Godley, 'Terminal Decay', *New Statesman and Society*, 15 March 1991)

Discussing the government's biggest failure – unemployment – has thus become almost taboo, as unemployment is presented as fluctuating like the weather and beyond government control. In 1991, the Chancellor of the Exchequer stated bluntly that rising unemployment was a 'price worth paying' for lower inflation. The concept of unemployment paying for price-stability is a critical one; 1980s government policy towards the economy has been dominated by the elevation of price-stability to the (sole) objective of government. In itself, price-stability is a worthy objective, particularly in ageing societies such as Britain where a growing proportion of people have to depend on fixed incomes. However, price-stability is not an end in itself; it must be weighed against the long-term and short-term costs incurred by single-minded pursuit of this objective. Even in the short term, is a 2 per cent fall in inflation worth half a million more people joining the registered unemployment count?

The problem has been that Conservative governments since 1979 have answered yes to this question. The election of the first Thatcher government in 1979 represented a fundamental stepwise shift in economic policy-making on a number of fronts, not least of which was the total abandonment of any kind of commitment to the management of labour demand. This involved the adoption of an exclusively supply-side interpretation of the causes of unemployment. 'Labour market rigidities' and 'barriers to growth' were identified as trade union power, centralized forms of collective bargaining and pay determination, high wages, generous social security benefits, employment protection legislation, high rates of income tax and an oversized public sector. All of these were held to produce malfunctions and distortions in the market place. The 1985 White Paper *Employment: the challenge for the Nation* exemplifies this perspective on unemployment.

As Deakin and Wilkinson point out (Chapter 11), it was the adoption of a brand of monetarism from across the Atlantic, based on nineteenth-century theories of how money moves in the economy, which provided the rationale for this approach to unemployment. According to orthodox monetarist economic theory, both wage differentials and unemployment are caused by impediments to the operation of a 'free' labour market, originating in the power of organized groups and in the extended regulatory role of the welfare state. The state is seen as contributing to the rigidity of the labour market, through social security programmes which make unemployment attractive by increasing out-of-work incomes (Minford 1986), and by the provision of certain non-cash benefits and services free to all (for example, health care and education), regardless of family and employment status. Similarly the state contributes to the rigidities of labour market organization through individual labour law regulating the contract of employment and through collective labour law supporting trade union rights (Rowley 1986; Hanson and Mather 1989). Taxation, in the form of social charges upon employers and regulation of the contract of employment which inhibits effective bargaining, acts as a disincentive to the creation of jobs by employers.

Employment and unemployment inequalities are then caused by exogenous non-market factors, the key culprits being individual 'choice', personal (in)efficiency, excessive labour power and the political intervention of the state. If the labour market was protected from these non-market factors, the market would be free to tend towards equilibrium and, concurrently, equality of exchange between workers and employers as market wage rates fell into line with individual effort and productivity. A programme of deregulation designed to remove market imperfections will therefore offer the most effective policy approach to the labour market. As Deakin (1989) argues, however, evidence which challenges the core tenets of the theory has been excluded and reclassified as 'non-economic' thus negating the need for significant modification to the central tenet – that the market allocates labour to its most efficient uses and rewards it accordingly.

It is within this framework that government labour market policy since

6

1979 becomes explicable, namely abandonment of attempts to regulate the level and nature of labour demand and deregulation of the supply side. This policy had three main thrusts: social security changes, promotion of low-paid work, and deregulation of the employment contract (see Chapter 11). Within the social security field, the 1980s were characterized by cuts in the levels of unemployment benefit relative to wages, lengthening of the qualification period for unemployment benefit, increases in the period of disqualification from benefit following 'voluntary' unemployment, widening of the range of jobs claimants were required to look for and accept, provision of proof that claimants were actively seeking work, and removal or reduction of social security rights for young people. Promotion of low-paid work has involved rebates of national insurance contributions for the low-paid and subsidies towards the employment of young people, together with an extension of in-work benefits targeted at the low-paid (particularly men) such as Housing Benefit and Family Credit. Deregulation of the contract of employment has occurred through, for example, withdrawal of employment protection from part-time and temporary workers, exclusion of many young workers from unfair dismissal and redundancy rights, abolition of fair wages legislation, curtailment of the powers of wages councils, outlawing closed shops and reducing the legal scope for strike action (see Chapter 11 for further discussion).

The pursuit of these labour market supply-side policies did result in a widening dispersal of pay and incomes in the 1980s. However, the growth in low pay and low incomes did not succeed in 'pricing' all the unemployed into work. How much further low wages and low incomes would have to fall before unemployment is 'cured' is rarely speculated upon by policy-makers and politicans. As Jackman argues (Chapter 3), the British experience (and that of other intermediate European countries [see Chapter 2]) does not accord with the standard macro-economic model. This holds that there is a reasonably stable equilibrium rate of unemployment, so long as non-market factors are removed, and deviations from equilibrium are typically small and self-correcting. The sharp changes that have occurred cannot be explained in terms of rapid jumps in factors affecting the underlying equilibrium rate. The enormous rise in unemployment in the early 1980s was the result of restrictive monetary policies leading to huge appreciation in the exchange rate. Likewise the decline in unemployment in the late 1980s was clearly attributable to a consumer spending boom. Neither of these sharp changes, one upwards and one downwards, were caused by supply-side factors. If the causes of the UK's poor unemployment record in the 1980s/early 1990s had been the welfare benefits system, the trade unions, high income tax rates, public-sector monopolies, and so on, then it would be reasonable to think that the energetic pursuit of policies specificially designed to remove these impediments would have resulted in at least lower and a more stable unemployment level. It did not, and it is not.

EMPLOYMENT AND TRAINING SERVICES IN THE 1980s/ EARLY 1990s

Alongside deregulation of the supply side of the labour market, government has been drawn towards increasing active labour market policies of a certain restricted kind in Britain and Northern Ireland since 1979. These policies and programmes have focused on restoring (a) the motivation and (b) the skills of unemployed individuals.

Motivating the unemployed

Whatever the merits of the monetarist interpretation of the causes of unemployment, monetarism has lent itself easily to the simplistic language of 'unemployed-bashing' by backbenchers and the popular media. Politicians have described the unemployed as to blame for their own predicament by not being fully mobile, by not taking one of the low-paid or part-time jobs on offer, or by not acquiring skills that would give them a greater chance of work. The media line has been somewhat different, feeding into an image of the unemployed as work-shy, feckless wastrels, dole scroungers, voluntarily unemployed people, living off the backs of the hard-working taxpayer, and probably supplementing their already too generous benefits with illicit work in the black economy.

As Hakim (Chapter 8) points out, such 'explanations' of unemployment have legitimised and justified the introduction of a two-pronged carrot and stick approach to unemployed people. The implication is that there is a more buoyant economy than is at first apparent, and that unemployment can be explained by the attitudes and behaviour of the unemployed. The stringent job-seeking regulations imposed on the unemployed, together with restrictions on benefit levels (as discussed in the previous section), have occurred alongside the more paternalist introduction of counselling and guidance services such as Restart interviews and courses, Claimant Advisors and Jobclubs. As Fryer (Chapter 6), Dilnot (Chapter 7) and Hakim (Chapter 8) show, there is little empirical evidence demonstrating that these developments need to be given the priority which they have enjoyed in employment policy.

Fryer's chapter does show that long-term unemployment leads to a sharp deterioration in mental, and possibly, physical health. Critically, however, through a careful appraisal of the social psychological literature over fifty years, Fryer argues that a major cause of this negative impact on well-being is the long-term material deprivation which unemployed people experience, rather than the removal of the integrative and supportive social

8

relationship of employment. It was only in the 1980s that the explanatory role of poverty in the distress and loss of activity evident among long-term unemployed people was minimized in the social psychological literature on unemployment.

As Fryer points out this must have been a convenient coincidence for policy-makers charged with the task of encouraging the job-seeking activity and attractiveness of long-term unemployed people at the same time as reducing their relative benefit income. Fryer's conclusion is that, within the limits imposed upon them by the material context of unemployment, unemployed people are active, try to control their own affairs, do not become 'work-shy', and do not live 'comfortably enough' on benefit income. Fryer shows that the extensive psychological research on unemployment has found that 'the most striking feature of this research is that almost everybody scores high on employment commitment measures'. The important explanatory role of poverty in the mental health deterioration shown by long-term unemployed people, suggests that benefit levels need to be increased in the interests of better mental health, and hence higher levels of proactivity among the long-term unemployed.

The mistaken belief that benefits themselves cause (registered) unemployment, the topic of Dilnot's Chapter 7, has of course meant that instead of redressing the negative effects of long-term unemployment on mental health, government since 1979 may have increased them by reducing and restricting benefits. Dilnot summarizes the extensive econometric work dealing with the effects of benefits on registered unemployment, and concludes that the level of unemployment benefit does have some impact on the duration of individuals' unemployment spells, but the effect is a rather small one. To have a dramatic impact on the level of unemployment, massive cuts in unemployment benefit levels would appear to be required. Were such cuts to occur, the regime would be so different from that under which the estimates of the effect of benefit levels on unemployment durations were derived, that their predictive usefulness would be very doubtful.

Accordingly, while there is little evidence to justify the restrictions in unemployment benefits which have occurred throughout the 1980s, both policy and most academic work has been guilty of concentrating on male benefit receipt and male incentives to take low-paid full-time work. As a result little attention has been paid to those aspects of the social security system which do exhibit disincentive effects of sizeable proportions. As Dilnot, Hakim (Chapter 8) and Metcalf (Chapter 9) point out, the social security system creates disincentives in relation to part-time and other forms of non-standard work. This particularly affects women living with unemployed men since more 'women's' than 'men's' jobs are offered on a part-time basis, and since women are more likely than men, even within unemployed couples, to be responsible for childcare and domestic work and hence accept part-time jobs. In addition, women's lower wages and a social security and fiscal system which does not take childcare costs into account, create disincentives in relation to full-time paid work for all women, but particularly lone mothers.

Hakim (Chapter 8) demonstrates the extent and growth, in the 1980s, of the kind of non-standard forms of paid work which the social security system fails to facilitate. This is one of the reasons why, contrary to popular assumptions, unemployed people do not constitute the most important source of recruits to the black economy. Indeed, they are the smallest source with the lowest incidence of such activity. Not, as Hakim points out, that all non-standard work is actually part of the black economy (most of it is legitimately outside the tax and national insurance nets), but rather that those attempting to guessestimate the size of the black economy have typically misconstrued such work as being part of this economy. Although the registered unemployed may have the time and motive to engage in such work and/or legal non-standard forms of work, in reality it is mainly the hidden unemployed, in Metcalf's terms (Chapter 9), who predominate. The inflexibility of the social security system, the highly publicized activities of benefit fraud investigators and lack of resources and social integration, together result in enforced inactivity among the registered unemployed. As Hakim concludes, insisting on complete inactivity as the price to pay for receiving unemployment benefits is far more likely to create a culture of welfare dependence than allowing unemployed people to take up whatever small scale opportunities come their way.

Reskilling the unemployed: training and retraining

The second arm of government policy on unemployment in the 1980s was training and retraining programmes for unemployed and young people. Despite a considerable level of political rhetoric about skilling unemployed people back into jobs, and although policies and provision in terms of counselling and remotivation appeared to proceed in excess of need, policies and provision on training and retraining have lagged behind need. Throughout the 1980s, government policy stated that employers should organise and finance the training of their own workers, while the government should take responsiblity for the unemployed and the young. However, funding of publicly funded training services for the unemployed and the young did not increase in line with rising unemployment.

The Youth Training budget was cut by £420 million in real terms between 1988 and 1991, and in cash terms from £1.02 billion to £833 million. Employment Training spending was cut from £1.34 billion to £1.06 billion over the same period. Both cuts were more severe taking into account inflation, so that, for example, real spending was cut by 52 per cent for each YT place between 1988 and 1991. Reductions in spending per training place are of particular concern since as White (Chapter 2) points out, the evidence is that high quality training 'works' but low quality does not.

These expenditure reductions in the face of rising unemployment resulted in thirty-five of the sixty Training and Enterprise Councils (out of a total of eighty-two) surveyed by the House of Commons Employment Select Committee in 1991 in England and Wales reporting that they could not fulfil the guarantee of a YT place for all 16–18-year-olds not in work or in full-time education, or ET places for all 18–24-year-olds out of work for between six months and one year. Training outside the guarantee groups appeared to have all but stopped by 1991, with the agencies reporting that they could not meet the needs of the disabled, the vulnerable (ex-offenders and people with literacy problems) and the valuable (people with shortage skills, *Guardian*, 28 May 1991).

Government policy has been to take responsibility only for those young people not in paid work or further education, and therefore the policy is relying on employers and the influence of the employer-led TECs to control the attraction of high wages. This means that 100,000 school-leavers go directly to jobs with little training. The 1991 White Paper on education and training states that 'A clear signal from the labour market is needed to persuade employers to provide and young people to . . . take up, training, particularly to higher levels of skill . . . Young people need to be able to see that acquiring skills opens up the prospect of progressing to higher levels of pay and to more rewarding jobs.' (*Education and Training for the 21st Century*, HMSO, 1991).

For two reasons this strategy seems unlikely to succeed. As White (Chapter 2) points out, there are motivation problems related to the low pay differentials between trainees and the fully skilled in Britain. Apprentices in Britain in their final year receive up to 90 per cent of the adult rate whereas in Germany they would be paid between 30 and 50 per cent. There is little evidence to suggest that employers will spontaneously reduce the relatively high wages available in the juvenile labour market and indeed these may increase in some geographical areas as the supply of young people declines in the 1990s.

Secondly, the low training qualifications of a large proportion of young people in Britain and Northern Ireland are in turn the result of low achievement levels in basic education. Low achievement in basic education constrains what can be achieved by subsequent training strategies and provision. Education's share of GNP declined from 5.5 to 4.6 per cent between 1979 and 1991, and overall represents a low proportion of GNP in European terms. While this decline was partially due to falling school rolls, in order to upgrade the quality of the labour force, it would have been profitable to take the opportunity to maintain education's share of GNP. This would have provided higher levels of resources per pupil, and higher levels of material incentives to young people to stay on at school for further and higher education.

Until 1991, Britain was one of the few industrialized countries not to have national training targets. Targets have now been set. By 1997, 80 per cent of young people should have four GCSEs or the equivalent National Vocational Qualifications (NVQs); by 2000, 50 per cent of young people should have A-levels or equivalent NVQs. The present figure is around 30 per cent. The low levels of public funding of both education and training for young people not in work must make attainment of these targets doubtful. The targets for those in work are that all employees should be provided with training by 1996 and half should reach the vocational equivalent of A-levels by 2000. The task of achieving this reskilling of the existing workforce is enormous, given that 34 per cent of women and 26 per cent of men of working age have no qualifications (*Training Statistics* 1991, HMSO). Many of those who most need job-related training to remain employed continue to miss out. The percentage of manual unskilled and low skilled workers receiving training is the lowest of all groups. Preliminary results of the 1990 LFS show that only 3 per cent of unskilled and 7 per cent of partly skilled workers receive any training, compared with 26 per cent of professional workers and 20 per cent of non-manual workers.

Without an active strategy to reach lower-skilled workers the structural weaknesses of the skills base will remain. At present the government's strategy is one of a limited range of programmes targeted at motivating individuals to take up training or retraining. The Education and Training White Paper stated that it is hoped to offer training credits (vouchers worth around £1,500 to spend with employers on in-house or day release courses) to all 16- and 17-year-olds by 1996. As regards registered unemployed people and the hidden unemployed (for example, women returning to employment), the government is to introduce six to ten pilot schemes, offering vouchers to buy guidance about training options. Finally, tax relief will be introduced for individuals on their costs of training towards a National Vocational Qualification. Realistically, tax relief is likely to be taken up mainly by those in better-paid jobs. The very lowest paid are unlikely to benefit from tax relief either because they earn too little to pay tax or because they cannot afford to pay for courses in the first place.

Although the scope and scale of training and special employment measures has grown in the 1980s, these have on the whole offered temporary relief to some individuals and to government by removing the numbers involved from the official unemployment count, at least temporarily. The scale of the resources which have been committed appears small in comparison with the numbers of unemployed and the extent of low qualifications in the population, as reviewed above. Of particular concern must be the quality of the training offered on these schemes and the targeting of these schemes. Retraining unemployed welders for electricians' jobs while simultaneously retraining unemployed electricians as welders does not constitute a well-planned and well-targeted national training programme. Yet that is very often the kind of programmes available at a local level. As Gordon commented: 'If [government-provided] training does lead to a job then it is rather more by good fortune than design' (1988: 114).

Similarly, the National Audit Office in a 1987 report to Parliament severely castigated the Department of Employment and the MSC for spending over £1 billion a year on training schemes without having any real idea of the current and future skill needs of industry. White's analysis of the needs created by new technology, consumer demand for higher standards of product and service quality and European integration, provides a basis upon which the future adequacy of training, retraining and education policy and provision can be judged. To date, the government's commitment, in terms of resources and political leadership, falls far short of what is needed to achieve the massive reskilling of the labour force required. Likewise, present policy initiatives do not seem likely to target effectively those most in need of training and retraining if they are to avoid high risks of unemployment, whether short-term, recurrent or long-term.

TOWARDS PROACTIVE LABOUR MARKET POLICIES

There has then been little in government policy towards unemployment in the 1980s and early 1990s which is likely to alter the UK's record of persistently high unemployment levels. The economic downturn of 1990–1 has served as a reminder that the most fundamental problems of the British economy have remained with us as we enter the 1990s. White (Chapter 2) argues that the foremost of these problems is the propensity to wage rigidity. Wage flexibility has been shown cross-nationally to be strongly related to high levels of growth and low levels of inflation. From the point of view of effective active labour market policies, what is important to note is that wage flexibility can be achieved in two very different ways: through strong central negotiating and planning mechanisms to achieve co-operation between state, business and trade unions on a wide range of economic policies; or through free-market strategies of low levels of unionization and lack of government intervention in wage-fixing. Since 1979, UK policy has been to shift towards the free-market model (Chapter 11), but by the acid test of wage flexibility, the policy has not succeeded. This is despite the availability of a large unemployed labour pool, themselves highly flexible in their willingness to change occupations and work for reduced wages.

This failure is largely accounted for by the behaviour of employers who have sought to develop policies of higher wages, higher productivity and higher labour force quality. This is not in itself an ineffective approach on a medium-term within-firm level, but in terms of alleviating unemployment, it has little to offer. This is primarily because of the incapacity of many workers, those currently unemployed and those at risk of recurrent unemployment, to move to a higher occupational level, and so move from the outside to the inside (Chapter 3). White argues that, because of this, upgrading the quality of the labour force, particularly at the lower occupational levels, may provide at least a partial route out of wage rigidity. However, government cannot rely on employers to do this either for unemployed people or for young people. As White and Jackson point out, left to their own devices employers will continue to pay unqualified school-leavers high rates. As long as this is true, young people themselves will see little reason to train. As regards the unemployed and those at high risk of future unemployment, Maguire (Chapter 5) and Metcalf (Chapter 9) show that employers' recruitment, training and promotion practices will perpetuate, not change, unequal economic opportunities structured by sex, race, disability, age and familial status. A 'free' British labour market is then inherently inefficient, and active government intervention in the labour market on both the demand and supply sides is required.

To counteract the malaise of unemployment in Britain and Northern Ireland requires active policies targeted at those groups feeling the effects of unemployment most severely and those most at risk of losing their jobs. We can identify just who the unemployed are, those most likely to lose their jobs and those most likely to stay in unemployment, as Pissarides and Wadsworth show in Chapter 4. Occupation is clearly a key explanatory variable, interlocking with qualifications and place of residence. Where you live and what you do (or did) for a living became increasingly important in the 1980s. The solution to occupationally caused unemployment must lie within a well-targeted, well-planned and well-resourced national retraining and educational programme and a renewed regional focus in employment policy.

Geographical unemployment policy

The importance of occupation interrelates with where unemployed people live since different geographical areas have built up different economic bases with consequently different occupational profiles. Most of the areas experiencing high unemployment rates are in the North and West and most of those enjoying low unemployment rates are in the South and East. Certainly there are parts of the South and East which have unemployment rates comparable to the high unemployment of many of the Northern and Western areas. It may then appear too simplistic to talk in terms of a North–South divide. The geographical distribution of employment and unemployment is dependent upon both urban/rural and North–South differences. Inner city areas have very different economic bases compared with conurbations as a whole, as do Northern and Southern conurbations from each other (Chapter 10). Despite this, the concept of a North–South divide is important as it points to the economic base of localities (bases which have developed differently over time) as providing a key cause of unemployment, rather than seeking explanation in terms of the personal characteristics of people in high unemployment areas.

The regions became a test-bed for the free-market approach to regeneration in the 1980s. The Labour administration was spending the 1991 equivalent of £1.83 billion on regional industrial policy in the late 1970s. This was halved to £989 million a year in the first half of the 1980s and slashed even further to reach an annual average of £242 million in the late 1980s (Elliott and Kelly, *Guardian*, 4 November 1991). Targeting too has changed from the regional aid budget to urban development agencies, but the depressed regions have seen no relative increase in the key Thatcherite indicators – competitiveness, business formation and self-employment. Net business formation grew by 20 per cent a year in the South-East during the 1980s but by only 7.7 per cent in the North, 7.2 in the North-West and 8.5 in Scotland. The gulf between North and South can also be seen in differences in employment growth. In the poorer regions growth was negative in 1979–88, reaching 10 per cent in the North-West and Wales, compared with expansion in employment of 8 per cent in the South-East, 10 per cent in the South-West and 26 per cent in East Anglia. In June 1987, the u/v (registered unemployed/registered 'Jobcentre' vacancies) ratio in Northern Ireland was 62.8 (even including the temporary job-creation scheme ACE vacancies) compared with 18.6 in Scotland and 7.7 in the South-East (both excluding temporary Community Programme vacancies). More recently, in the first eleven months of the 1990–1 recession, unemployment rose by 2.2 per cent in Wales, a rise almost equalled in the Northern, North-West, Northern Ireland, Yorkshire and Humberside, and the West Midlands regions. At the same time, and starting from a much lower base, the number of people out of work rose by less than one per cent in the South-East, South-West and Greater London.

How to address these continuing regional and other geographical differences in unemployment and employment rates is hardly a new concern but it as pressing as ever, given that the free-market regeneration approach of the 1980s has clearly failed to alter these differences. As Townsend points out (Chapter 10), for decades up to 1979 it was accepted that government should assist regions and urban areas with severe economic problems through grants and fiscal stimulus. This consensus has now gone. The 1985 White Paper on employment policy (*Employment: the challenge of the Nation*) almost completely ignored regional inequalities in employment and unemployment. The National Economic Development Office's 1991 report on reducing regional inequalities made no mention of such traditional policies as direct government grants to depressed regions and subsidies to reward the relocation of capital to those areas. Instead, nearly all the discussion paralleled the tenor of Conservative social and economic policy in the 1980s by focusing on the supply side – how to remove distortions to the working of the market, especially for labour and housing.

In contrast, Pissarides and Wadsworth (Chapter 4) show that, at an individual level, the unemployed are more likely to move than the employed, while Townsend (Chapter 10) argues that the literature of the 1980s underestimated some periods of success for active regional policy and some significant transfers of manufacturing which occurred. For example, in the 1971–8 period, regional policy overcame the North's disadvantage originating from its industrial structure. Without government intervention the free play of market forces frequently leads to increased regional disparities within countries. The evidence that government intervention can work positively in areas of high unemployment, and that, without higher levels of intervention in the 1990s, Scotland and Northern Ireland may stagnate economically, while Wales and Northern England will enjoy some growth but less than that of the South/South-East, provides a good case for a renewed regional focus in UK labour market policy.

Sex, race and unemployment

Moving beyond the important interlinked factors of occupation, qualifications and place of residence, both race and sex can be described as having 'pure' effects on unemployment rates. These pure race and sex effects are the result of the way that employers structure the entry to work and constrain movement within the labour market given their control over the recruitment process. It is not just criteria of suitability but also criteria of acceptability which employers use when matching people to jobs. Both Maguire (Chapter 5) and Metcalf (Chapter 9) argue that it is therefore as appropriate (and indeed even more necessary) for government to intervene in the attitudes and practices of employers as it is to intervene in the attitudes and practices of unemployed people.

In contrast, in neo-classical economics, low pay and unemployment are held to reflect low skills and personal inefficiency on the part of employees or job-seekers rather than reflecting employers' attitudes and practices. For example, the concentration of unemployment amongst the old, the young, women, ethnic minorities and those low-paid in their last job, is taken as evidence of a lack of skills and abilities among the jobless. Neo-classical economic theory assumes that individuals vary in earning power because of differences in investment in human capital (training and education) and in personal work efficiency and aptitude. Individuals are assumed to vary in their innate ability, in their attitude to risk and in their preferences for the use of time, so that they acquire variable amounts of human capital to bring to the market (Becker 1975). In this way the relatively low pay of women is accounted for by their 'choice' of forgoing time spent in training for waged employment in favour of child-rearing and family responsibilities (Polacheck 1981). The costs of training for specific skills together with hiring and turnover costs give rise to wage differentials.

The difficulty with this analysis is that it takes the level of pay of a job as an objective measure of its worth in terms of skill. An examination or evaluation of job content is avoided and the result is an argument of impregnable circularity in which the outcome, low pay and unemployment, is used as the only evidence for the supposed cause – low skill and personal inefficiency. Employers' use of criteria of acceptability, dependent on stereotypes of race and sex, together with the poor fit between employers evaluations of jobs, the skill content of those jobs, and the accumulated human capital of the people performing those jobs, can explain the 'pure' race and sex wage and unemployment differentials which neo-classical models cannot.

Empirical studies have repeatedly shown that levels of skill and experience are only incompletely related to the wages paid for jobs and to the employment histories of individuals (see, for example, McLaughlin and Ingram 1991 and Craig, Garnsey and Rubery 1985). The return on human capital varies greatly for different groups. Years of formal training may explain why white males reach top positions but, as Pissarides and Wadsworth's analysis shows (Chapter 4), the benefits from education are much reduced for women and racial minorities. In the lower strata of the labour market, and in particular for those returning after unemployment, illness and family responsibilities, the returns on education and training are low for all groups (Wilkinson 1981).

It is necessary then to look beyond the dominant market paradigm of orthodox economics if an attempt is to be made to explain structural inequalities in unemployment and economic opportunities. This is of fundamental importance with respect to the efficiency of the labour market and the appropriate role of the state. The labour market does not function to discipline both capital and labour towards the most efficient allocation of resources, and economic opportunities for individuals are structured in a way which is independent of both their productivity and their preferences. Under these circumstances, institutional forms of regulation and government action play a crucial role in counteracting the effects of endemic labour market inefficiencies and inequalities.

Labour market regulation in some form should be seen as an essential prerequisite of a productive and competitive economy. The alternative is both high unemployment and social security budgets and continued growth of an undercompetitive industrial structure, kept afloat only by low pay and the continued use of low-quality labour. As Deakin and Wilkinson argue (Chapter 11), low pay serves as a substitute in terms of competitiveness for more effective strategies in marketing and production. Dependence on low pay and low-qualified labour to contain costs, serves to limit the ability of firms to respond to new technology, organizational and product innovation and the increased demands for quality identified by White (Chapter 2). 'The long-term cost to the national economy will be measured in terms of the growth of an unproductive tail of low-paying firms and industries, continued decline in international competitiveness and renewed vulnerability to recession and structural unemployment' (Deakin and Wilkinson, Chapter 11).

THE WAY FORWARD

Deakin and Wilkinson (Chapter 11) show that other European countries have taken an alternative approach to that in Britain in the 1980s. Against a background of basic statutory rights, continental systems have sought to introduce flexibility in (a) the form of the contract of employment and (b) working time, through the technique of controlled derogation. In contrast to Britain, where deregulation has meant the dismantling of social and employment protection without new forms of employer control or obligation, continental derogation has involved:

1 the permission of a greater range of exceptions to labour standards if these can be justified in terms of a positive job creation effect;
2 legalization of forms of part-time and temporary work which were previously unlawful in continental countries (but not in the UK);
3 equal treatment of part-time and fixed-term contract workers with their full-time permanent equivalents;
4 devolution of rule-making power from courts and government agencies to the collective bargaining process; and
5 schemes which permit the unemployed to retain part of their benefit entitlement after they take part-time work, and in some countries topping up to a notional minimum full-time wage.

It is these derogation policies which form the basis of the EC Social Charter and Action Programme of 1989 and which the UK alone in the EC has been unable to endorse.

These differences between labour market policies in the UK and the other EC member states in the 1980s are important for two reasons. Firstly, the evidence presented in this and subsequent chapters suggests that the UK approach is not as effective as that of the other EC member states. The evident vulnerability of the UK economy to cyclical recession and large-scale job loss at the beginning of the 1990s is a case in point. Secondly, the experience of the United States since 1945 suggests that if the Single Market proceeds without harmonization of the social dimension, then the result could be a destructive competition between EC states, each cutting labour and social standards in an attempt to attract inward investment.

Consequently what is required for the UK in the 1990s is the adoption of more proactive labour market policies. Such policies must act on both the demand and supply sides of the labour market. White (Chapter 2) argues that injecting demand into the economy can still work in terms of generating more employment and reducing unemployment, despite criticisms levelled against this approach by monetarists. The 1980s have seen a range of alternative policies on unemployment put forward by economists, policy-makers and the political parties. Some have been fairly conventional in approach, arguing for expansionist job-creation measures funded through government borrowing and/or sometimes increased taxation. With this in mind, it is noteworthy that of the twenty-four OECD countries, only Britain is spending no more as a percentage of GDP than it did in the late 1960s (Johnson, 1991). Despite the £6 billion discretionary increase in spending announced in the public expenditure round of November 1991 (which will amount to a small net increase even after public-sector pay settlements), the gap between Britain and the other OECD countries will remain. In the early 1980s the Government said that the fruits of economic growth would be spent on public services; instead it was used to pay off the national debt, now the lowest in Europe. There is a positive role for increased borrowing if the resources so raised are targeted effectively within integrated and proactive labour market policies. There are also, however, a number of ways in which demand could be stimulated, not all of which involve increased public sector borrowing and not all of which are inflationary. Elliott, for example, has suggested that the abolition of mortgage tax relief and the reduction in UK defence expenditure to the European average could provide up to £20 billion a year to improve the productive capacity of the economy while bearing down on consumer-led inflation (Elliott, *Guardian*, 2 April 1991).

Integrated, proactive demand-side policies must include a regional and urban policy component in order to reduce the structuring of individuals' economic opportunities by where they happen to live. The structural causes of unemployment must also be addressed through supply-side interventions. Improved and forward-looking education, training and retraining policies are necessary, particularly targeted at disadvantaged groups to enable them to regain entry to the labour force and to remain in employment. However, training and retraining will not on their own solve the institutional problems of sexism, racism and ageism endemic in the labour market. Simultaneously employers need incentives or requirements or both to recruit the long-term unemployed, registered, unregistered and hidden, while social policies relating to the costs of caring for dependants urgently need new government attention and resources (see Chapters 7 and 9). Apart from the more obvious possibilities of strengthened anti-discrimination legislation and policies (Chapter 5), the introduction of job guarantees for those who have been out of employment for lengthy periods is an attractive proposal, as Jackson (Chapter 3) argues, particularly if coupled with strong, well-resourced, integrated training and education programmes. The Conservative government's opposition to a role for the state in job creation and job guarantees is ideologically based and has had little to do with the pragmatic economics of cost-effectiveness. A job in the public services can be 'bought' by government for little more than the net cost of maintaining someone on benefits.

Finally, and also with regard to the supply side, present medium-term policies must take account of the 1980s legacy of the rise in the proportion of long-term unemployment corresponding with increases in temporary, part-time and self-employed forms of work (OECD 1991; McLaughlin 1991). Social security policy in the 1980s has done nothing to reduce the rigidities in relation to non-standard forms of work which are inherent in British social security (see Chapters 7 and 8). Instead 1980s policy has focused on supposed supply-side rigidities in relation to full-time, low-paid work, whilst simultaneously reducing pro-activity among long-term unemployed people by reducing and restricting benefit levels (Chapter 6) and enforcing full-time inactivity as a requirement for benefit (Chapter 8).

The need for new active labour market policies identified by all the contributors to this book is one for which there is growing support, among both the academic community and the general population. For example, Worswick (1991), of the National Institute for Economic and Social Research, has recently argued that if government carry on using interest rates as the sole instrument to manage the economy, unemployment may remain high for many years, and that such unemployment cannot be regarded as 'caused' by unemployed people themselves: 'Unemployment is not a reflection on the unemployed, it is a reflection on all of us.'

Meanwhile, the annual British Social Attitudes Survey has shown that public opinion on unemployment and management of the labour market and economy, has shifted ever further away from that of government throughout the 1980s (Jowell et al. 1991). In 1983, 32 per cent wanted government to raise more in taxes and increase public expenditure; by 1990 this had risen to 54 per cent. Only a tiny minority of the population support a reduced role for government through lowering taxes and public spending – 9 per cent in 1983 and just 3 per cent in 1990. There has also been consistently high support – 83 per cent in 1990 – for Keynesian policies of fighting unemployment through investment in construction projects; for more government subsidy of industry (56 per cent); and for a government guarantee of jobs for all who want them (60 per cent), coupled with a decline in support for policies of privatization (down to just 16 per cent in 1990). As Taylor (in Jowell et al. 1991) concludes, 'We have continually found widespread enthusiasm for active government intervention in the economy.'

Public enthusiasm and academic argument thus join forces to urge for

20

new government and policy perspectives on how to address the long-running crisis of unemployment in Britain and Northern Ireland. In the chapters that follow, more detailed analyses of major areas of research and policy are presented; on the nature of labour supply and demand in the 1980s and 1990s, employer recruitment processes, the effect of unemployment on individuals and families, the role of the black economy, social security, regional differences and the potential impact of European harmonisation on UK labour market policy. The chapters are deliberately diverse in form and style, as well as in content and disciplinary framework. Several are bold overviews (for example, White, Jackman, Deakin and Wilkinson); others are up-to-date research reports (Pissarides and Wadsworth, Maguire); still others are literature reviews (Fryer); and some review research agendas or criticize conceptual approaches to research issues (Dilnot, Hakim, Metcalf, Fryer). At the very least, these interdisciplinary perspectives on unemployment and the role of the state in the labour market, demonstrate the clearly contested nature of almost all the 'knowledge' which the academic and policy communitites accumulated on unemployment in the 1980s. At best, taken together, they offer new and positive perspectives on understanding unemployment and the nature of effective active labour market policies.

REFERENCES

Becker, G. (1975) *Human Capital: a theoretical and empirical analysis*, Chicago: NBER.

Craig, C., Garnsey, E. and Rubery, J. (1985) *Payment Structures in Smaller Firms: women's employment in segmented labour markets*, Research Paper no. 48, London: Dept of Employment.

Deakin, S. (1989) *Contract, Labour Law and the Developing Employment Relationship*, Ph.D. thesis, University of Cambridge.

Education and Training for the 21st Century, May 1991, London: HMSO.

Gordon, A. (1988) *The Crisis of Unemployment*, Bromley: Christopher Helm.

Hanson, C. and Mather, G. (1989) *Striking out Strikes*, London: Institute of Economic Affairs.

Hayek, F. (1984) *1980s Unemployment and the Unions*, London: Institute of Economic Affairs.

Johnson, C. (1991) *The Economy under Thatcher*.

Jowell, R., Brook, L. and Taylor, B. with G. Prior (eds) (1991) *British Social Attitudes: the 8th report*, Dartmouth: Dartmouth Publishing Company.

McLaughlin, E. (1991) 'Work and Welfare Benefits: social security, employment and unemployment in the 1990s', *Journal of Social Policy*, 20, 4: 485–508.

McLaughlin, E. and Ingram, K. (1991) *All Stitched Up: Sex-segregation in the Northern Ireland Clothing Industry*, Belfast: EOC (NI).

Minford, P. (1986) *Unemployment: Cause and Cure*, Oxford: Basil Blackwell.

National Economic Development Office (1991) *Reducing Regional Inequalities*, London: NEDO.

OECD (1991) *The OECD Employment Outlook*, Paris: OECD.

Polacheck, S. (1981) 'Occupational Self-selection: a human capital approach to sex differences in occupational structure', *Review of Economics and Statistics*, February: 60–9.

Rowley, C. (1986) 'The relationship between economics, politics and law in the formation of public policy', in R. Matthews (ed.) *Economy and Democracy*, New York: St. Martin's Press.

Wilkinson, F. (1981) *The Dynamics of Labour Market Segmentation*, London: Academic Press.

Worswick, G. (1991) *Unemployment: a problem of policy*, London: NIESR.

2

LABOUR SUPPLY AND DEMAND IN THE NINETIES

Michael White[1]

THE NINETIES – A DECADE OF CHANGE?

The 1990s have begun in a ferment of political change. In 1990, the advent of the Single European Market seemed momentous enough to fill one decade, but even this has been crowded out of attention by events in the former USSR, Eastern Europe and South Africa. At home, meanwhile, the political certainties of the 1980s have collapsed, leaving the field open to whoever can correctly read or mould the new mood of the electorate. The most obvious way that these changes will affect labour markets is through the different economic maps they draw. There will be new markets, new partnerships, new competitors, new economic opportunities for the international movement of labour. This will lead to both opportunity and risk. Harder to predict are the changes in attitudes and motives which both propel and are shaped by the changes in the political climate. The workings of the labour market, and the scope for policies to make labour markets work in particular ways, depend on what people think and do in regard to such matters as wages, profits, welfare, equity, effort, innovation and enterprise. The more willing they are to change their stance on these matters, the greater is the scope for economic change.

The starting point for this chapter then is that there may be great pressures for change coming from both outside and within. This climate of change will also provide opportunities for new policies towards the most intractable problems of labour markets in Britain. But too much talk of change can lead quickly to over-optimism. All manner of changes can be envisaged at a detailed level, but ultimately the figures have to add up and the books have to balance. In particular, change is constrained by the available resources, including human resources. One of the main themes of this chapter is the tension between change and constraint.

The first part of this chapter looks at the labour market in Britain in the aggregate – employment and unemployment trends over the 1980s. The second part of the chapter examines the quality of labour supply and demand in the context of the needs of the 1990s economy, while the final section offers some conclusions about the need for policy change of certain kinds.

TOWARDS FULL EMPLOYMENT OR RECESSION?

The results of the 1989 LFS (*Employment Gazette*, 1990a), summarized in Figure 2.1, show the British labour market's recovery in the late 1980s – a recovery which has since fallen back (see Chapter 3). Compared with 1979, which was the previous employment peak, employment first fell by roughly 2 million in the early 1980s, but subsequently grew by 3 million, so that the net increase in the 1980s was about a million, similar to that of the 1970s.

The course of unemployment over the decade is less easy to encapsulate because the definition of unemployment has been inconsistent and controversial. But it would not be greatly misleading to say that by 1989 it had fallen to around half of its peak level of 1983. Most of the employment gain, and unemployment fall, evident at the end of the 1980s, had taken place since the start of 1987. From June 1990 onwards unemployment rose sharply again so that the gains of the late 1980s were not as solid as political rhetoric of the time suggested. Consumption ran ahead of output in the late 1980s, partly funded by private dis-saving. High and rising inflation at the beginning of the 1990s led to an intensification of the regime of high interest rates and the early 1990s recession. How well had the 1980s experience prepared the British economy for this setback? Will recovery be long and painful, as in the 1980s, or relatively smooth and rapid? Will goverment policies remain much as they were throughout the 1980s/early 1990s?

A number of arguments can be found for a relative degree of optimism. Recent experience seems to show that injecting demand into the economy can still work, in terms of generating more employment and reducing unemployment, despite all that has been said against it by monetarists (for example, Brittan 1977). According to economic historians such as van der Wee (1986) and Madison (1982), demand management was abandoned too precipitately, and the impact of the oil shocks on the international economic order was overestimated by the Western governments. We can also turn to the example of Sweden, the European country which, over the 1970s and 1980s, has run its economy with most consistent effectiveness. There, the use of demand stimulation has always formed an important part of policy, despite the extreme openness of the economy. I would expect to see demand stimulation becoming more widely used as a policy instrument in the 1990s partly because policies, too, have their cycles of fashion. In addition, the Single European Market purports to offer a growth spurt around the middle of the decade in which Britain could reasonably expect to share (Cecchini 1988).

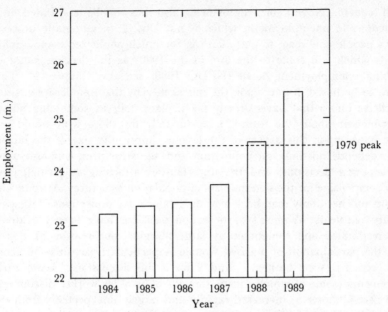

Figure 2.1a Employment, 1984–9 Great Britain (LFS)
Source: *Employment Gazette*, 1990a
Note: Excludes those on government schemes.

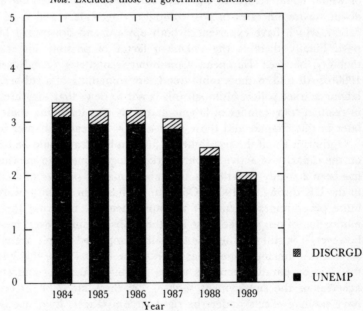

Figure 2.1b Unemployment, 1984–9 Great Britain (LFS)
Source: *Employment Gazette*, 1990a
Note: ILO definitions for unemployment and for discouraged workers.

25

Of course, growth in employment also has to be translated into reductions in unemployment, which is not always an automatic process. Many people now seem to place faith in the much-publicized demographic trends which will come to the fore in the 1990s as the decisive factor in pushing unemployment down (NEDO 1989; see also Chapter 9). This seems to be based in part upon the mistaken view that demography, since it reflects births that have already taken place, tells us something highly deterministic about the future. Unfortunately for those who would pin their hopes upon this aspect of the labour supply, the size of the labour force depends not only on population and age structures, but also upon participation decisions; and the uncertainties attaching to participation fully compensate for the determinism of population structures. Anyone who doubts this need only read back over the labour force projections of the past twenty-five years. Women's participation decisions have been repeatedly underestimated and sometimes by large margins; one reason for this is that the participation of married women is particularly sensitive to economic returns (see Chapters 7 and 9 for a full discussion). Again early retirements (some of which can be thought of as older worker discouragement; see Chapter 5) increased rapidly and largely unexpectedly from the mid-1970s. There is still scope for forecasts of women's participation rates to be too low; there is a large pool of economically inactive over-55s, many of whom could return to the fray; and there is considerable uncertainty about staying-on rates in post-compulsory secondary and third-level education, which have experienced both upward and downward blips in the past. Finally there is the unknown factor of possibly increased labour mobility between European Community countries (*Employment Gazette*, 1990b). All told, demographic trends are something of a rubber crutch for labour market policy, although this is not to deny that they are important in relation to a number of labour market issues, including some discussed later in this chapter and those discussed by Metcalf (Chapter 9).

Optimism about the possibility of full employment would be better based on the capacity of active labour market programmes and measures. There has been a steady growth of active labour market policies of a certain kind in the UK during the 1980s. Government has been drawn towards offering more programmes to combat unemployment by restoring the skills and motivation of people who have lost their jobs. Despite government pledges, however, it is still not the case that all unemployed people are offered such services. As unemployment has risen in the early 1990s, this has not been matched by parallel increases in the funding of training and employment agencies or the employment service. Yet these kinds of interventions do have positive effects under the right circumstances. Evidence is available that high-quality training for unemployed people is effective, though low-quality training is not (Payne 1990). Young people in long-term unemployment do appear to benefit from getting information about job openings

(White 1990). The Youth Training Scheme, for all its limitations, could be said to be better than no scheme (Bosworth and Hasluck 1989). Restart counselling interviews have had substantial effects imputed to the programme (Dicks and Hatch 1989; Layard 1989) though the results of direct research are still awaited. Active labour market measures can no longer be dismissed as merely a means of stirring the unemployed pool. Provided that the political priorities, and hence the funding, are right the lessons learned in the 1980s could provide the basis for better programmes and better results in the 1990s.

The measures outlined above all assume a background of reasonable levels of labour demand. They will not do, at least not on their own, when labour demand is very weak, as in the early 1990s. The most fundamental problems of the British economy seem to have remained with us as we enter the 1990s. In pride of place, there is the propensity to wage rigidity which in turn leads to persistent inflationary pressures. Indeed during the 1980s, Britain stood out from other advanced industrial countries for the extraordinary unresponsiveness of wages to the level of unemployment (see also Chapter 3). The best evidence for the general importance of wage fixing, in relation to national economic performance, comes from a large body of cross-national research conducted chiefly by political scientists and macrosociologists (Schmidt 1982; Crouch 1985; Bornschier 1989). This research has shown that there are long-term differences in national performance which have become particularly marked since 1973. Wage flexibility (the responsiveness of average wages to unemployment levels) has been shown to be strongly related to high levels of growth and low levels of inflation. However, from the point of view of active labour market interventions, it is vital to note that not all countries which achieve wage flexibility do so in the same ways.

The countries with high levels of wage flexibility are commonly divided into two groups: the Scandinavian countries and Austria on one hand, and Japan, Switzerland and the USA on the other. Quite detailed statistical evidence (for example, OECD 1989a) has been adduced to show that the two groups have highly contrasting features, with the remaining industrialized countries falling somewhere between. Scandinavia/Austria are generally referred to as the 'corporatist' economies, because of the strong central negotiating and planning mechanisms which they have established to achieve co-operation between the state, business, and trade unions on a wide range of economic policies including wage fixing. Japan, Switzerland and the USA are characterized as 'free-market' economies because of their low levels of unionization or large non-union sectors and because of the lack of government intervention in wage fixing. The two groups also differ markedly in the proportions of the labour force employed by the public sector and in other characteristics, including fiscal policies.

The corporatist and free-market economies, different though they are, can be thought of as sharing a certain consistency or coherence of political stance which is sanctioned by the long-term support of the electorate. By contrast the intermediate economies (for example, the UK, France, The Netherlands) acquire the unattractive label of 'inconsistent' or 'incoherent'. They have, for example, strong unions, but lack the institutions and the social consensus to get unions to put aside sectional interests. The result is that intermediate economies suffer wage rigidity (see OECD 1989a, Diagram 2.6A and B).

Since 1979 the policy of the UK government has been to shift the economy's institutions towards the free-market model (see Chapter 11 for a detailed discussion). It is now clear that, by the acid test of wage flexibility, this has not succeeded. High wage increases occurred throughout the 1980s and, in the final years of the decade, pulled away from the underlying rate of productivity. The availability of an unemployed pool, itself highly flexible in its willingness to change occupations and to work for reduced wages (Moylan, Millar and Cooke 1984; White and McRae 1989; Millar, Cooke and McLaughlin 1989; McLaughlin, Millar and Cooke 1989), appears to have had very little impact on the general trend of wages and hours. (See Chapter 3 for a discussion of theoretical perspectives on why this should be so.) Trade union membership appears to have changed only in a structural way (Gallie 1989; Edwards and Bain 1988) leaving underlying attitudes and allegiances unaffected. Moreover, union influence over wage determination appears to have increased both in the public sector and in small and medium-sized firms (Brown and Wadwhani 1990). Most fundamentally, employers themselves have shown few signs of wishing to break away from their traditional relations with trade unions. Indeed, I would argue that it is employers' own policies, rather than trade union pressures, which kept wages moving up during the 1980s (White 1991). Large manufacturing employers, in particular, have sought to develop policies of higher wages, higher productivity and higher labour force quality. Nor is it obvious that these policies should be discouraged, in a country trying to drag itself up to the productivity levels of its leading competitors.

Could all this change in the 1990s so that Britain finally cracks its wages problems? The idea that Britain is going to become a USA, a Japan or a Switzerland, in terms of how wages are fixed, now seems far-fetched. The effect of European integration, and of developments in the Social Charter (see Chapter 12), are more likely to increase worker protections and, given present wage fixing arrangements, to cement wage rigidity. Could Britain, and perhaps Western Europe in general, veer towards a Scandinavian corporatist approach to wage fixing? A Labour government in particular could well be attracted towards a Social Charter Mark II. The central organizations of both employers and trade unions are weak and this tells against a revitalization of corporatist policies. Yet institutions and cultures can be changed. Australia is an interesting example of a country which has made determined efforts to move towards a more centralized approach from an unpromising initial position (OECD 1988b).

On balance, however, by far the most likely scenario in this area remains one of 'no change'. This means that wage-rigidity and wage-push will remain persistent problems for the development of the British labour market. Employment growth will be less than would otherwise be the case, although it may still be sufficient given expanding external opportunities. The more worrying problem is that the resilience of the labour market will be limited. Britain has to place its hopes for the 1990s on a favourable environment for growth rather than on capacity to overcome adverse circumstances.

THE QUALITY OF LABOUR SUPPLY AND DEMAND

The second part of this chapter turns to qualitative aspects of labour supply and demand in Britain. It considers what the needs of the economy are likely to be in terms of levels of qualifications (that term being used in the broad sense). And it assesses the chances of meeting those needs, with education and training provision as now planned or under development.

There are several reasons for giving more weight to labour quality than has conventionally been the case in the past. Labour quality is likely to be closely related to wage-rigidity if higher-qualified groups are in short supply and substitutability between qualification levels is difficult or costly. Wage rigidity may be, at least in part, an expression of the incapacity of (many) workers to move to a higher occupational level. The willingness of British firms to make high wage settlements under conditions of high unemployment can be read in that way, especially as workers in long-term unemployment have been found to come chiefly from the less qualified sections of the labour force (or rather from those occupations which are generally low-qualified; see Chapter 4; White 1983; White and McRae 1989). One of the reasons for giving attention to labour quality is that improved labour supply may provide a way of outflanking the impasse of wage rigidity.

Labour quality has considerable importance, over and above its influence on wage fixing, for international economic competitiveness. Appreciation of this has grown during the past decade (Hayes and Fonda 1984; OECD 1989a) so that the assertion no longer seems controversial. To compete with other advanced industrial countries, an economy needs considerable powers of innovation, in services as well as in products, and the ability to provide high standards of quality. These competitive characteristics can best be achieved through investment in human resources.

Perhaps the most important reason for emphasizing the quality dimension of labour supply is its bearing on equity for individuals. Without an adequate preparation in terms of education and training, individuals will be placed at a disadvantage in relation to both opportunities and to economic hazards during their working lives (see Chapter 4).

The demand for labour quality

Demand for different sorts of labour over the next decade can be assessed partly by extrapolating the established trends and partly by considering the major developments likely to be continuing or taking place over the period. The trends are clear, although it must be emphasized that these represent the interaction of supply and demand rather than demand as such. The 1989 Labour Force Survey (*Employment Gazette*, 1990a) shows that nearly four-fifths of the employment growth in 1984–9 was attributable to non-manual occupations, and about one-half to what may loosely be called 'higher' occupations. The manual occupations accounted for a little over one-fifth of total employment growth; but most of that growth came in 1988–9 (see Figure 2.2) and its durability proved weak in the early 1990s.

Bearing in mind that most of the job losses of the late 1970s and early

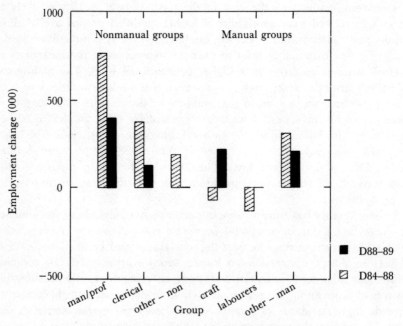

Figure 2.2 Occupation groups, 1984–9 Great Britain (LFS)
Source: Employment Gazette, 1990a

1980s were in manual occupations, one can see that the 1980s have continued the shift to the higher non-manual occupations identified in previous research on social mobility (for example, Goldthorpe *et al.* 1980). The growth in clerical occupations (half a million extra jobs) has also been surprisingly strong in view of earlier predictions that routine white-collar jobs would start to be cut back through information technology.

This picture suggests, at a rather simple level of inference, that the trend of demand for labour quality is in an upward direction. But one should not be over-hasty in accepting this inference. Sociologists examining social mobility over long time-periods and numerous countries have failed to identify any law of development of the occupational structure: changes of direction do occur from time to time (Ericson and Goldthorpe 1988).

That being the case, there is no substitute for a careful analysis of current and future influences upon the qualitative demand for labour. There are some salient developments which provide a reasonable basis for such an analysis. These were, for the most part, already having important effects during the 1980s or before. It is convenient, first of all, to list those which are likely to have substantial effects in the 1990s across all levels of the labour force:

1 changes in consumer tastes, especially those which reflect high and rising affluence in both domestic and major overseas markets;
2 European integration and the Single European Market; and
3 the impact of new technology and especially of information technology and of microelectronics.

In addition, there are two developments which have come to the forefront more recently; these have fairly definite implications for some groups/levels of workers, but their likely impact elsewhere is less clear:

1 the abatement of East/West hostilities, with its connotations of an extended European Community and a reduction in defence expenditure; and
2 the new priority likely to be given to national and international environmental protection.

These broad developments act upon labour quality requirements through their specific change implications – implications which vary between levels of qualification or occupation.

The dominant theme across all levels and occupations is the importance of developments in the markets for products and services. This is led by the revolution in consumer tastes brought about partly by rising affluence and partly by the technical capacity of industry to stimulate and satisfy a thirst for variety, innovation and quality. In short, the affluence of markets has led to the growing importance of non-price factors of competition. Recent research indicates that while price competition leads firms to cut

31

labour, non-price competition leads firms to introduce a much wider range of measures to increase the performance both of methods and of labour; and similarly non-price competitive pressures are related to certain types of 'skill shortages' (Wilkinson and White forthcoming). Rising standards of product quality exemplify these trends; the remarkable success of BS5750 (the British Standard for quality assurance systems) illustrates the potential impact of quality demands on firms' labour force policies.

Particularly important for labour quality at a more basic level is the continuously changing division of labour between households and services. Increasing income, coupled with the innovations of manufacturers, permits households to use consumer durables and DIY when they would previously have purchased a service (Gershuny 1978; Gershuny and Miles 1983). To re-create markets, services then have to innovate and raise quality standards. The evidence of this can be seen, by casual observation, in the construction industry, where much of the recent effort has moved up-market into fitted kitchens, conservatories, conversions, etc., and into higher levels of pre-fitments in new housing. In the past decade, not surprisingly, unskilled construction labour has neared extinction while there has been a remarkable intensification of skilled employment in the industry (Institute for Employment Research 1989). Similar up-market movement is surely required if Britain's tourist industry is not to go further into trade deficit (NEDO 1990).

In addition to non-price impacts, markets are becoming more extensive and more complex. The Single Internal Market, which in turn can be seen as part of the global evolution of markets, is stimulating businesses towards new marketing, financial and organizational strategies. This higher level of market complexity will create (is creating) an expanding demand for corporate managers, for sophisticated business services (law, finance, consultancy, property), and for product-market innovators. There are also substantial implications for technological organization and for the position of small businesses. The addition of an East European dimension promises greatly to increase the complexity of market strategies and organization by adding to the diversity of conditions faced by international business.

Cross-cutting these market developments are the continuing and intensifying effects of new technology, especially information technology (IT). Not long ago the effects of IT on demand for labour quality were controversial. The evidence of large-scale research now weighs heavily in favour of the view that IT requires increased skills at every level of the organization, in the great majority of organizations which introduce it or extend it (Daniel 1987). From more scattered indications, it is also becoming clear that the skill requirements are often less in the form of technical specialization or deepening, and more in the form of widening. They include such matters as literacy in machine operators, system understanding in managers, multi-skilling in maintenance, and the ability to communicate, coordinate, and think across boundaries in complex forms of co-operative innovation (von Hippel 1988; Rigg, Christie and White 1989). These observations help to explain why businessmen and women are now taking the lead in demanding reforms of education to provide broader, rather than academically specialized, capacities.

The conclusion from this brief review of the demand side is that the tendencies during the 1990s are likely to be predominantly towards increases in the qualification or quality requirements of labour. These quality requirements will operate within each of the main occupational or skill levels; higher, intermediate and basic. Early confirmation of the strongly rising trend within the most highly qualified group, in the early 1990s, is contained in the results of a recent survey of employers (Elias and Rigg 1990), although the 1990–1 recession may have imposed a temporary standstill.

The supply of labour quality

In discussing the supply of labour quality, I will deal explicitly with the three broad levels of qualifications or occupations already referred to, namely higher, intermediate and basic. In each case, the situation leading up to the beginning of the 1990s has to be taken into consideration in assessing the prospects for the 1990s.

The higher level

Britain's production of graduates and others with higher qualifications compares quite favourably with major competitors in Europe (OECD 1989a). Substantial expansion has taken place since around 1970. This means that the stock of highly qualified people is heavily weighted towards under-40s, which will be an advantage when faced with the 'demographic pinch' of the 1990s. During the 1980s continued growth took place, almost wholly through the polytechnics. In addition recent information from the Department of Education and Science suggests that there has been a strong surge of entrants to higher education at the end of the 1980s, leading to a bullish forecast for the 1990s (Report of an Interdepartmental Review 1990). Early results also suggest that the proportion of young people going forward to A-levels and hence to higher education may increase considerably as a result of the introduction of the GCSE examination. A breaking down of the rigidities caused by A-levels themselves, for instance through wider use of AS-levels and BTECs, will doubtless contribute further to this increase.

All things considered, the British higher education system seems well on the way to delivering the doubling of graduate numbers which has been called for by some prescriptions (Ball 1989; White 1988b), if not by 2000, then by 2010. There could nevertheless be some shortfall during the 1990s, either in aggregate terms or in particular sections of the higher-qualified labour market. A temporary shortfall would not be a bad thing, however, if it resulted in employers paying higher salaries and improving their utilization of human resources; both would probably help to assure the longer-term growth of supply, and there is evidence that both are under way (Elias and Rigg 1990).

The main anxiety concerns the supply of engineers and other technical and scientific specialists to manufacturing industry. During the 1980s, the numbers employed within this group have remained static while the reported level of shortages has risen; special funding to the higher education system by government and by large employers has failed to sustain a growth in the numbers of these specialist graduates. Manufacturing faces increasing competition from service industries, particularly financial and business services, in the recruitment of numerate graduates. Meanwhile the innovative performance of British manufacturing, outside of pharmaceuticals and one or two specialized branches, has been declining (Narin and Olivastro 1987). A lack of technical strength in manufacturing could, by the end of a decade of increasing openness to European competition, affect employment prospects at all levels.

Other anxieties concern the supply of graduates to smaller enterprises and, in the longer run, to the public sector. Smaller enterprises needing graduates to a large extent rely on obtaining them from large firms after they acquire experience. If, in response to a tightening market for graduates, large firms considerably strengthen their retention of graduates, then small firms will be adversely affected. As for the public sector, it has already levelled out its demand for graduates in the 1980s, and is clearly at some disadvantage in a competition with the private sector. In the long run, the supply of qualified labour throughout the economy is clearly dependant upon adequate staffing in education at all levels. At present, however, the longer planning horizons of the public sector and its greater use of policies such as the employment of qualified women returners, are enabling it to hold its own (Elias and Rigg 1990).

Basic and intermediate levels

While there is reason for optimism in the case of higher qualification levels, Britain's chief problem has been, and continues to be, the qualification level for basic skills. That problem expresses itself in:

1 a high proportion only completing a basic education to the age of 16 (OECD 1989a);
2 a large proportion of 16-year-old school-leavers having low educational attainments; and

3 a low proportion of these early school-leavers going on to obtain vocational qualifications.

A crucial question for the 1990s is what progress is likely to be made with this problem.

To make a qualitative projection for the 1990s, it is necessary as before to begin with the 1980s. At the beginning of the 1980s, the picture was bleak. Apprenticeships, the main path to qualifications for (male) 16-year-old school-leavers, had all but disappeared. There was no alternative scheme for school-leavers to obtain vocational qualifications. Youth unemployment was rising to mass proportions. Against that background, progress was made during the 1980s. The Youth Training Scheme (YTS) absorbed youth unemployment, provided a route to vocational qualifications which did not, at least formally, depend on educational attainment, and propped up the remnants of the apprenticeship system. It also acted as a vehicle for some radical and controversial innovations in vocational training methodology, such as work-based learning and certification by competence. By the second half of the 1980s, around half of 16-year-old school-leavers were entering YTS. In addition, there was a considerable increase in the proportions staying on at school or going to further education, to pursue non-advanced education for a time.

These achievements, however, did little to dent the more fundamental problems of qualification at basic level. The proportions leaving school without any qualification, or with only the lowest level of qualification, altered little over the decade. Early indications are that these attainment levels were not improved by the introduction of the GCSE examination. The effectiveness of YTS was impaired by high rates of leaving before completion, which in turn reflected a preference for employment opportunities over the achievement of qualifications (Grey and King 1986). Although no full account is yet available, it might be estimated that YTS led no more than 30 per cent of its entrants, or 15 per cent of the age cohort, to vocational qualifications. Furthermore, YTS schemes varied in quality, and there is strong evidence that those entering better schemes and attaining qualifications also tended to be those with relatively high prior educational attainments (Roberts and Parsell n.d.).

At the beginning of the 1990s, we have apparently reached another watershed, and there is a new set of vocational training strategems beginning. In the tight youth labour markets of the late 1980s in the South, YTS had shrunk and the old pattern of immediate employment at 16 has been reasserted; this similarly led to a contraction of the non-advanced staying-on rate (this emerges particularly clearly from the different development of the youth labour market in Swindon by comparison with Kirkcaldy, Sheffield and Liverpool, as described in Roberts, Parsell and Connolly n.d.; see also Raffe and Willms 1989). The impending demographic reduction of the inflow of 16-year-olds indicates a still tighter juvenile labour market; indeed by the end of the 1990s the economically active 16–24 age group is expected to have shrunk by more than one million (*Employment Gazette*, 1990b). The outlook, if no action is taken, would probably be a virtual demise of YTS except in the most economically depressed areas; the chances of creating a better qualified labour force would recede.

However, new actions are being taken. YTS is becoming YT, a less rigidly defined training resource, delivered to suit local conditions by the Training and Enterprise Councils (TECs). The performance of YT, and TECs, is to be judged in terms of outputs, that is of what they deliver. Flexibility is to be welcomed; the value of an output-based approach will depend upon what the output targets are. In parallel, the work of the National Council for Vocational Qualifications (NCVQ) is continuing, now firmly committed to 'Level Two' as the norm for a basic vocational qualification, and to work-place competence testing as one of the chief routes to certification. Finally there is the adoption of vocational training vouchers which permit young people to 'purchase' training either from their employers or from providers such as further education colleges, and hence give young people a degree of choice and control (CBI 1989).

All these developments are commendable and constructive, but the bottom line is whether basic qualifications will rise in the way that competitive pressures require. One's answer to this question will depend on one's explanation of the underlying problem. I have argued that the problem of basic-level qualification does not lie within vocational training systems, but within education itself. At the same time, the difficulty in raising educational standards at the basic level lies not within education institutions, but within the institutions and expectations of the youth labour market. Training cannot make up for the deficiencies of education, but neither can education solve its own problems without the support of the labour market. The reason for this is that young people's motivation to achieve qualifications depends upon their seeing a chain of connection between qualifications, training and worthwhile jobs (White 1989; see also Gambetta 1987). What is required, therefore, is an integrated set of policies for education, training and the labour market.

Low educational attainments among a substantial proportion of its clientele have made it virtually impossible for the YTS to deliver high vocational qualification levels. For example, it has been estimated that 18 per cent of YTS entrants have no educational qualifications (Gray, Jesson, Pattie and Sime 1989). As I have noted above, YTS has tended to lead to worthwhile vocational qualifications for those who had already made a good start in education. Making vocational training into a three-year scheme, an idea with the support of government, employers, providers and trade unions, will only marginally alter the position; a serious three-year training scheme cannot be based upon low educational attainments. To put this in perspective, about half of British 16-year-old school-leavers would not obtain entry to the German apprenticeship system. Progress within the pre-16 educational system is, therefore, essential for the development of more successful vocational training.

Similarly, desirable though it is to make increased and better-quality provision for adult training, the prior educational level may set practical limits on what can be achieved by this path. There are numerous indications that adult training increased during the 1980s, but this was mainly received by those with relatively higher qualification and skill levels (Rigg 1989; Keep 1989). A poor basic level of education for an economy limits what it can achieve through adult training, while a higher basic level gives it far more flexibility to use adult training and gain further advantages.

The central motivational problem for the educational system has been, and continues to be, the high juvenile wages available for entrants to the labour market (Jones 1984). These wage rates, a product of the post-war era (Wells 1983), inevitably make young people who discount the long term, careless of school qualifications and anxious to get into a job at the first opportunity. They also contribute to employers' reluctance to incur training costs. Other disincentives are created by the lack of financial support for those who remain in education post-16 (Micklewright, Pearson and Smith 1989); the lack of any entry requirements to YTS; and the absence of any conditions linking YTS funding, for individuals and employers, to progress with training. Recent research, moreover, has shown how, during the mid-1980s, school-leavers had to face more complex transitions into the labour market (with YTS and other options) and also much more uncertainty about a lasting job being the eventual outcome (Roberts and Parsell n.d.; Grey and King 1986). Under these circumstances, it was not surprising that young people grabbed at the chance of a job whenever it arose rather than sticking things out for a qualification.

The labour supply conditions of the 1990s, moreover, with the large reduction in the stock of 16–24-year-olds, will increase competition among employers to offer more juvenile jobs and to increase juvenile wages. This will weaken the attraction to young people of seeking qualifications and tempt some employers to cut training costs yet again.

The prognosis for the 1990s on present form, accordingly, is one of rather modest improvement in the qualifications at basic level. These improvements are likely to consist of rather little at the basic educational level, but probably accompanied by wider distribution of moderate (say, Level Two) vocational qualifications – already strongly criticized in some quarters as being inadequate (Prais 1989). Unlike the position with regard to higher level qualification, the supply to employers will not be enhanced by the existing stock of qualified labour at the basic level. On the contrary, the disruption caused by the economic recession in the early and mid-

1980s means that the basic qualification level among 20–30-year-olds is particularly low.

The analysis of basic-level qualifications and trends also has implications for the intermediate level. Weaknesses at this level have been noted by commentators as frequently as those at basic level. Strengthening supply at this level would not only be valuable in itself but would also contribute to an easing of the pressures of demand on the higher education system. Opportunities for expanding provision seem ready and waiting, since further education advanced courses are in many cases filled much below capacity and often suffer from high drop-out rates. However, successful use of intermediate level education depends upon the prior educational attainments of entrants. If the supply from basic education is not of sufficient quality to make possible a high-quality basic training scheme, then it can hardly be sufficient for an expansion of intermediate-level education and training. On the contrary, with higher education expanding into the ranks of those who would formerly have gone to intermediate level qualifications, it is the latter which will be squeezed. The growth of intermediate level education, training and skills would best be served by a raising of basic educational standards and hence the creation of a substantially larger pool of ability. As things stand, the numbers simply do not add up to an expansion at this level.

Could a further political initiative emerge during the 1990s, to tackle the issue of motivation through an integrated set of policies for education, training and the youth labour market? This seems far more feasible than a similar initiative in relation to wage fixing. The issues are less obviously politicized and less entrenched and the CBI and TUC have shown themselves to be close together in their thinking about the training element. It is even conceivable that, faced with increasing international competitive pressures in the quality dimension, employers themselves will move decisively away from employing underqualified teenagers.

CONCLUSIONS

Quantitatively, there are some grounds for optimism that, during the 1990s, labour supply and demand could become well balanced. But this would have to depend on a favourable external economic context unless more active labour market intervention is adopted by government. Under benign conditions, Britain's problems of wage rigidity and inflationary pressures would restrain growth but not too seriously. Under recessionary conditions, however, they would result in substantial lack of resilience. The prospects for tackling wage rigidity do not appear good since large employers, as well as trade unions and employed workers, have their reasons for not restraining wages. Institutionally the path seems blocked both in the direction of a US-style free market arrangement and in the direction of a

Swedish-style corporatist arrangement. Meanwhile, we are left a system with free-market leanings, as the result of three Conservative administrations, but now under pressure from our European partners, as well as from other political forces within, to move towards semi-corporatism.

Government interventions to improve the quality of labour supply might offer an alternative path to a more flexible, less unemployment-prone, economy. Apart from that, an analysis of some major developments, and of their implications for the demand side, suggest how important increases in labour quality will be for competitiveness in the 1990s. Consumer tastes, the Single Market, and new technologies all point in the same direction.

What improvements in the supply of labour quality can be expected? At the level of higher qualifications for higher occupations the prospects for considerable expansion appear to be good. Britain already has considerable strengths at this level, and all the trends seem positive. Some shortfalls may occur in the 1990s but this should help, rather than hinder, further longer-term expansion.

At the levels of basic and intermediate qualifications, the conclusions cannot be so optimistic. Basic levels of qualifications are low, and this is likely to handicap all efforts to improve vocational training, as it handicapped YTS in the 1980s. The recent policy initiatives of 1990–1 do not confront the central problems of motivating young people at school, and after, to improve their levels of qualifications. The prognosis is for continuing low basic-level qualifications. This will also hinder the expansion of intermediate level qualifications, especially in combination with the expansion of the higher level. There is a clear need for new policies which integrate education, training and youth labour market provisions and practices. Even if the 1990s turn out to be, as many speculate, a decade of growth and opportunity, failure to address this fundamental need for new integrated policies in education, training and the labour market will demand a heavy price in the early 2000s or whenever the next major recession arrives.

NOTE AND REFERENCES

Note

1 This chapter has been facilitated by work previously carried out as part of the PSI 2010 Project funded by the Joseph Rowntree Foundation and a consortium of government departments and companies.

References

Ball, C. (1989) *Aim Higher: widening access to higher education*, London: Royal Society of Arts.
Bornschier, V. (1989) 'Legitimacy and comparative economic success at the core

of the world system: an exploratory study', *European Sociological Review*, 5, 3: 215–30.

Bosworth, D. and Hasluck, C. (1989) *YTS and the Labour Queue: an econometric analysis of the labour market effects of participation on the YTS*, Sheffield: Training Agency Research and Development Series, No. 54.

Brittan, S. (1977) *The Economic Consequences of Democracy*, London: Temple Smith.

Brown, W. and Wadwhani, S. (1990) 'The economic effects of industrial relations legislation since 1979', *National Institute Economic Review* No. 131, February 1990.

CBI (1989) *Towards a Skills Revolution*, London: CBI Vocational Education and Training Task Force.

Cecchini, P. (1988) *The European Challenge 1992: the benefits of a Single Market*, London: Wildwood House.

Crouch, C. (1985) 'Conditions for Trade Union Wage Restraint', in Lindberg, L. and Maier, C. (eds), *The Politics of Inflation and Economic Stagnation*, Washington: Brookings Institution.

Crowley-Bainton, T. and White, M. (1990) *Employing Unemployed People: how employers gain*, Sheffield: Employment Service.

Daniel, W. (1987) *Workplace Industrial Relations and Technical Change*, London: Frances Pinter.

Dicks, M. and Hatch, N. (1989) *The Relationship between Employment and Unemployment*, London: Bank of England.

Edwards, P. and Bain, G. (1988) 'Why are unions becoming more popular? Trade Unions and public opinion in Britain', *British Journal of Industrial Relations*, 26, 3: 311–26.

Elias, P. and Rigg, M. (eds) (1990) *The Demand for Graduates*, London: PSI.

Employment Gazette (1990a) '1989 Labour Force Survey preliminary results', April 1990.

—— (1990b) 'Labour Force Outlook to 2001', April 1990.

Ericson, R. and Goldthorpe, J. (1988) 'Trends in class mobility: a test of hypotheses against the European experience', CASMIN-Working Paper No. 13, Institut fur Sozialwissenschaften, Universitat Mannheim.

Gallie, D. (1989) 'Trade Union Allegiance and Decline in British Urban Labour Markets', ESRC Social Change and Economic Life Initiative, Working Paper 9, Nuffield College, Oxford.

Gambetta, D. (1987) *Were They Pushed or Did They Jump?*, Cambridge: Cambridge University Press.

Gershuny, J. (1978) *After Industrial Society: the emerging self-service economy*, London: Macmillan.

Gershuny, J. and Miles, I. (1983) *The New Service Economy: the transformation of employment in industrial societies*, London: Frances Pinter.

Goldthorpe, J. with Llewellyn, C. and Payne, C. (1980) *Social Mobility and Class Structure in Modern Britain*, Oxford: Clarendon Press.

Grey, D. and King, S. (1986) *The YTS: the first three years*, London: MSC Research and Development No. 35.

Grey, J., Jesson, D., Pattie, C. and Sime, N. (1989) 'Education and Training Opportunities in the Inner City: the experiences of 16–19 year olds', Educational Research Centre, Sheffield University, mimeo.

Hayes, C. and Fonda, N. (1984) *Competence and Competition*, London: NEDO/MSC.

Institute for Employment Research (1989) *Review of the Economy and Employment: occupational assessment*, Coventry: University of Warwick.

Jones, I. (1989) 'Pay relativities and the provision of training', Conference Paper,

NEDO Policy Seminar on Incentives for the Low Paid, mimeo, IRRU, University of Warwick.

Keep, E. (1989) 'Training for the Low Paid', Conference Paper, NEDO Policy Seminar on Incentives for the Low Paid, mimeo, IRRU, University of Warwick.

Layard, R. (1989) 'European Unemployment: cause and cure', Centre for Labour Economics, Discussion Paper 368, London: LSE.

McLaughlin, E., Millar, J. and Cooke, K. (1989) *Work and Welfare Benefits*, Aldershot: Avebury.

Maddison, A. (1982) *Phases of Capitalist Development*, Oxford: Oxford University Press.

Micklewright, J., Pearson, M. and Smith, S. (1989) 'Has Britain an Early School-leaving Problem?', *Fiscal Studies*, 10, 1: 1–16.

Millar, J., Cooke, K. and McLaughlin, E. (1989) 'The Employment Lottery: risk and social security benefits', *Policy and Politics*, 17, 1: 75–81.

Moylan, S., Millar, J. and Davies, R. (1984) *For Richer, For Poorer: the DHSS Cohort Study of Unemployed Men*, London: DHSS/HMSO.

Narin, F. and Olivastro, D. (1987) *Identifying Areas of Strength and Excellence in UK technology*, London: Department of Trade and Industry.

NEDO (1989) *Defusing the Demographic Time-bomb*, London: NEDO.

OECD (1988a) *OECD Economic Surveys: Sweden 1986/87*, Paris: OECD.

—— (1988b) *OECD Economic Surveys: Australia 1987/88*, Paris: OECD.

—— (1989a) *Economies in Transition: structural adjustment in OECD countries*, Paris: OECD.

—— (1989b) *OECD Employment Outlook 1989*, Paris: OECD.

Payne, J. (1990) 'Effectiveness of adult off-the-job skills training', *Employment Gazette*, March 1990.

Prais, S. (1989) 'How Europe would see the new British initiative for standardising vocational qualifications', *National Economic Review*, 129, August 1989.

Raffe, D. (1979) 'The "Alternative Route" reconsidered: part-time further education and social mobility in England and Wales', *Sociology*, 13, 1: 47–73.

Raffe, D. and Willms, J. (1989) 'Schooling the discouraged worker: local labour market effects on educational participation', *Sociology*, 23, 4: 559–81.

Report of an Interdepartmental Review (1990) *Highly Qualified People: Supply and demand*, London: HMSO.

Rigg, M. (1989) *Training in Britain: individuals' perspectives*, London: HMSO.

Rigg, M., Christie, I. and White, M. (1989) *Advanced Polymers and Composites: creating the key skills*, Sheffield: Training Agency.

Roberts, K. and Parsell, G. (not dated) 'The Stratification of Youth Training', ESRC 16-19 Initiative Occasional Papers No. 11, Social Statistics Research, City University, London.

Roberts, K. and Parsell, G. (not dated) 'Opportunity Structures and Career Trajectories from age 16–19', ESRC 16-19 Initiative Occasional Papers, No.1, Social Statistics Research, City University, London.

Roberts, K., Parsell, G. and Connolly, M. (not dated) 'Britain's Economic Recovery, the New Demographic Trend and Young People's Transition into the Labour Market', ESRC 16-19 Initiative Occasional Papers No. 8, Social Statistics Research, City University, London.

Schmidt, M. (1982) *Wohlfahrtsstaatliche Politik unter burgerlichen und sozialdemokratischen Regierungen*, Frankfurt: Campus.

van der Wee, H. (1986) *Prosperity and Upheaval: the world economy 1945–1980*, New York: Viking.

von Hippel, E. (1988) *The Sources of Innovation*, Oxford: Oxford University Press.

Wells, W. (1983) *The Relative Pay and Employment of Young People*, London: Department of Employment Research Paper No. 42.

White, M. (1983) *Long-term Unemployment and Labour Markets*, London: PSI.

—— (1988) 'Educational Policy and Economic Goals', *Oxford Review of Economic Policy*, 4, 3: 1–20.

—— (1989) 'Motivating Education and Training', *Policy Studies*, 10, 1: 29–40.

—— (1990) 'Information et chomage des jeunes', *Sociologie du Travail*, 32, 4: 529–41.

—— (1991) *Against Unemployment*, London: PSI.

White, M. and McRae, S. (1989) *Young Adults in Long-term Unemployment*, London: PSI.

Wilkinson, F. and White, M. (forthcoming) 'The Responses of Employers to Product Market Pressures', in J. Rubery and F. Wilkinson (eds) *Employers' Policies* (provisional title), Oxford: Oxford University Press.

3

AN ECONOMY OF UNEMPLOYMENT?

Richard Jackman[1]

INTRODUCTION

The title of this chapter poses the paradox of continuing high levels of unemployment in an economy even though, at times, the demand for labour has been buoyant. Why, in the absence of a general deficiency of demand, does the labour market not appear to 'work' to create job opportunities for all who want them? Or why, as Robert Hall put it in the title of a paper twenty years ago, is the unemployment rate so high at full employment (Hall 1970)? At the time Hall was writing, the unemployment rate in the United States was 5 per cent, not very different from the average American unemployment rate of 5.5 per cent recorded in 1990. Going even further back, one may recall that in the late 1930s, Keynes regarded 6 per cent as the minimum unemployment rate safely attainable through demand expansion alone, with progress to lower levels of unemployment having to depend on reducing structural imbalances and the like (Keynes 1937).

Economists have two main answers to the question why an efficiently functioning labour market does not 'clear', to leave no one unemployed and no job vacancies, in the way that the market for oranges or ICI shares clears:

1 The heterogeneity of jobs and workers creates incentives for careful matching of the one to the other. Unemployed workers do not apply for every available job nor do firms take on any applicant. Each side may search actively for what they want, or, failing that, may at least wait until something or someone suitable turns up. During this matching process jobs are temporarily vacant and workers temporarily unemployed. There is nothing inefficient in this outcome. Nor, contrary to what is sometimes alleged (Beveridge 1944), need it imply that in equilibrium the number of vacant jobs ought to be equal to the number of unemployed workers. If the characteristics of jobs differ to a greater extent than the productivity of workers, it will be sensible for workers to search for longer than firms, and so there will be more unemployed people than job vacancies (Reder 1969).

43

2 Unlike commodities or financial assets, people have preferences and they do not necessarily want to work continuously. Thus, people may choose to take casual, temporary or part-time work, precisely because they do not wish to work all the time. When one job comes to an end they may look for another, though not necessarily with great urgency. In the United States, arguments of this type have been used to explain why youth unemployment rates are so much higher than those of older workers (Clark and Summers 1979).

The post-war performance of the United States labour market does give support to the idea of there being a relatively stable underlying equilibrium unemployment rate, in the 5–6 per cent range, with the fluctuations in unemployment around this level normally small and short-lived. Were one asked to explain the 6.8 per cent unemployment rate in the United States at the time of writing (October 1991), up from 5.5 per cent a year ago, one might easily argue that it represents the impact of a small recession superimposed on an underlying equilibrium in the labour market, with the main causes of unemployment those listed above.

This type of explanation seems inadequate for the British economy. Unlike the United States, though in common with many European countries, Britain has found it possible to achieve very much lower unemployment rates for long periods of time. If, in the twenty-five years after the war, the unemployment rate was generally less than 2 per cent and never as high as 3 per cent, why need it now (October 1991) be 8.5 per cent? Or, from a different perspective, if unemployment had apparently settled down at a level in excess of 3 million during the 1980s, how could it have fallen so sharply, to only 1.6 million by spring 1990? And does the current (1991) sharp increase suggest a return to 3 million unemployed, or does the fact that inflation is now falling mean that the current level of unemployment (of around 2.5 million, late 1991) is above the equilibrium rate?

How are these major medium- to long-term fluctuations in unemployment to be explained? The approach I take is the following. By way of background, I first note how the level of unemployment has changed since the 1987 election in Britain and of how perceptions of what is possible have changed more or less in step. The next section of the chapter offers some explanations for this recent history, drawing on recent theories concerning the causes of persistence or 'hysteresis' in unemployment. The main elements of such theories involve the role of insider power in wage bargaining, the problem of the labour market ineffectiveness of the long-term unemployed, and structural imbalances in the labour market. Though none of these theories is entirely satisfactory, taken together they do suggest why the spontaneous forces equilibrating the labour market after a shock may be very weak.

The final section discusses prospects and policies. My conclusion is that any sustainable progress in bringing down unemployment cannot be based on more skilful macro-economic management but must depend on a serious commitment to well-designed supply-side policies to reduce long-term and structural unemployment. Many existing policies can be expected to have a helpful effect, but much remains to be done.

BACKGROUND: THE UNITED KINGDOM LABOUR MARKET 1987–91

At the time of the General Election in May 1987 the number of people registered as unemployed was 2.99 million. At the time this figure was regarded almost as commendable: unemployment had fallen for eleven months in succession and the May 1987 count was the first below three million since June 1983. Nevertheless the prospects for further reductions in unemployment at that time were thought negligible. Most forecasting groups projected a stabilization of the number registered as unemployed at around 2.9–3 million over the medium term.

In the 1987 election campaign, both opposition parties put forward ambitious programmes of direct job-creation measures to tackle the perceived problem of persistent mass unemployment. Both parties stressed that their policies involved selective and carefully costed interventions rather than indiscriminate demand expansion which might well have been branded as inflationary. Labour's plan, which involved higher spending on the infrastructure, health, education and the social services, together with an expansion of training, was projected to reduce unemployment by one million over two years at a gross cost of around £6 billion a year. The Alliance programme similarly involved public spending and training initiatives but also recruitment subsidies to encourage private employers to take on unemployed people. The package was particularly focused on improving prospects for the long-term unemployed. It was costed at around £4 billion a year and projected to reduce unemployment by one million over three years.

In the out-turn, no such direct employment-creation measures were adopted by the Conservative government elected yet the fall in unemployment exceeded even the ambitious targets of these opposition plans. By May 1989 the number registered as unemployed was 1.80 million, a fall of 1.19 million over the two years since May 1987, and by May 1990 the figure was 1.61 million (or 5.7 per cent of the labour force). But by May 1991 unemployment had again risen to 2.24 million, so that the Conservative government's achievement in reducing unemployment, though greater than anyone had thought possible, turned out also to have been more ephemeral.

Clearly the immediate cause of the rapid fall in unemployment was the equally rapid, and largely unanticipated, growth of demand. This 'Lawson boom' was the result not of expansionary government policy so much as of a very rapid growth of consumer spending financed by easy credit and supported by rising asset prices. Fiscal policy had in fact been quite tight over the period (the surplus in the government budget being the result of the higher tax revenues generated by rapid growth). Monetary policy (as measured by real interest rates) had also been tight with the exception of the contentious period in early 1988 when interest rates were held down in an attempt to prevent an excessive appreciation of the pound against the Deutschmark.

But was the fall in unemployment between 1987 and 1990 simply the product of a temporary and unsustainable boom in demand? As the spending boom has come to an end, as a result of restrictive monetary policies and falling real asset prices, unemployment has again been rising sharply.

In spring 1990, as in 1987 when unemployment was 3 million, neither government nor private-sector forecasters were projecting any very large change in unemployment (in either direction). In their immediate post-budget forecast, for example, Goldman Sachs (the most sophisticated and successful of City forecasting groups) projected unemployment to rise from 1.65 million in the fourth quarter of 1989 to 1.68 million by the fourth quarter of 1990, and then fall again to 1.66 million in the fourth quarter of 1991. While other forecasting groups were more pessimistic (for example, the National Institute) none predicted more than a marginal increase and certainly not a return to 3 million.

During the first six months of 1990, there was little evidence that the rate of unemployment was unsustainably low. If that had been the case, the labour market would have been seen as a source of inflationary pressures within the economy. Forecasting groups would have been projecting either a rapid acceleration of inflation or a significant rise in unemployment to contain wage pressure.

Even when unemployment was at its lowest, in the spring of 1990, other labour market indicators cast doubt on the idea that the labour market was overheating. The number of vacancies was below 200,000, and historically periods of demand-driven inflation have always been associated with vacancies well in excess of 200,000. The proportion of firms reporting shortages of unskilled labour was below 5 per cent, and though this was high for the 1980s, it was well below the average of the past thirty years. Shortages of skilled labour have been more of a problem. Nearly 25 per cent of firms now report shortages of skilled labour, the highest figure since 1973, though below the average of the 1960s (see Figure 3.1). The underlying index of average earnings, which had grown at a steady rate of about 7.5 per cent per year from 1983 to 1987 increased to 9 per cent by the end of 1988, to 9.5 per cent in the first months of 1990, and peaked at 10.25 per cent in July 1990. This reflects the rapid growth in demand for

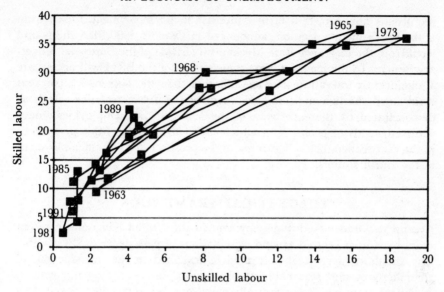

Figure 3.1 Percentage of firms reporting labour shortage in Britain, 1963–91
Source: CBI Industrial Trends Surveys

labour during 1988 (when vacancies topped 250,000 for the first time since 1979).

Even if the labour market was subdued, there were other sources of inflationary pressure. The headline increase in the retail price index during 1990 was largely the consequence of higher interest rates and various fiscal decisions, in particular the policies surrounding the introduction of the poll-tax. The underlying increase in price inflation was in large part due to a decline in productivity growth, the reasons for which are not entirely clear, and which may not persist. These faster rates of wage and price inflation would clearly get built into people's expectations and make a return to the lower inflation rates of the mid-1980s more difficult to achieve, but conditions in the labour market of themselves seemed unlikely to set off an inflationary spiral.

In summary then the inflationary pressures in the UK economy in 1990 appear to have derived from the financial markets, initially from the demand effects of credit deregulation and subsequently from the 'cost' effects of high interest rates. The labour market does not appear to have been an independent source of inflationary pressure, and this in turn suggests that the rate of unemployment at that time was not unsustainably low.

The breaking of the credit boom in 1990 has led to a sharp fall in demand and a sharp rise in unemployment. As a result, in 1991, wage and price inflation are both falling and this gives support to the view that unemployment in 1991 is above its equilibrium level. None the less forecast-

47

ing groups now project a further increase in unemployment. One reason is the government's decision, announced in October 1990, that the pound would join the Exchange Rate Mechanism (ERM) of the European Monetary System. In the medium term, membership of the ERM will necessitate a significantly lower rate of wage inflation than the floor of 7.5 per cent maintained throughout the worst years of the 1980s recession. And, as demonstrated by the experience of the 1980s, high unemployment, once achieved, tends to persist. I discuss some of the causes of this persistence in the next section, before returning to the prospects for UK unemployment in the fourth section.

THEORETICAL FRAMEWORK

Attempts to understand unemployment in the United Kingdom in recent years have been centred around explanations of persistence or 'hysteresis'. The standard macro-economic model, described in the introduction, of an underlying and reasonably stable equilibrium rate of unemployment, deviations from which are typically small and self-correcting, simply fails to accord with the experience of Britain and of most other European countries. The sharp changes in unemployment that have been observed cannot plausibly be explained in terms of sharp jumps in the factors affecting the underlying equilibrium rate. The enormous rise in unemployment at the beginning of the 1980s, for example, was common to all sectors, regions and occupations. It was clearly the result of restrictive monetary policies leading to a huge appreciation of the exchange rate. Likewise, the decline in unemployment around 1988 is clearly attributable, as noted above, to a consumer spending boom. Not only is it difficult to point to possible supply-side factors that could have had so enormous an effect in so short a space of time, but if the change in unemployment had been caused by an adverse supply-side shock we would have expected to see inflation rising in the early 1980s as unemployment rose, as had happened in 1974–5. If the fall in unemployment at the end of the decade had been caused by positive supply-side factors it would have been accompanied by falling inflation rates rather than by an increase in inflationary pressure.

Equally, however, we cannot simply regard the observed levels of unemployment as continuing deviations from some stable underlying equilibrium. Even with unemployment in excess of three million people between 1982 and 1987, money wages rose steadily at 7.5 per cent per year. If the labour market were in acute disequilibrium, a clear sign of it should be a continuing tendency for money wage increases to decline as shown in 1981 and again in 1991. Without a decline in the growth rate of money wages, the 'automatic' self-correcting mechanisms of the market cannot even start to work. So the key theoretical question is what enables the labour market apparently to settle down in a sort of quasi-equilibrium which seems to be determined primarily by the current unemployment rate and without much reference to any underlying long-run equilibrium. Three types of factors have been suggested in this context:

1 the 'insider' power of wage bargainers;
2 the ineffectiveness of the long-term unemployed; and
3 structural imbalances.

Insider power

The term 'insider power' derives from the work of Lindbeck and Snower (for example, 1988) who have stressed that wages are determined with the interests of current employees ('insiders') only taken into account. The unemployed ('outsiders') have minimal influence on wage determination because the insiders can effectively prevent them from competing for their jobs in conditions of excess supply in the labour market. Lindbeck and Snower focus on the mechanisms insiders can use to insulate themselves from competition (for example, harrassment or threats of non-co-operation with new recruits). The economic consequences of such behaviour have been elegantly modelled by Blanchard and Summers (1986).

The crucial point is that insiders will choose to fix wages at the highest level consistent with their continued employment. If this idea were taken literally, and there were no uncertainty and no labour turnover, the level of employment would never change. Those in work would keep their jobs, and those out of work would never get a job because wages would be set such that each firm had reason neither to reduce its labour force nor to take on new workers.

In practice, of course, there is uncertainty and wage bargainers may not anticipate economic developments very well. For example, the recession of the early 1980s may have been unexpectedly severe, and was therefore not fully taken into account in wage settlements. As a result, firms were forced to lay workers off. But in subsequent rounds of wage bargaining, only those who kept their jobs were represented so employment remained at the lower level even after the unexpected deflation had come to an end.

Similarly an unexpected boost to demand would cause employment to rise, and this again would be permanent, because people taken into employment would then become insiders and wages thereafter would be set to preserve their jobs as well as those of the original workforce. This again seems to fit in with the interpretation of the current evidence set out in the previous section.

While the exact details of the various insider/outsider models are not important, the main underlying ideas do have force. They are:

1 that unemployment affects wages through the fear that those in work

have of losing their jobs rather than through the threat posed to existing employees from competition from the unemployed, and

2 that the risk of job loss to existing workers is not very great except when unemployment is rising sharply. Even when unemployment is high, as long as it is not rising most workers can regard their jobs as secure and the level of unemployment is thus not an important influence on their wage claims.

There are none the less two pieces of evidence which seem at odds with the general thrust of the insider/outsider approach.

1 In micro-economic (panel data) studies of firms, it is possible to examine the effect on wages of (i) lagged employment within the firm and (ii) the unemployment rate in the outside labour market. The evidence is that outside unemployment has a powerful effect whereas lagged inside employment has a weak effect, if any at all (Nickell and Kong 1988; Nickell and Wadhwani 1990). Thus, there is little evidence that unions moderate wage claims in firms where employment is high in order to secure their members' jobs.

2 There has been huge movement of the unemployment–vacancy (u/v) curve in most countries where unemployment has risen sharply. If the insider model were correct, a large rise in unemployment should have no effect on the location of the u/v curve but should simply lead a collapse in the vacancy rate. Yet in Britain there was an enormous outward shift of the u/v curve up until the mid-1980s, while the fall in unemployment in the late 1980s was accompanied by a significant inward shift of the u/v curve. As argued by Jackman et al. (1989), a shift in the u/v curve is evidence of changes in the efficiency with which unemployed people are matched to vacancies in the labour market, rather than of changes in the overall pressure of demand for labour.

Long-term unemployment

A key fact in this context has been the growth of long-term unemployment. There is also clear evidence that in all countries the rate at which unemployed people find work is at any instant much lower for long-term than for short-term unemployed. In Britain the rate is but one-tenth of its initial value for those who have been unemployed for over four years. Psychological evidence suggests that there is a serious adverse effect of prolonged unemployment on workers morale, motivation and expectations (Warr and Jackson 1985), though as Fryer (Chapter 6) points out, this may be due as much to the effects of material deprivation as to the absence of a job itself. Whichever is the case, time-series evidence on the movement of exit rates at different durations does show that over time, unemployed people are increasingly less likely to re-enter employment (Jackman and Layard 1991).

Long-term unemployment and/or the material deprivation accompanying it seems to reduce the 'effectiveness' of unemployed people as job-seekers – lowering their expectations, morale and skills and their quality as perceived by employers. Given this, it is easy to see how the u/v curve can shift out if the unemployed include a higher proportion of long-term unemployed people as the unemployment stock rises. Econometric evidence supports the view that this has been an important mechanism shifting out the u/v curve (Budd, Levine and Smith 1987; Franz 1987). For the same reason unemployment exerts less downwards pressure on wages if a high proportion of the unemployed have been out of work for a long time (Layard and Nickell 1987).

We have here a mechanism generating persistence. An adverse shock reduces employment. This reduces the outflow from unemployment. In consequence, a higher proportion of the unemployed have experienced long spells without work. This means that wage pressure at given unemployment is higher than it would otherwise be, or equivalently that more unemployment is required to restrain wage pressure. Long-term unemployment is best regarded as a phenomenon which amplifies the adverse consequences of economic shocks. If economic conditions are bad, many of those who become unemployed will not find work and thus enter long-term unemployment. If the economy recovers, fewer people will enter long-term unemployment and so the number of long-term unemployed people will gradually decline. One cannot explain the higher unemployment rates of the 1980s purely by reference to the ineffectiveness of the long-term unemployed, because on average during the mid-1980s there were about 1.8 million unemployed people with durations of less than a year. Even if the long-term unemployed had become completely detached from the labour market one still has to explain why the level of short-term unemployment was almost twice as high as it had been during the late 1970s.

Structural imbalance

A third possibility is that the big movements in unemployment are the consequence of major structural shifts in the economy leading to a situation where the unemployed are less well matched to the jobs that are available. As with long-term unemployment, however, it is difficult to determine to what extent increased imbalance is the cause of higher aggregate unemployment and to what extent it is the consequence. If one measures imbalance in terms of the variance of unemployment rates, the measure of imbalance moves very closely in line with the aggregate unemployment rate (Figure 3.2). When unemployment in aggregate doubles, the unemployment rate for each region, skill and industry tends approximately to double, increas-

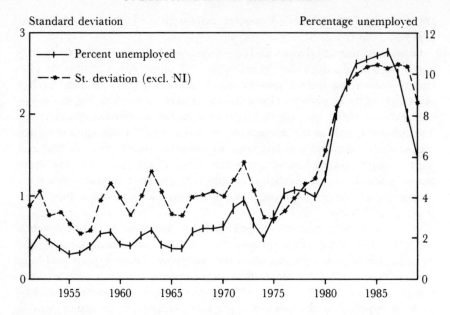

Figure 3.2 Regional unemployment disparities and percentage unemployed in the
UK, 1951–89

Source: Taylor, J., 1990, 'Regional economic disparities: causes and consequences', Lancaster
University

Note: Unemployment data for 1961–73 based on old method of measuring unemployment;
1974–89 data based on new method.

ing the percentage point dispersion between the better off and the less
prosperous sectors. Similarly, during a recovery, the absolute gap in unemployment rates tends to narrow.

While it is not entirely clear why this is so (but for one theory see
Jackman, Layard and Savouri 1991), the practical implication seems to be
that any increase in imbalance which simply matches an increase in aggregate unemployment can be expected to melt away when unemployment
declines and hence cannot be an explanation of the higher aggregate rate.
The question then is whether imbalances increased over and above this
purely proportional effect. At the beginning of the 1980s there is evidence
of increased mismatch by industry (Jackman and Roper 1987; see also
Chapter 4). Employment in manufacturing fell by nearly 30 per cent, from
about 7 million to about 5 million people, at the beginning of the 1980s
and has remained at the lower level ever since. It is unfortunately difficult
to gauge to what extent this structural shock is continuing to affect unemployment since there have been no figures collected on unemployment by
industry since 1982. The structure of employment by industry has, however, remained reasonably stable since the traumas of the early 1980s and
it seems unlikely that it remains a major cause of higher unemployment.

The evidence in general suggests that most unemployed people are in any case quite flexible with regard to the industry in which they work.

Regional disparities seem to be largely a reflection of the higher aggregate unemployment rate rather than an independent cause of it. But the situation with regard to skills seems to show some, though perhaps not very pronounced, signs of getting worse. Here it is convenient to refer back to Figure 3.1. This shows that shortages of skilled labour have always been a more serious concern than shortages of unskilled workers but the two have tended to move together. The figure for 1989, however, seems to be outside the normal range of co-variation, with shortages of skilled labour being somewhat higher (or of unskilled labour somewhat lower) than one would expect given the normal relationship between the two.

It may be noted, however, that it is only in 1989 that this apparent break from the previous relationshp has been observed. There are perennial complaints about shortages of skills but it is hard to explain variations in the unemployment rate by features of the economic landscape that are unchanging over time.

PROSPECTS AND POLICIES

The main conclusions to be drawn from the argument so far are:

1 that in the short run, fluctuations in unemployment are driven by changes in aggregate demand, but that
2 unlike what happens in the United States (or in the simple textbook models), equilibrating forces in the labour market are very weak. The level of unemployment tends to settle down to whatever its current level happens to be, until subject to a new demand shock.
3 But equilibrating forces, even if weak, are not non-existent. In the long run, the sustainable level of unemployment depends on supply-side factors (the efficiency with which the labour market operates and individual decisions on labour force participation and job search).

At the time of writing (October 1991), price inflation is falling sharply and wage inflation more gradually and it may thus be anticipated that a recovery of demand cannot be long delayed. None the less, unemployment is bound to go on rising and could easily reach 2.75 or even 3 million before growth in demand catches up with the growth of productive potential.

But does this suggest that the first half of the 1990s may be a re-run of the early 1980s, with output growing but unemployment stuck stubbornly at close to the 3 million mark? I would argue that such a projection could prove too pessimistic. Since 1979, the Conservative government has introduced a number of policy measures which can be expected to reduce the extent of hysteresis in the labour market. Whether or not high unemployment persists in the early 1990s may be regarded as the first true test of the extent to which these reforms can reduce hysteresis.

The key reforms that can be expected to reduce hysteresis are:

1 changes in the law relating to trade unions, and other measures to enhance competition in the labour market, which will have weakened the powers of insiders in wage bargaining;
2 improvements in the effectiveness of job-matching procedures in the labour market, including more pressure on the unemployed to find work; and
3 reduced structural imbalance (at least by industry and by region) in the economy.

It may be worth elaborating the second and third of these points in more detail. On the second, the measures taken to improve the supply side of the labour market include (Meadows 1990 and see Chapter 11):

- a stricter benefit regime
- more intensive counselling and guidance
- help in job search
- the offer of training opportunities
- efforts to make the long-term unemployed more effective job seekers and more desirable as potential employees.

With regard to the long-term unemployed, these measures have been brought together in the Restart programme of regular interviews of long-term unemployed people with the objective of assisting them to find work. While the Restart programme appears to have had some effectiveness in reducing long-term unemployment (Disney *et al.* 1992), the programme appears to have been more successful in encouraging unemployed people to undergo training and to take part in employment programmes (and in weeding out benefit claimants who either had a job already or were unwilling to look for one) than in leading to jobs (Dicks and Hatch 1989). The reason is that even when the labour market has been generally buoyant (as it was during the first two or three years after the introduction of Restart) the long-term unemployed are often hard to place for reasons set out in the previous section.

The more difficult labour market conditions likely to prevail over the next few years threaten to make the task of the Restart programme very much more difficult. It is one thing to help long-term unemployed people to take advantage of the opportunities available when there are indeed opportunities available, but quite another to encourage them to search more actively when job opportunities are scarce. If the Restart programme is not simply to arouse expectations which it cannot then fulfil it is necessary to assist not only with guidance but with some form of job creation to provide the opportunities for the long-term unemployed to take up. This is, of course, the way in which the Labour Market Board in Sweden has kept unemployment below 3 per cent in that country, and proposals along similar lines, involving a Job Guarantee for the long-term unemployed, have been worked out for the United Kingdom.

It can be argued that active labour market policies in Sweden have worked well because centralized wage bargaining (see Chapter 2) has been successful in moderating wage claims and this has ensured that unemployment in the economy as a whole has remained low (Meadows 1990). Clearly it is true that the scale of the problem is much greater in Britain than in Sweden, and to exactly replicate Swedish procedures in the British context would be to place enormous and unrealistic demands in terms both of money and administrative resources on the Employment Service. But this does not mean that the basic principle should be abandoned, rather it means that the coverage of the guarantee and the nature of the programmes themselves have to be modified in line with the resources that can be made available. (For further consideration of these issues, see Jackman and others 1986; Layard and Philpott 1991; Meacher 1990; Philpott 1990.)

Turning to the third heading, that of structural imbalance, much has been made of the fact that the 1990–1 downturn, unlike that of the early 1980s, has been most acute in the previously most prosperous sectors (for example, finance and other professional services) and regions (in particular the South East; see also Chapter 10). Some have attributed this to a new found supply-side vitality in manufacturing industry and in the North, but it is more plausible to think that it has been the sectors and industries built up on the back of the credit boom which have suffered most from its collapse. As many of these sectors had become 'overheated', their collapse may contribute to a better structural balance in the economy, at least with regard to regions and industries.

In one dimension, however, imbalances do appear to be getting worse. The skills of the workforce are continuing to fall short of those that employers require. The weakness of current arrangements for education and training in the UK have been discussed by White (Chapter 2). It is well known that the British workforce is the least educated and least qualified of any advanced industrialized country. Government policy seems at present guided mainly by stinginess and it can only be hoped that the business leaders who are to run the TECs will have a better grasp of what is required.

The main conclusions are these:

1 That joining the Exchange Rate mechanism requires the adoption of restrictive demand-side policies to force the underlying rate of inflation down to the level of other European nations. The result will be, and already has been, a rise in unemployment.

2 A number of policies introduced since 1979 give some, albeit limited, grounds for hope that the high unemployment of the early 1990s will be less persistent than that of the early 1980s.

3 There none the less remain a number of supply side weaknesses in the labour market. There is still no effective policy for reintegrating long-term unemployed people into the labour market, and skill imbalances may become a serious obstacle to any recovery. A sustainable reduction in unemployment towards levels that were taken for granted in the 1950s and 1960s (or even to those achieved during the 1970s) requires a much more energetic approach by the government to these remaining supply-side weaknesses.

NOTE AND REFERENCES

Note

1 I am grateful to the Department of Employment, the Economic and Social Research Council and the Esmee Fairbairn Charitable Trust for financial support.

References

Beveridge, W.H. (1944) *Full Employment in a Free Society*, London: Allen & Unwin.

Blanchard, O. and Summers, L.H. (1986) 'Hysteresis and the European Unemployment Problem', in S. Fischer (ed.) *NBER Macroeconomics Annual 1986*, Cambridge, MA: MIT Press.

Budd, A., Levine, P. and Smith, P. (1987) 'Long Term Unemployment and the Shifting U/V Curve: A Multi-Country Study', *European Economic Review*, 31: 1071–91.

Clark, K.B. and Summers, L.H. (1979) 'Labour Market Dynamics and Unemployment: A Reconsideration', *Brookings Papers on Economic Activity*, 1: 13–60.

Dicks, M.J. and Hatch, N. (1989) 'The Relationship Between Unemployment and Employment', London: Bank of England, Research Paper No. 39.

Disney, R., Bellmann, L., Carruth, A., Franz, W., Jackman, R., Layard, R., Lehmann, H. and Philpott, J. (1991) *Helping the Unemployed: Active Labour Market Policies in Britain and Germany*, London: Anglo-German Foundation.

Franz, W. (1987) 'Hysteresis, Persistence and the NAIRU: An Empirical Analysis for the FRG', in R. Layard and L. Calmfors (eds), *The Fight against Unemployment*, Cambridge, MA: MIT Press.

Hall, R. (1970) 'Why is the Unemployment Rate so High at Full Employment', *Brookings Papers on Economic Activity*, 3: 369–402.

Jackman, R. and Layard, R. (1991) 'Does Long-Term Unemployment Reduce a Person's Chance of a Job?: A Time-Series Test', *Economica*, 58: 93–106.

Jackman, R., Layard, R. and Pissarides, C. (1989) 'On Vacancies', *Oxford Bulletin of Economics and Statistics*, 51: 377–94.

Jackman, R., Layard, R. and Savouri, S. (1991) 'Mismatch: a Framework for Thought', in F. Padoa-Schioppa (ed.) *Mismatch and Labour Mobility*, Cambridge: Cambridge University Press.

Jackman, R. and Roper, S. (1987) 'Structural Unemployment', Special Issue on

Wage Determination and Labour Market Flexibility, *Oxford Bulletin of Economics and Statistics*, 49: 9–36.

Jackman, R., Cahill, J., Cornelius, M., Disney, R., Haskel, J., Layard, R. and O'Brien, R. (1986) *A Job Guarantee for the Long-Term Unemployed*, London: Employment Institute.

Keynes, J. (1937) quoted in R. Kahn 'Unemployment as seen by the Keynesians', in G.D.N. Worswick (ed.) *The Concept and Measurement of Involuntary Unemployment* (1976) London: Royal Economic Society.

Layard, R. and Nickell, S. (1987) 'The Labour Market', in R. Dornbusch and R. Layard (eds), *The Performance of the British Economy*, Oxford: Oxford University Press.

Layard, R. and Philpott, J. (1991) *Stopping Unemployment*, London: The Employment Institute.

Lindbeck, A. and Snower, D.J. (1988) 'Cooperation, Harassment and Involuntary Unemployment: An Insider–Outsider Approach', *American Economic Review*, 78, 1: 167–88.

Meacher, M. (1990) 'Adopting the Employment Principle: A Green Paper', Campaign for Work, *Research Report*, 2, 1, February.

Meadows, P. (1990) 'Notes on "An Economy of Unemployment" ' presented to the ES-SPRU 'Understanding Unemployment' Conference, May 1990, York, mimeo.

Nickell, S. and Kong, P. (1988) 'An Investigation into the Power of Insiders in Wage Determination', Oxford: University of Oxford Institute of Economics and Statistics, Applied Economics Discussion Paper No. 49.

Nickell, S. and Wadhwani, S. (1990) 'Insider Forces and Wage Determination', *Economic Journal*, 100: 496–509.

Philpott, J. (1990) *A Solution to Long-term Unemployment: The Job Guarantee*, London: The Employment Institute.

Reder, M. (1969) 'The Theory of Frictional Unemployment', *Economica*, 36, 1: 1–28.

Warr, P. and Jackson, P. (1985) 'Factors Influencing the Psychological Impact of Prolonged Unemployment and of Re-employment', *Psychological Medicine*, 15: 795–807.

4

UNEMPLOYMENT RISKS

Christopher Pissarides and Jonathan Wadsworth

INTRODUCTION

Unemployment is a key variable. The performance of the labour market, and sometimes the entire economic record of governments, are judged by what happens to unemployment. Why should this be so? The answer most frequently given by economists is that unemployment is associated with loss of output – if the unemployed had jobs, domestic output would be higher. Another aspect, often neglected in aggregate approaches to policy, is that some groups in the population suffer much more unemployment than others. To talk of the loss of national output as the main cost of unemployment tells only part of the story. For the individuals most exposed to the risk of becoming and remaining unemployed this is not an important consideration. Furthermore, the loss of income associated with unemployment is often accompanied by loss of skill and work habits, which can further damage an individual's chances of finding new work.

This chapter quantifies the extent to which different groups in the population are exposed to different unemployment risks. We do not attempt to explain fully why these differential risks exist. Our interest is merely in finding out the facts, by making use of the most comprehensive data source on unemployment available in Great Britain, the Labour Force Survey (LFS). However, identification of who is most likely to suffer unemployment should facilitate the task of policy makers seeking to alleviate unemployment.

We adopt the LFS definition of unemployment, which is close to that recommended by the International Labour Office and the OECD. The LFS definition is used by the Statistical Office of the European Communities for the calculation of comparable unemployment rates in member countries and is reported regularly in the Department of Employment *Gazette*.

A person is unemployed on the LFS definition if:

1 the person did not work during the survey reference week (usually the week prior to interview);
2 if he or she is available to start work immediately; and

3 if he or she looked for work during the reference week or was waiting to start work in a job already found.

The LFS definition of unemployment is still not widely used. The measure in common use, which, unlike the LFS, is available monthly, is the 'claimant count'. The claimant count includes all persons without a job and eligible to receive unemployment-related benefits.

Persons without a job need to satisfy certain conditions to be entitled to unemployment benefit, which, at least until 1989, did not include the condition of actively looking for work. Thus, there are individuals out of work who are not job seekers but who satisfy all the conditions for receipt of unemployment benefit. There are also individuals who are job seekers but are not entitled to benefit. The two definitions of unemployment need not, and in general do not, coincide. In Table 4.1 we report the LFS and claimant count unemployment rates for 1979, 1986 and 1989. The two definitions of unemployment give different rates, especially when we consider men and women separately. In 1979 the two aggregate rates were very similar, with the LFS rate slightly exceeding the claimant count. In 1986 the claimant count exceeded the LFS rate, but by 1989, the latest year for which data are available, the order was again reversed. In all years, the claimant count gives a higher male unemployment rate than the LFS definition. Men who lost their jobs are almost automatically entitled to unemployment benefit, even if they are not looking for work. For women the reverse holds, because women normally have less entitlement to benefit than men, due to the nature of their previous employment and employment history.

Up to 90 per cent of men unemployed on the LFS definition claim benefit. The 10 per cent not in the claimant count are mostly new entrants. In contrast, only about 40 per cent of unemployed women are claimants. The high number of women re-entrants, not entitled to benefit because of insufficient National Insurance contributions or means-tested income requirements, partly explains this. Women job losers are also less likely to be entitled to benefit than their male counterparts.

Table 4.1 Unemployment rates, 1979, 1986 and 1989, LFS and claimant count

Definition	1979			1986			1989		
	Men	Women	Total	Men	Women	Total	Men	Women	Total
LFS	4.6	6.0	5.1	10.3	9.8	10.1	7.2	6.9	7.1
Claimants	5.9	3.4	4.9	13.5	9.1	11.7	8.0	4.2	6.4
%LFS who are claimants	n.a.	n.a.	n.a.	88.8	44.1	70.9	89.8	38.5	68.3

Source: Department of Employment *Gazette* and LFS 1979, 1986

We concentrate on the LFS definition because it is both closer to the economic concept of unemployment than the claimant count, and, like the LFS definition itself, our analysis is based on survey information. We calculate average unemployment rates for some key groups in the population. We then break down unemployment differentials, according to personal characteristics. Thus, we are able to say, for example, how much unemployment is suffered because of different education qualifications, occupation, age, race, etc. We report separate results for men and women from two surveys, one at a time of low unemployment – 1979 – and one taken when unemployment was at its highest in the post-war period – 1986. We consider three aspects of unemployment: overall incidence, long-term unemployment and recurrent unemployment.

THE INCIDENCE OF UNEMPLOYMENT

We run logit regressions of the probability of being unemployed on a set of personal characteristics (a similar analysis for men with the General Household Survey was conducted by Nickell 1980). A respondent in a survey either is or is not unemployed, and either has or does not have any particular characteristic. Thus all the variables in our regressions take two values, one if the respondent has the characteristic (including unemployment) and zero otherwise.

The regressions are not meant to identify causalities, but simply offer a compact way of cross tabulating the incidence of unemployment against personal characteristics. Since our objective is to identify the unemployed, they serve our purposes well.

The regressions for men and women are reported in Table 4.2. If a variable has a positive coefficient, individuals with that characteristic are more likely to be unemployed than individuals without it; and conversely for negative coefficients. Moreover, if a personal characteristic has a larger coefficient than another, the former contributes more to the incidence of unemployment than the latter. Since the regressions are non-linear, the actual coefficients reported are not particularly meaningful. We therefore discuss the incidence of unemployment by first translating these estimates into unemployment differentials, following the transformations described in the methodological note at the end of this chapter. We consider the effect of several characteristics, which can conveniently be divided into four groups.

Education and occupation

We distinguish between four categories of educational attainment, university degree, GCE 'A' or 'O' level, other post-compulsory schooling qualifications (including technical training, apprenticeships, etc.) and no qualifications. Occupations are classified into five groups, professional,

Table 4.2a Unemployment incidence (men) 1979 and 1986 (logit regression)

	1979		1986	
Variable	Sample mean	Estimate	Sample mean	Estimate
No. obs.	57,712		18,356	
Dependent	0.044		0.094	
Intercept		−3.72		−1.85
Age 16–19	0.070	0.25	0.063	0.42
Age 20–24	0.107	0.19	0.100	0.42
Age 25–34	0.249	0.14*	0.241	0.25
Age 50–64	0.258	0.02*	0.237	−0.05*
Single	0.251	0.73	0.254	0.45
Degree	0.112	−0.65	0.154	−0.29
GCE	0.246	−0.51	0.346	−0.30
Other	0.071	−0.17	0.107	−0.12*
Race	0.038	0.59	0.048	0.76
Cncl tnt	0.318	0.72	0.183	1.16
Prvt tnt	0.088	0.61	0.090	0.67
Dep chd	0.476	0.25	0.503	0.07*
Move rgn	0.013	0.44	0.029	0.48
Move hse	0.097	0.68	0.118	0.45
Professional	0.260	−1.35	0.343	−1.50
Clerical	0.062	−1.22	0.045	−1.28
Other non-man	0.047	−1.12	0.067	−0.93
Skilled manual	0.291	−0.87	0.258	−0.96
North	0.062	1.01	0.056	0.79
Yorks	0.099	0.35	0.090	0.54
East mdls	0.066	0.14*	0.075	0.35
East angl	0.034	0.01*	0.038	−0.07*
Sth west	0.078	0.34	0.079	0.13*
West mdls	0.108	0.21	0.098	0.42
Nrth west	0.121	0.76	0.111	0.67
Wales	0.051	0.74	0.046	0.76
Scotland	0.088	0.68	0.090	0.28

Source: LFS
Note: The dependent variable takes value one if the respondent is unemployed and value zero if he is employed. All variables are zero–one dummies. A star (*) denotes not significant estimate.

group and our calculated unemployment differential due to that attribute clerical, other non-manual, skilled manual and unskilled manual. It is appropriate to discuss together the effect of educational attainment and occupation because of the high degree of correlation between them. For example, degree holders are employed mostly in the professions, whereas unskilled manual workers usually have no educational qualifications. The statistics reported in Tables 4.3 and 4.4 are: the percentage of LFS respondents who have each attribute, the average unemployment rate of that

Table 4.2b Unemployment incidence (women) 1979 and 1986 (logit regression)

Variable	1979		1986	
	Sample mean	Estimate	Sample mean	Estimate
No. obs.	37,268		13,156	
Dependent	0.059		0.093	
Intercept		−2.85		−2.90
Age 16–19	0.094	0.68	0.081	0.84
Age 20–24	0.126	0.86	0.118	0.88
Age 25–34	0.230	0.70	0.238	0.69
Age 50–59	0.202	0.11*	0.173	0.21*
Single	0.300	0.35	0.315	0.26
Degree	0.075	0.08	0.099	−0.72
GCE	0.275	−0.22	0.371	−0.44
Other	0.113	0.06	0.129	0.09*
Race	0.034	0.66	0.044	0.59
Cncl tnt	0.327	0.14	0.178	0.75
Prvt tnt	0.088	0.11*	0.083	0.51
Dep chd	0.437	0.26	0.489	0.70
Move rgn	0.012	0.83	0.027	0.23*
Move hse	0.097	0.58	0.117	0.59
Professional	0.198	−1.89	0.248	−1.60
Clerical	0.303	−1.77	0.280	−1.48
Other non-man	0.092	−1.29	0.098	−1.15
Skilled manual	0.056	−0.97	0.043	−0.86
North	0.060	0.34	0.057	0.36
Yorks	0.096	0.17	0.092	0.27
East mdls	0.062	0.01*	0.077	0.06*
East angl	0.031	0.21*	0.038	−0.18*
Sth west	0.077	0.06*	0.076	−0.04*
West mdls	0.106	−0.11*	0.094	0.19*
Nrth west	0.130	0.29	0.116	0.42
Wales	0.049	0.61	0.044	0.36
Scotland	0.092	0.46	0.089	0.12*

Source: LFS
Note: The dependent variable takes value one if the respondent is unemployed and value zero if he is employed. All variables are zero–one dummies. A star (*) denotes not significant estimate.

(highest educational qualification in Table 4.3 and current or, for the unemployed, past occupation in Table 4.4).

Taking degree holders as an example, we find that in 1979 men with degrees had an average unemployment rate of 1.3 per cent. Men with no qualifications had more than four times this unemployment rate − 5.6 per cent. Thus the average unemployment differential between degree holders and unqualified men was 4.3 per cent. This could be due to a number of factors. Most importantly, degree holders are likely to be in different occupations from those men with no qualifications. Other characteristics, such as age, may also differ between the two groups. Such differences are likely to influence the average unemployment rate of each group. We calculate that when the unemployment effect of all the variables in our regressions, except for educational attainment, is removed, there remains an unemployment differential between the two groups of 2.6 per cent. We attribute this to the holding of a degree; the remainder of the average differential (1.7 per cent) is due to other factors.

Table 4.3 Education and unemployment, 1979 and 1986

Qualifications	% in sample		Unemployment rate		Differential due to education	
	1979	1986	1979	1986	1979	1986
Men						
Degree	10.9	14.8	1.3	2.3	−2.6	−4.2
GCE	24.8	35.1	2.5	4.3	−2.2	−4.4
Other	7.2	11.1	4.3	6.7	−0.8	−1.7
None	57.1	39.0	5.6	19.8	−	−
Women						
Degree	7.6	9.5	3.1	5.8	0.4	0.5
GCE	27.6	37.3	4.3	9.0	−1.3	−0.1
Other	11.2	13.0	6.5	12.8	0.3	2.8
None	53.6	40.2	6.8	10.5	−	−

Source: LFS

In general higher educational qualifications are associated with lower unemployment (see also Nickell 1979). The relation, however, is not as simple as the unadjusted data suggest. There are also substantial differences between men and women, which are not easy to explain.

Although male unemployment rates rise uniformly as education falls, the big rise at a time of high unemployment takes place when we move from the groups with some qualifications to those with none. This rise however, appears to be due to some other factor that characterizes those with no qualifications. Secondly, after controlling for occupation (and the other attributes in our regressions) the education groups can be split into two; those with GCE or above and those without. The pure effect of education on unemployment in the former group is about 2.5 points in 1979 and just over four points in 1986 – both of which are less than the total unemployment differential between the two groups.

For women the picture is different. Although higher education is again associated with lower unemployment, the differentials are not as large as for men. More strikingly, education does not appear to affect unemployment once occupation and the other variables are controlled for.

Thus the lesson for women in particular, is that higher education qualifications do not by themselves insulate one from the risk of unemployment.

On average they help, but only because higher qualifications make it easier for the holders to obtain more secure jobs.

The latter point emerges more clearly when we examine occupation in Table 4.4. Although unemployment rates rise as we move down the occupational scale, the big jump takes place when we move from skilled manual to unskilled. The recession of the early 1980s affected unemployment in all occupational groups more or less equally, with all nearly doubling between 1979 and 1986. What is remarkable, however, is that even after controlling for various personal characteristics, the observed differentials in average unemployment rates remain occupation-specific. On average, two women with similar education and other labour-market characteristics, but in different occupations, will be exposed to different unemployment risks because of their occupations. For example, a secretary with a degree will have a higher risk of unemployment than a similar degree holder in a professional job.

Table 4.4 Occupation and unemployment, 1979 and 1986

Occupation	% in sample		Unemployment rate		Differential due to occupation	
	1979	1986	1979	1986	1979	1986
Men						
Professional	26.0	34.4	1.2	3.0	−6.2	−17.0
Clerical	6.2	4.4	2.0	3.8	−5.9	−15.5
Other non-manual	4.7	6.7	2.1	7.9	−5.6	−12.6
Skilled manual	29.1	25.8	2.9	6.4	−4.8	−12.8
Unskilled manual	34.0	28.7	8.6	23.3	–	–
Women						
Professional	20.0	24.9	1.8	3.9	−9.8	−14.6
Clerical	30.3	27.9	2.4	4.9	−9.5	−14.0
Other non-manual	9.2	9.8	3.5	7.3	−8.2	−12.1
Skilled manual	5.6	4.3	4.8	9.8	−6.9	−10.0
Unskilled	14.9	33.1	11.7	19.1	–	–

Source: LFS

Something similar is true of men but to a lesser extent. Thus, unemployment is a bigger problem for unskilled (male) manual workers than it is for women. Although all occupational unemployment rates increased between 1979 and 1986, the increase was far greater for unskilled manual workers than for the rest. Occupation alone cannot explain the observed differences in the average occupational unemployment rates. For example, in 1986 unskilled male manual workers had 20 points of unemployment more than professional men. Belonging to the latter occupational group accounted for about 17 of those points; the remainder was accounted for by other factors, which as Table 4.3 suggests are almost certainly related to education: most men in professional jobs have at least GCE.

Age, family and race

The relation between age and unemployment is shown in Table 4.5. Average unemployment rates decline uniformly with age for both men and women. The differentials in the last two columns of Table 4.5, removing all but the pure age effect, show that in 1979 age did not appear to exert an independent influence on male unemployment, but in 1986 there was some effect. Men under 25 had on average 3.7 points more unemployment than the prime age group and men aged 25–34 about two points more. The pure age effect disappears after the mid 30s for both men and women.

Table 4.5 Age and unemployment, 1979 and 1986

Age	% in sample		Unemployment rate		Differential due to age	
	1979	1986	1979	1986	1979	1986
Men						
16–19	7.1	8.4	8.7	19.0	0.9	3.7
20–24	10.7	11.9	6.2	16.8	0.6	3.7
25–34	24.9	24.1	4.3	10.4	0.5	2.1
35–49	31.8	33.5	3.3	8.1	–	–
50–64	25.5	22.1	3.5	7.5	0.1	−0.2
Women						
16–19	9.6	10.2	10.1	18.2	3.6	8.3
20–24	12.7	13.4	8.4	13.7	4.9	6.9
25–34	23.0	22.9	7.0	12.0	3.7	5.5
35–49	34.7	36.1	4.0	6.9	–	–
50–59	20.0	17.4	3.7	5.0	−0.4	0.1

Source: LFS

In general one can say that age appears to be much more important for women than men. The differentials in average unemployment rates are higher for women. What is more important, however, is that the observed differentials in the case of women can be attributed almost entirely to pure age effects. This is not the case for men. We cannot tell whether this is the result of pure age discrimination, or missing factors that are important for women but not for men (for example, the childrearing responsibilities more typically borne by women than men). We can say, however, that the factors included in our analysis explain some of the observed age-specific male unemployment differentials but none of the female ones.

The unemployment differentials associated with family background and race are given in Table 4.6. Marital status has a larger effect on the unemployment of men than on women. The effect is substantial in both cases and increased from 1979 to 1986, more so for women. The differential attributed solely to marital status is slightly less than the observed differential in the unemployment rates of married and single persons. The remainder may be accounted for by age and education, both of which are likely to be different for single and married individuals.

The presence of young children does not appear to have any effect on the unemployment of the father, though mothers with young children have higher unemployment. When the effects of marital status and children are combined, married women with children have about the same unemployment rate as single women, higher than the unemployment rate of married women without children. The highest unemployment rates are suffered by single mothers. The high cost of childcare facilities, when compared with the average earnings of women, may be a factor behind these differentials. Women with children can afford to accept only jobs with high hourly earnings or fewer hours of work or, more likely, both, especially if there is no male wage-earner in the household to share childcare expenses (see also Chapters 7 and 9). Such jobs are more difficult to come by.

Race has a large effect on unemployment. Table 4.6 indicates that non-whites have higher unemployment rates than whites. Although women non-whites suffered the average rise in unemployment between 1979 and 1986, male non-whites have much more. For men, race causes a bigger unemployment differential than found in the average unemployment rates, implying that the other characteristics of non-whites are less likely to be

Table 4.6 Family background, race and unemployment, 1979 and 1986

Attribute	% in sample		Unemployment rate		Differential due to attribute	
	1979	1986	1979	1986	1979	1986
Men						
Single	25.1	30.7	7.5	14.7	3.2	4.1
Married	74.9	69.3	3.2	8.4	–	–
Children	47.6	49.3	4.5	10.5	1.1	0.6
None	52.4	50.7	4.1	i0.3	–	–
Non-white	3.8	4.8	5.5	15.1	3.2	8.8
White	96.2	95.2	4.2	9.1	–	–
Women						
Single	30.1	35.2	8.1	13.3	1.9	3.3
Married	69.9	64.8	4.8	7.8	–	–
Children	44.7	47.6	7.4	12.2	1.3	3.7
None	55.3	52.4	4.5	7.6	–	–
Non-white	3.3	4.6	10.7	17.7	4.7	6.6
White	96.7	95.4	5.6	9.4	–	–

Source: LFS

associated with high unemployment than those of whites. The reverse holds for women.

Residence

In Table 4.7 we report statistics related to the housing situation of the unemployed. Individuals who own their house (either outright or through a mortgage) are much less likely to be unemployed than those in council accommodation or in private rental. On average, men in council accommodation in 1979 had more than six points higher unemployment than men in owner-occupier housing. Of this, only two points can be attributed to housing tenure. For women the pure effect of housing tenure is even lower, being almost zero in 1979.

The striking change between 1979 and 1986, is that whereas the unemployment rates of those not in council accommodation doubled, the rate of those in council accommodation increased by a factor of four. Moreover, the fraction of all individuals in council accommodation fell from a third to just under a fifth. This was the direct outcome of the Conservative Government's policy of encouraging council tenants to purchase their properties under favourable terms. What our analysis suggests is that purchases took place on a large scale but only by the employed, leaving only poorer families, a third of which had unemployed heads, in council properties.

As in 1979, only a small fraction of the observed 1986 unemployment differential between council tenants and the rest can be attributed to housing tenure. Council tenants have higher unemployment rates because of other characteristics (such as low education, manual occupations, etc.), not because they live in council properties. Hughes and McCormick (1985) show that council tenants are less likely to move outside their direct area to look for a job than persons in owner-occupier housing. This factor may well contribute to the observed higher unemployment of council tenants. The last two columns in Table 4.7 give an estimate of the unemployment that may be due to such factors.

The second set of results in Table 4.7 concern mobility. Individuals who recently moved either house or region have higher unemployment rates than individuals who made no move. Pissarides and Wadsworth (1989) show that the unemployed are more likely to move than the employed. Thus recent movers have higher unemployment rates but, had they stayed behind, their unemployment rates may have been even higher. The results below for long-term unemployment confirm that mobility is good for employment.

Women movers, however, appear to have higher unemployment rates than men. The reason for this may partly be that the primary force behind

Table 4.7 Residence and unemployment, 1979 and 1986

Residence type	% in sample		Unemployment rate		Differential due to education	
	1979	1986	1979	1986	1979	1986
Men						
Council tenant	31.7	19.7	8.3	32.1	2.0	7.7
Private rental	8.5	9.1	5.5	12.3	1.6	3.5
Owner occupier	59.8	71.2	2.0	4.0	–	–
Moved house	9.6	11.8	7.3	14.1	3.6	4.8
Moved region	1.3	3.0	7.9	13.9	2.2	5.4
No move	89.1	85.2	4.0	9.9	–	–
Women						
Council tenant	33.0	19.4	8.2	17.1	0.6	4.3
Private rental	8.9	8.4	6.3	13.3	−0.5	3.3
Owner occupier	58.1	72.2	4.3	7.4	–	–
Moved house	9.8	11.4	9.5	15.0	4.8	5.9
Moved region	1.1	2.8	17.9	16.4	6.5	2.3
No move	89.1	85.8	5.5	9.3	–	–

Source: LFS

the move in the household is the husband, with more women moving into unemployment in their new area of residence than their male counterparts.

Regional unemployment

Much has been written about regional unemployment differentials and the apparent emergence of a 'North–South divide' (see also Chapter 10). This is evident in the average unemployment rates reported in Table 4.8. The regions in the table are ordered North to South. Unemployment rates in the three southern regions are much less than in the rest of the country both for men and women, especially in 1986.

These regional unemployment differentials may be due to the occupational distribution of employment, differences in the other personal characteristics in our regressions, or to something else. Amongst the important factors in the latter group we might include the industrial distribution of employment, differences in the regional cost of living, especially housing, and other unquantifiable regional effects. The last two columns of Table 4.8 show the impact of such differentials.

Most regions do not have significantly higher unemployment than the South East. Moreover, the 'unexplained' regional unemployment differentials did not increase between 1979 and 1986, despite the big increase in the observed average differentials. The three southern regions have the same unemployment, the two Midland regions and Scotland (which benefited from North Sea oil between 1979 and 1986) have about 2.5 percentage points of unemployment more and the other regions have again as much. For most of the regions, however, most of the observed differentials is accounted for by the other variables in our regressions.

Table 4.8 Region and unemployment, 1979 and 1986

Region	% in sample		Unemployment rate		Differential due to region	
	1979	1986	1979	1986	1979	1986
Men						
Scotland	8.7	9.1	6.4	13.3	2.3	2.3
North	6.2	5.7	8.5	14.1	4.2	6.8
North West	12.3	11.2	5.3	13.4	2.8	5.2
Yorkshire	9.9	9.1	4.2	11.6	1.1	3.5
Wales	5.0	4.8	5.2	14.3	2.7	6.2
West Midlands	10.9	9.8	4.1	11.1	0.6	2.6
East Midlands	6.7	7.5	3.5	9.8	0.4	2.4
South West	7.8	7.9	4.0	7.7	1.0	0.9
East Anglia	3.4	3.7	2.6	6.7	0.0	−0.2
South East	30.0	31.2	2.6	7.5	–	–
Women						
Scotland	9.6	9.1	7.5	11.3	2.6	1.3
North	5.8	5.8	8.0	12.0	2.1	2.8
North West	13.0	11.7	6.3	11.7	1.5	2.6
Yorkshire	9.6	9.2	6.6	11.3	0.9	1.6
Wales	4.9	4.6	6.9	12.2	3.6	3.6
West Midlands	10.7	9.3	5.2	10.6	−0.4	0.9
East Midlands	6.1	7.8	4.8	9.4	0.0	0.1
South West	7.9	7.6	5.8	7.2	0.3	−0.9
East Anglia	2.8	3.8	5.1	7.3	−0.9	−1.7
South East	29.7	31.1	4.7	8.3	–	–

Source: LFS

LONG-TERM UNEMPLOYMENT

We now ask whether, within the group of unemployed workers, long-term unemployment is evenly spread, or whether some of the unemployed are more likely to suffer than others. We define long-term as unemployment of at least one year's duration. Table 4.9 presents logit coefficients on the incidence of long-term unemployment. In the first and third columns of Table 4.10, we give the average long-term unemployment rate of the group of workers who have each attribute. Taking age as an example, the first column shows that in 1979, 14.5 per cent of unemployed workers aged 16–19 had durations of at least one year. By 1986 this ratio rose to 27.4 per cent. The average long-term unemployment ratio was 31 per cent in 1979 and 51 per cent in 1986, so the rise in unemployment between the

69

two years was associated with a large increase in long-term unemployment (see also Chapter 3).

In columns 2 and 4 we calculate the differential in the long-term unemployment ratio attributable solely to each particular characteristic. Thus, men aged 16–19 had a ratio 32.2 points less than men aged 35–49. The uncontrolled differential is therefore 25.8 in this case.

Considering education, we find that it is a less important influence on long-term unemployment than we might expect, especially since we are obliged to restrict occupation, because of data limitations (workers with over three years duration of unemployment are not asked about previous occupation in the LFS). The holding of a degree appears to make no difference to the duration of unemployment in 1979, but this result is statistically unreliable. Generally, unemployed workers with more

Table 4.9a Long-term unemployment incidence (men), 1979 and 1986

Variable	1979		1986	
	Sample mean	Estimate	Sample mean	Estimate
No. obs.	2,385		4,108	
Dependent	0.309		0.511	
Intercept		−1.44		0.12*
Age 16–19	0.144	−2.04	0.155	−1.49
Age 20–24	0.154	−0.66	0.194	−0.36
Age 25–34	0.251	−0.42	0.243	−0.25
Age 50–64	0.207	0.34	0.173	0.05*
Single	0.437	0.30	0.487	0.02*
Degree	0.033	−0.03*	0.051	−0.47
GCE	0.146	−0.55	0.263	−0.35
Other	0.072	−0.60	0.135	−0.16*
Race	0.049	0.18*	0.077	0.17*
Manual	0.868	0.20*	0.829	0.88
Cncl tnt	0.613	0.65	0.485	0.78
Prvt tnt	0.109	0.43	0.114	0.69
Dep chd	0.501	0.01*	0.489	−0.09*
Move rgn	0.024	−1.73	0.043	−0.55
Move hse	0.162	−0.18*	0.163	−0.47
Redundancy	0.438	−0.04*	0.261	−1.33
Temp job	0.074	−0.47*	0.148	−1.29
New entrant	0.080	1.08	0.111	−0.35

Source: LFS
Note: The dependent variable takes value 1 if the respondent has been unemployed for at least one year and value zero if he has been unemployed for less than a year. All variables are zero–one dummies. A star (*) denotes not significant estimate.

Table 4.9b Long-term unemployment incidence (women), 1979 and 1986

Variable	1979		1986	
	Sample mean	Estimate	Sample mean	Estimate
No. obs.	1,775		2,828	
Dependent	0.194		0.309	
Intercept		−2.62		−1.05*
Age 16–19	0.167	−1.45	0.189	−1.28
Age 20–24	0.184	−0.58	0.188	−0.36
Age 25–34	0.280	−0.39	0.281	−0.25
Age 50–59	0.128	0.18*	0.089	0.26*
Single	0.422	0.75	0.481	0.53
Degree	0.040	−0.08*	0.056	−0.40*
GCE	0.205	−0.09*	0.343	−0.03*
Other	0.126	−0.16*	0.170	0.16*
Race	0.061	0.14*	0.083	0.27*
Manual	0.759	1.01	0.677	0.80
Cncl tnt	0.469	0.07*	0.339	0.39
Prvt tnt	0.097	0.26*	0.114	0.38
Dep chd	0.573	−0.42	0.592	−0.70
Move rgn	0.034	−0.35*	0.047	−1.34
Move hse	0.160	−0.42*	0.175	−0.50
Redundancy	0.127	0.06*	0.125	−0.58
Temp job	0.111	−0.32*	0.109	−0.13*
New entrant	0.116	0.28*	0.138	0.11

Source: LFS
Note: The dependent variable takes value 1 if the respondent has been unemployed for at least one year and value zero if she has been unemployed for less than a year. All variables are zero–one dummies. A star (*) denotes not significant estimate.

education are less likely to be in long-term unemployment than those with less education but these differentials are small.

The effect of the broader occupational decomposition on long-term unemployment is important in 1986, but not as important as in 1979. We argued in our discussion of overall incidence that the increase in unemployment between 1979 and 1986 was heavily concentrated in manual occupations. The same appears to be largely true for the increase in long-term unemployment. Non-manual workers suffered only fractionally more long-term unemployment in 1986 than in 1979, most of the increase in the average long-term unemployment ratio being the result of the increase in the long-term unemployment of manual workers.

Looking at the effect of age, teenagers in 1979 were unlikely to be found in long-term unemployment because of their age. Although 14.5 per cent of them were in long-term unemployment, about half this number were there for other reasons. Long-term unemployment increased rapidly with age. In 1986, when the average long-term unemployment ratio went up, teenagers were again the least likely group to be in long-term unemployment. Age became generally less important in 1986, with men over twenty having similar incidences of long-term unemployment.

Marital status is not an important influence on long-term unemployment, especially at a time of high unemployment. The presence of young children in the family is unimportant for male long-term unemployment, as it was for overall unemployment incidence. Race has very little effect on long-term unemployment, in contrast to its sizeable effect on the overall incidence of unemployment.

Individuals in all tenures experienced significantly higher long-term unemployment in 1986 than in 1979. Council tenants are worse off than other unemployed workers. The long-term unemployment differential, however, does not appear to be as substantial as the overall unemployment differential.

The relation between mobility and long-term unemployment provides an interesting contrast to the relation between mobility and unemployment as a whole. Recent movers are more likely to be unemployed than other workers. We attributed this to the fact that mobility is higher among the unemployed. The analysis of long-term unemployment shows that recent movers are less likely to be long-term unemployed than those who did not move. Thus, mobility appears to improve the prospects of finding a job. Those unemployed that moved are likely to have shorter durations than those who stayed behind.

Regional mobility is more relevant to this argument than house mobility and its effect was far greater in 1979, when unemployment was low. This latter fact may partly explain why the unemployed are less likely to move at a time of high unemployment (a result found in Pissarides and Wadsworth 1989).

We also considered the reason for entering unemployment. Unemployed workers of less than three years' duration are asked in the LFS whether they lost their previous job because of redundancy, because the job was temporary, or because of voluntary quitting. The average long-term unemployment ratios for each of these groups and for new entrants are similar in both 1979 and 1986, with the exception of the last group in 1986. As that group includes all those not asked this question, mostly workers of more than three years' duration, their average ratio is bound to be higher than the rest by construction. In 1986 some 27 per cent of unemployed workers had more than three years' duration. Thus, we conclude that the computed average long-term unemployment ratios indicate that the duration of unemployment is largely independent of the reason for entering unemployment. Our coefficient estimates, however, give a high and signifi-

72

cant estimate for new entrants in 1979, which we suspect is spurious and due to the small number of independent observations in that category.

Long-term unemployment is on average lower among women than men, the average ratios for women being 19 per cent in 1979 and 31 per cent in 1986. The regression analysis reported in Table 4.10 shows that in 1979 only personal characteristics and occupation contributed significantly to the observed differentials in long-term unemployment ratios. Long-term unemployment was almost exclusively a feature of women who lost manual jobs, other women experiencing very little. Younger women experienced

Table 4.10a Long-term unemployment differentials (men), 1979 and 1986

Attribute	1979		1986	
	Long-term unemployment rate	*Differential due to attribute*	*Long-term unemployment rate*	*Differential due to attribute*
Age 16–19	14.5	−32.2	27.4	−35.0
Age 20–24	23.7	−14.4	47.5	−9.1
Age 25–34	27.1	−9.6	53.5	−6.2
Age 35–49	40.3	–	61.1	–
Age 50–64	43.8	8.5	59.5	1.2
Single	28.0	8.5	45.3	0.5
Married	33.1	–	56.6	–
Degree	26.7	−0.7	35.2	−11.6
GCE	17.8	−11.4	39.6	−8.8
Other	16.6	−12.3	47.3	−4.1
None	35.0	–	59.0	–
Non-white	29.1	4.1	50.8	3.9
White	31.0	–	55.2	–
Manual	32.4	3.6	55.6	20.5
Non-manual	21.2	–	29.5	–
Council tenant	35.5	12.8	62.1	19.0
Private tenant	29.2	8.2	52.4	16.9
Owner occupier	21.4	–	37.4	–
Dependent child	29.4	0.2	51.7	−2.4
None	32.4	–	50.5	–
Move region	5.0	−24.0	29.7	−13.6
No move	31.6	–	52.1	–
Move house	23.3	−3.8	40.5	−11.7
No move	32.4	–	53.2	–
Redundancy	33.5	−0.9	35.1	−32.2
Temporary job	21.4	−9.0	33.5	−31.1
New entrant	26.2	−25.9	41.9	−8.1
Quit	30.9	–	67.4	–

Source: LFS

73

Table 4.10b Long-term unemployment differentials (women), 1979 and 1986

Attribute	1979		1986	
	Long-term unemployment rate	Differential due to attribute	Long-term unemployment rate	Differential due to attribute
Age 16–19	12.5	−17.1	22.6	−20.8
Age 20–24	16.8	−8.8	34.4	−7.6
Age 25–34	15.7	−6.2	25.3	−5.4
Age 35–49	23.6	–	34.9	–
Age 50–59	32.6	3.4	47.0	6.2
Single	24.0	12.8	36.1	11.3
Married	16.1	–	26.0	–
Degree	13.9	−1.4	17.7	−8.7
GCE	14.3	−1.5	25.5	−0.7
Other	14.7	−2.6	30.9	4.1
None	22.4	–	36.8	–
Non-white	18.5	2.3	30.7	3.4
White	19.5	–	33.3	–
Manual	22.5	13.0	37.2	14.7
Non-manual	9.6	–	17.7	–
Council tenant	21.7	1.0	39.3	7.9
Private tenant	20.8	4.0	32.9	7.8
Owner occupier	16.6	–	25.2	–
Dependent child	16.1	−6.8	24.6	−15.1
None	3.0	–	39.9	–
Move region	9.8	−5.1	9.0	−21.0
No move	19.8	–	32.0	–
Move house	12.3	−6.1	20.8	−10.0
No move	20.7	–	33.0	–
Redundancy	23.1	1.0	23.4	−11.3
Temporary job	13.1	−4.6	26.7	−2.9
New entrant	12.2	3.8	32.3	2.4
Quit	19.6	–	32.8	–

Source: LFS

less long-term unemployment, like their male counterparts. Finally, unlike men, single women had more long-term unemployment, but women with dependent children had less. These results contrast with the analysis of overall unemployment incidence, where women with dependent children were found to experience more unemployment.

Results are little changed in 1986, when the higher long-term unemployment ratios enable more precise estimates of the various effects in the regression analysis. The manual/non-manual differential remains important but does not widen. Thus, in contrast to men, women in non-manual

74

occupations suffered as much from the rise of long-term unemployment as women in manual occupations. As in 1979, education is unimportant.

The age differentials do not widen between 1979 and 1986. The same is true of marital status but women with dependent children suffered less from the rise in long-term unemployment.

Women in council accommodation or private rentals have higher long-term unemployment ratios than other women, but the differentials are not big. In contrast, recent movers have less long-term unemployment than women who did not move, confirming the results of the analysis of mobility and unemployment obtained for men.

RECURRENT UNEMPLOYMENT

We now analyse the relation between recurrent unemployment and individual characteristics. The definition of recurrent unemployment is con-

Table 4.11 Recurrent unemployment incidence, 1979 and 1986

Variable	1979		1986	
	Sample mean	Estimate	Sample mean	Estimate
No. obs.	1,288		1,199	
Dependent	0.147		0.381	
Intercept		−3.37		−0.77*
Female	0.335	0.32*	0.370	−0.04*
Age 16–19	0.132	0.39*	0.203	1.70
Age 20–24	0.223	0.23*	0.263	1.21
Age 25–34	0.275	0.30*	0.241	0.39*
Age 50–ret.	0.135	0.14*	0.102	−0.44*
Single	0.418	0.61	0.540	0.19*
Degree	0.033	−0.22*	0.069	0.46*
GCE	0.191	−0.56	0.334	−0.35*
Other	0.102	−0.21*	0.158	−0.53
Race	0.058	0.78	0.083	1.04
Manual	0.718	0.76	0.695	1.43
Cncl tnt	0.520	0.38*	0.343	0.69
Prvt tnt	0.125	0.42*	0.117	0.64
Dep chd	0.488	0.25*	0.461	−0.25*
Move rgn	0.044	−0.77*	0.044	0.42*
Move hse	0.195	−0.30*	0.174	−0.69
Redundancy	0.426	−0.53	0.285	−1.41
Temp job	0.111	0.67	0.158	−0.39

Source: LFS

Note: The sample is restricted to unemployed persons of less than three months duration. The dependent variable takes value 1 if the respondent was unemployed one year prior to interview and value zero otherwise. All variables are zero–one dummies. A star (*) denotes insignificant estimate.

strained by data limitations. LFS respondents are only asked whether they were unemployed twelve months prior to interview. We define the recurrent unemployed as those who are currently unemployed with duration of three months or less and who were also unemployed twelve months previously.

The regression results are given in Table 4.11 and the differentials in Table 4.12. Because of the small sample size, we group men and women and introduce a new variable for gender. Thus we allow for differences in

Table 4.12 Recurrent unemployment differentials, 1979 and 1986

Attribute	1979		1986	
	Recurrent unemployment rate	Differential due to attribute	Recurrent unemployment rate	Differential due to attribute
Women	16.5	4.2	36.0	−0.1
Men	13.7	–	39.3	–
Age 16–19	22.8	4.8	64.3	35.9
Age 20–24	14.6	2.7	53.3	23.7
Age 25–34	14.4	3.6	26.6	5.9
Age 35–49	12.2	–	17.1	–
Age 50–ret.	11.5	1.6	13.0	−5.4
Single	19.3	7.6	51.8	3.4
Married	11.3	–	22.1	–
Degree	9.3	−2.9	31.3	11.2
GCE	8.5	−6.4	33.9	−8.3
Other	14.3	−2.6	36.0	−12.2
None	16.7	–	43.2	–
Non-white	21.3	12.3	58.0	25.3
White	14.2	–	36.3	–
Manual	17.2	7.9	49.0	25.8
Non-manual	8.3	–	13.4	–
Council tenant	17.5	3.9	52.1	15.6
Private tenant	16.2	4.4	45.0	14.5
Owner occupier	10.0	–	27.8	–
Dependent child	16.0	3.2	35.3	−6.0
None	13.3	–	39.9	–
Move region	5.3	7.5	37.7	10.2
No move	15.1	–	38.1	–
Move house	11.2	3.6	29.2	−15.3
No move	15.5	–	40.0	–
Redundancy	10.7	−5.9	15.5	−30.8
Temporary job	25.9	10.9	33.2	−10.0
Quit	15.6	–	51.1	–

Source: LFS

the incidence of recurrent unemployment between men and women but not for variations in the effect of their characteristics. Our estimates, however, show that there is no significant gender difference.

In 1979 only 15 per cent of unemployed workers experienced recurrent unemployment. Our regression analysis identifies only two attributes as significant. First race, where non-whites appear to be more likely to experience recurrent unemployment than whites. Second, as with overall and long-term unemployment, recurrent unemployment is more frequently observed amongst manual workers than amongst non-manuals. In 1986, both these effects continued to be dominant, especially the manual/non-manual differential, which widened substantially. Recurrent unemployment in 1986 increased to 38 per cent on average. Non-manual workers experienced hardly any increase, the burden of the higher unemployment falling almost entirely on manual workers.

Two other attributes become significant in 1986. Workers under 25 experience more recurrent unemployment than older workers. When contrasted with our findings on long-term unemployment, this diminishes the apparent privileged position of young workers identified earlier. The percentage of younger workers who experience recurrent unemployment is of the same order of magnitude as the percentage of older workers who experience long-term unemployment. Thus, the difference between young and old workers is that the former are more likely to be found in jobs which may be temporary or dead-end. In contrast the latter are more likely to leave unemployment for a regular job. Secondly, housing tenure becomes important in 1986. Tenants in council or private properties experience more recurrent unemployment than owners occupiers, in line with our earlier results.

CONCLUSIONS

In this chapter we have examined the incidence of unemployment and the incidence of long-term and recurrent unemployment amongst men and women, making use of information in the 1979 and the 1986 Labour Force Surveys. The analysis of the relation between characteristics of employed and unemployed workers shed light on aspects of incidence in two years with substantially different overall unemployment rates. We found that the most important influence on unemployment incidence is occupation. Unemployment is mainly concentrated amongst manual workers in the Midland and Northern regions of the country. Council properties have particularly high concentrations of unemployed workers, especially after many employed workers in council accommodation bought their properties in the early 1980s. After controlling for all these factors, workers from non-white ethnic backgrounds still face higher unemployment rates than others.

Long-term and recurrent unemployment are also mainly features of manual occupations. Within the group of unemployed workers the incidence of these two types of unemployment is not as differentiated as the incidence of overall unemployment within the entire workforce. An interesting finding is that youths have high recurrent unemployment but very little long-term unemployment. In contrast adult workers experience more long-term unemployment but little recurrence.

Hence policies needed to alleviate unemployment and its associated problems need to vary both over the course of the economic cycle and across specific groups in the population. In bad times, the needs of a large stock of unemployed workers take precedence over longer-term labour market planning. What is apparent from our analysis, however, is that the same groups of individuals are at risk, whatever the state of the country's economic performance. Only the severity of the risk fluctuates. As the economy enters the 1990s, with aggregate unemployment rising once more, it becomes important to recognize that whilst the risk of unemployment amongst the entire population is increasing, those at either end of the age spectrum and the unskilled will suffer disproportionately. Policies to rectify the problem should specifically address these issues.

Since occupation is a primary explanatory variable behind unemployment incidence, then policy-makers could seek to establish appropriate active labour market interventions. For example, schemes for the unskilled in high-risk occupations and economic sectors could be established, specifically intended to provide these workers with the skills to enable them to participate more effectively in the labour market. This would help reduce both the incidence of recurrent unemployment amongst the young and long-term unemployment amongst older workers (see also Chapter 2 on the importance of basic skills training). A recognized skill-training scheme could make workers more attractive to employers and also help avoid the potentially damaging consequences of a protracted spell without work. A trained workforce are also less likely to enter jobs with limited prospects or duration and hence avoid the costs of recurrent unemployment. Policy-makers should seek to target any training schemes at those vulnerable groups – the young, older workers, non-whites and women – for whom the risks of unemployment are most severe.

NOTE AND REFERENCES

Methodological Note

The regressions presented in this paper estimate the likelihood that an individual i will be observed in state j (e.g. unemployment) as a function of a set of personal and environmental characteristics, X_i.

(1) $$Y_{ij} = BX_i + u$$

The dependent variable, Y_{ij}, takes the value one if the individual is unemployed and zero otherwise. Assuming that the error term, u, is logistically distributed, then the probability of being unemployed is given by

$$(2) \qquad Pij = \frac{1}{1 + EXP\ (-bXi)}$$

where b are the maximum likelihood parameter estimates

Taking natural logs

$$(3) \qquad Log\left[\frac{Pij}{1 - Pij}\right] = bXi$$

The differential propensity of individual i to experience the state j from the rest of the population is therefore

$$(4) \qquad Log\left[\frac{Pij}{1 - Pij}\right] - Log\left[\frac{Pj}{1 - Pj}\right] = b\ (Xi - X)$$

where Pj is the population average probability of being observed in state j and X are the population average characteristics.

In order to calculate the unemployment differential attributable to a specific characteristic xi, (e.g. age), then we assume individual i is identical to the rest of the population except for the variable xi. Hence (4) reduces to

$$(5) \qquad Log\left[\frac{Pij}{1 - Pij}\right] = \frac{Pj}{1 - Pj} + bXi$$

We calculate Pij from (4) and estimate the specific unemployment differential as the difference between Pij and the unemployment rate ud of the default group for each variable x, where ud is given by

$$(6) \qquad ud = \frac{Ud}{Ld} = \frac{Ud}{U} * \frac{U}{L} / \frac{Ld}{L}$$

The right-hand side components of (6) can be calculated from Tables 4.2, 4.6 and 4.8.

References

Hughes, G. and McCormick, B. (1985) 'Migration Intentions in the UK: Which Households want to Migrate and which Succeed?', *Economic Journal*, 95: 113–23.

Nickell, S. (1979) 'Education and Lifetime Patterns of Unemployment', *Journal of Political Economy*, 87: 117–32.

—— (1980) 'A Picture of Male Unemployment in Britain', *Economic Journal*, 90: 776–94.

Pissarides, C. and Wadsworth, J. (1989) 'Unemployment and the Inter-Regional Mobility of Labour', *Economic Journal*, 99: 739–55.

5

THE ROLE OF EMPLOYERS IN THE LABOUR MARKET

Malcolm Maguire[1]

INTRODUCTION

Those responsible for recruitment in employing organizations effectively act as gatekeepers to the labour market. They are able to structure the entry to work and to constrain movement within the labour market by virtue of their control over the recruitment process. Their particular requirements must be met before individuals are able to gain access to jobs. This chapter will focus on the part played by employers in determining the distribution of job opportunities, the constraints under which employers operate in exercising control over that distribution, and their attitudes towards the employment of unemployed people.

Government policies in the 1980s were targeted at the unemployed themselves, with underlying assumptions that the problem of unemployment is a problem of unemployed people (their attitudes, behaviour, and so on). However, the importance of employers' role in the labour market means that unemployment is also a problem of employers' attitudes and behaviour and it will be the argument of this chapter that it is as appropriate for government to intervene in employers' attitudes and behaviour as it is for government to intervene in unemployed people's attitudes and behaviour, and that indeed doing the latter without the former is not only misguided but neglectful.

The chapter begins with a discussion of the factors which determine the level of employment and the type of labour demanded by employers. The research findings on which this discussion is based stem from previous work carried out by the Centre for Labour Market Studies at the University of Leicester, supplemented by data from two very recent pieces of research carried out at the Centre[2].

THE DETERMINANTS OF EMPLOYMENT LEVELS

From our earlier research (see Ashton, Maguire and Spilsbury, 1990), discussions with senior management about the factors they perceived as determining the level of employment in the firm, revealed that the main concerns were the size of the product market and the firm's share of the market, the degree of competition in the market and the employment–output relationship. These are discussed below.

Product market

The product market was invariably seen by senior managers as the most important determinant of the level of employment in firms in the private sector. The size of the workforce in a firm operating in a predominantly British market will be influenced by the general level of demand and by the ability of the firm to obtain a larger share of that market, subject to import penetration. For firms operating in international markets, while the overall level of world demand sets limits to employment levels, individual firms operating in Britain can increase their share of world markets.

The employment–output relationship

The capacity for changes in the demand for a firm's product to generate alterations to a company's demand for labour is largely dependent on the character of the employment–output relationship. Many organizations experienced considerable changes in this relationship during the recession. We distinguished two types of employment–output relationship. The first is where capital is assumed to be infinitely divisible and is depicted as a smooth employment–output curve. To produce more output, further employment of labour is required. Firms in the traditional manufacturing industries of footwear, clothing and furniture and those in retail and catering most closely approximate this type. In the second type, capital is not infinitely divisible but comes in large blocks. A factory can operate with a minimum number of people to run it and output can be varied along a range of levels without requiring a dramatic rise in employment.

Technology

Technology plays an important part in determining the character of the employment–output relationship, while also influencing the type of labour recruited. The speed and sophistication of modern manufacturing equipment, such as CNC machines and Flexible Machining Systems, now mean that considerable increases in output can be achieved by introducing such machinery, although it may lead to a reduction in staff, as fewer operatives are required. In most cases the new equipment is capable of coping even with a major expansion of product demand. Where new technology has reduced the labour input required, companies must expand their market share or enter new markets if employment levels are to be sustained or increased.

OTHER FACTORS AFFECTING EMPLOYMENT LEVELS

Ownership and political factors are also significant determinants of employment. They are both external to the firm and tend to be underestimated in the current debates.

Political factors

Political factors may affect employing organizations in different ways. A firm's product market, or their ability to compete in a product market, can be greatly influenced by government legislation and policy or decisions taken outside Britain. Perhaps the best example of legislation making a direct impact on a company's product market has been the de-regulation of the financial sector which has taken place in recent years and has created intense competition between banks, building societies and insurance companies.

Ownership

Patterns of ownership may also be important in determining employment levels, particularly where ownership, and perhaps the head office, is based outside the United Kingdom. In a multinational company, decisions about investment in particular products and hence employment levels may be beyond the control of the British subsidiary, and may be made on the basis of the competitiveness, in terms of labour or production costs, of a subsidiary in another part of the world. Even if production is maintained in Britain, the company's policy towards the training of staff may play a significant part in determining the type of labour to be recruited, whether it be fully trained or 'green' labour, and the way that labour is deployed.

TYPE OF LABOUR RECRUITED

All the above factors may significantly influence the general demand for labour within the firm. Some of them, such as the particular technology in operation, or decisions about the product market, can also influence the type of labour recruited. The thrust of the argument in the latter half of this chapter is, however, that the type of labour recruited is also highly dependent on employers' perceptions of, and stereotyping of, particular groups in the population. Effectively, these groups encounter direct or indirect discrimination from employers. In addition, the type of labour recruited may be dependent on the supply side. It is the interaction of

82

demand-side and supply-side factors which leads to decisions about which group is recruited. On the supply side, important factors are wage rates, the domestic household structure, local labour market conditions and customs, and political constraints.

Wage rates

With regard to the part played by wages, labour-intensive organizations are conscious of the need to keep down labour costs in order to remain competitive. Thus, firms in the clothing and footwear and hotel and catering industries are under pressure to keep labour costs down by employing youths or adult females. However, the extent to which firms deliberately discriminate in favour of youths because of their low wage costs depends upon a number of factors, such as the extent of competition in the product market, the share of wages in the total cost of production, the payment system, and the strength of organized labour.

In capital-intensive organizations production costs are dependent to a lesser extent on labour costs. The crucial factor is often the continuous operation of the extremely sophisticated and expensive machinery. An employer is mindful that the key workers required to ensure this are dependable, responsible and feel a commitment to the organization. Recruitment is therefore likely to be focused on individuals who have demonstrated their capacity to work conscientiously and have family responsibilities which will prohibit them from behaving irresponsibly.

Domestic household structure

The organization of the household is very important in influencing the type of labour recruited. The family responsibilities of married males are seen as important in ensuring commitment. Married females are seen as attractive in jobs where possible domestic commitments do not conflict with the employers' requirements. They are regarded as particularly attractive for part-time jobs, where work and domestic commitments can be more easily managed, or in firms where high labour turnover can be seen as advantageous in helping the firm adjust to fluctuations in output. Single females are seen as less attractive in jobs where there is a considerable investment in training on the part of the employer, because they may break their career for marriage or the start of a family. These stereotypes are important in that they inform the mechanisms by which differences in the social location of the sexes are transformed into different opportunities in the labour market. They also explain why labour substitution between adult males and married females is difficult in certain parts of the labour market.

Local labour markets

The significance of local labour markets in structuring the demand for labour is well established (see Ashton, Maguire and Spilsbury 1990). This demand will be highly dependent on the industrial distribution of firms within a local labour market, and those firms' occupational structures, as well as the level of unemployment and availability of a pool of labour in the locality.

Political constraints

Political factors again play an important role in influencing the type of labour recruited, either directly through legislation, such as the Health and Safety at Work Act, or indirectly through training schemes, such as YTS (now YT), which has encouraged some employers to substitute youths for adults. Political pressure has also been important in enhancing the demand for part-time labour, whether, for example, through the imposition of cash limits on local authorities or through the privatization of services.

Factors which structure the supply of workers

Further constraints are placed on the behaviour of employers by factors which structure the supply of workers. Of great significance here are the institutional structures which regulate this supply. Foremost among these are the educational and training systems, which provide external constraints and influence employers' recruitment practices and the types of labour recruited for different types of job (see Chapter 2 for a discussion of education and training in the UK). However, employers are not passive agents. Their interpretation of worker characteristics, and especially the position of the person in the family, are also important forces which serve to differentiate labour. The interplay of these two sources of differentiation leads to the segmentation of the labour market.

Our earlier research (Ashton, Maguire and Spilsbury 1987) identified four distinct occupational groupings, by which the labour market is segmented:

1 professional, managerial, administration and technician jobs;
2 clerical jobs;
3 skilled manual jobs; and
4 semi-skilled and unskilled manual jobs and sales jobs.

Within each of these segments, access to jobs, and the career chances they provide, differs for males and females.

Wider characteristics

When deciding from which groups to recruit, employers' assessments will often be influenced by their perceptions of worker characteristics. Through their control over the recruitment process, they are able to impose their own, sometimes idiosyncratic, definitions, which effectively determine the access of different groups to jobs. It is the ability of employers to enforce their definitions of worker characteristics that provides one of the most important mechanisms linking the position a person occupies in the family and society as a whole to their position in the labour market.

Among the factors which are of major importance here are gender, age, race, disability and employment status, and there is substantial evidence that stereotyping and discrimination, on the part of employers, profoundly affect their recruitment decisions. However, before considering the factors referred to above it is necessary to say something about the context in which employers' recruitment decisions are made. Richard Jenkins (1990 and subsequent personal communication) rightly points up some of the complexities of this decision-making. He has argued that, in recruiting the 'best' person for the job, there is a

> subtle distinction which can be drawn between selection criteria of suitability and of acceptability. Suitability concerns the applicant's ability to perform the tasks that are entailed in the job and may embrace a range of criteria, from physique to formal qualifications to relevant experience. Acceptability, on the other hand, concerns the recruiter's assessment of whether or not the applicant will 'fit' and may include a wide range of social, cultural and individual factors, from personal hygiene to appearance, from marital or family circumstances (which are thought to relate to reliability) to gender, and from age to ethnicity or 'race'; a very mixed bag indeed. In some situations, such as jobs dealing with the public, for example, the distinction between acceptability and suitability is blurred. This is also often the case for 'women's work', in all of its different forms.

Jenkins also cites the possibility of decisions being influenced by 'managerial politics and conflict', and direct and indirect discrimination, as well as

> the cultural context, both inside and outside the workplace (it is, for example, still socially respectable in many contexts to discriminate against black people); the economics of the situation, in particular, estimations of who is cheapest to recruit; the psychological dynamics of the interview; and traditional or customary stereotypes of the appropriate workers for specific jobs.

His conclusion that 'the selection process, for many jobs and in many companies, may be summed up as complex, something of a lottery, and involving multiplex criteria for decision-making', supports the findings of our earlier research which emphasized the apparent lack of rationality in recruitment decisions.

Gender

The extent of sex segregation in the labour market has been well established (Hakim 1979; Martin and Roberts 1984; Dex 1985; Walby and Bagguley 1990). Employers' perceptions of the characteristics of males and females as potential recruits, are related to traditional values about domestic circumstances, notably about the domestic division of labour. Males who have family responsibilities in the form of mortgage repayments and children to maintain, are regarded as the most desirable recruits for routine operative jobs, as it is felt that their domestic commitments will ensure that they work regularly and in a disciplined manner. A standard response to requests to define the 'ideal' manual worker is: 'a male aged between 25 and 35, married with two kids, a mortgage and repayments on a car'. By contrast females are seen as more committed to their domestic role. In the event of a clash of loyalties, such as when a child is ill, the domestic role is expected to have first claim on the mother's loyalties. For this reason employers perceive females as being less committed and hence less stable employees than males. Consequently, an employer recruiting labour for a capital-intensive plant which requires a series of cohesive work groups, which have to work shifts to ensure continuity of production, will deem the extra cost of the labour of prime age males worthwhile. On the other hand, in industries such as hosiery and footwear, where the work is individual-machine-based, and where high rates of labour turnover can allow adjustments to be made to the size of the workforce to match seasonable fluctuations in demand, the perceived personal characteristics of females, in addition to their lower wages, can be seen as advantageous.

For higher status professional, administrative and management jobs, adult males have traditionally been stereotyped as being more committed to a career in the organization than are females. In the eyes of employers the possibility of females interrupting their career to have children renders them potentially less likely to repay fully any investment made in their training, especially if they decide to return to work only on a part-time basis.

Thus for many years banks and other financial institutions used to make a distinction between males as career employees and females as non-career employees. For this reason males were recruited into career grades as future managers and technical experts, while females predominantly entered non-career grade jobs as cashiers and clerks. In recent years, the combined influence of equal opportunities legislation and a fear of future labour shortages at the career level, has led to the diminution in importance of this division. Increasingly females are being accepted into career positions. This change coincides with a trend amongst female workers to spend less time out of the labour force for the purpose of childbirth and child-rearing (Martin and Roberts 1984; Dex 1987).

However, the very fact that there appears to have been a shift in employers' perceptions of females as 'acceptable' recruits for some occupations, highlights one of the underpinning themes of this chapter, namely that employers' perceptions of the characteristics of particular groups may be shown by research to be inaccurate or unfounded, or, when faced with difficulties in recruiting, may suddenly cease to be relevant.

Some writers have expressed scepticism about the degree to which employers will significantly change their recruitment practices, in terms of the characteristics of those recruited, even if there are shifts in the channels of recruitment used (Wood and Manwaring 1988). By contrast, other studies have shown employers' practices to be sensitive to shifts in the availability of labour, so that, in times of recession, members of disadvantaged groups will find it difficult to get jobs, because of increased competition from a greater number of job-seekers (Meager and Metcalf 1987; Bevan and Fryatt 1988). In Jenkins' terms it may be that, as suggested by Jewson *et al.* (1990), the criteria for acceptability are raised.

Age

Age segmentation is a recognized phenomenon of the labour market. Our own previous research has focused on how young people's early experience of the labour market is structured by age requirements for entry to many jobs, which effectively differentiate the youth labour market from the adult labour market (see Ashton, Maguire and Garland 1982; Ashton and Maguire 1986).

Employers were found to have many reasons, such as the perceived lack of responsibility of young people, their lack of training, and the regulations governing shift working, for not recruiting 16-year-old school-leavers for a great many semi-skilled and unskilled jobs. By contrast, entry to apprenticeship training is confined almost entirely to 16- and 17-year-olds, due to employers' recruitment practices, and the institutional arrangements for training.

As far as older workers (over-50s) are concerned, their acceptability for recruitment generally tends to fluctuate with changes in the relationship between the supply of, and demand for, labour. During the first half of the 1970s, concern was expressed about the difficulties the older unemployed were experiencing in returning to employment, as employers preferred prime-age workers, who could potentially offer greater longevity in a job.

At a time when there were suggestions that this conventional wisdom was being questioned by some employers, that is, as they began to realise that there was greater stability among the over-50s, the whole issue was relegated to relative unimportance by steeply rising levels of youth unemployment, and the onset of the recession. Soaring unemployment rates transformed perceptions of the 'problem' of older workers. The Job Release Scheme sought to encourage the early retirement of male workers over the age of 62 in order to create more opportunities for the young unemployed. In addition, a widely canvassed suggestion, supported by the TUC, among others, to alleviate high levels of unemployment, was to lower the retirement age. In 1983 a change in benefit regulations went part way towards this by allowing males over 60 who had been unemployed for more than one year to transfer to a higher rate of supplementary benefit, while being regarded as having left the labour market.

Even those firms which survived the recession and began to recruit again were not necessarily prone to take on older workers in large numbers. Many firms, particularly in manufacturing industry, had shed labour, or, at best, frozen recruitment for a time, and, post-recession, were aware of an age imbalance in their workforces which was unfavourable to younger age groups. In order to redress this imbalance, any recruitment was likely to be targeted at these younger age groups, and certainly not at the over-50s. Equally important, during the same period, was the rapid pace of technological change which radically altered the content of many occupational tasks. Popular perceptions of the capabilities of older workers are that they are less trainable than younger people, who are more likely to have had some 'hands on' experience of new technology.

In the latter part of the 1980s an increasingly buoyant economy, coupled with demographic trends which were drastically reducing the numbers of 16–19-year-olds entering the labour market, generated fears about labour shortages. As a consequence, employers in some parts of the country, notably the South East of England, began to reassess their recruitment strategies. The shortfall in young people began to be tackled by targeting alternative sources of recruitment, such as females who have been out of the labour market, and older (sometimes even retired) people. This has been referred to as a 'wrinklies' policy.

ETHNIC MINORITIES

A substantial body of literature has focused on the position of ethnic minorities in the labour market (see, for example, Jewson et al. 1990; Jewson and Mason 1986; Jenkins 1986; Lee and Wrench 1987; and see Chapters 4 and 9). Jenkins has pointed to employers' use of informal, often word-of-mouth, methods of recruitment, effectively leading to discrimination against those groups which do not have access to the appropriate information networks. Jewson *et al.* have shown how the use of such recruitment channels can result in the characteristics of a firm's current workforce being reproduced, often to the disadvantage of ethnic minorities. As with other groups of job-seekers, employers' stereotyping can inhibit their ability to gain entry to jobs. Fevre (1984) goes further and contends that attributing the outcomes of employers' recruitment decisions to stereotyping masks what is, in truth, discrimination.

UNEMPLOYED JOB-SEEKERS

The segmentation of the labour market, and the stereotyping of employers both in terms of the desired characteristics for recruits to specific occupations, and the perceived characteristics of particular groups of workers (for example, male/female, older/younger) severely restrict the range of job opportunities to which many job-seekers have effective access. This problem is made worse for unemployed job-seekers where their unemployed status is, of itself, regarded as an undesirable characteristic (see Crowley-Bainton 1987). In a study of employers, Meager and Metcalf (1987) found that the recruitment channels they used for many lower level jobs, notably word-of-mouth methods, militated against the long-term unemployed who were unable to gain access to these channels. They were also found to be less likely to be short-listed for jobs where such a process existed.

Our own research revealed that employers' interpretations of what constituted an 'acceptable' length of unemployment, varied according to the overall level of unemployment in a locality. Thus, employers in a depressed area of the North-East were prepared to consider employing someone who had been unemployed for twelve months, as it was accepted that this did not reflect badly on an individual, due to the dearth of job opportunities locally. In contrast, employers in an economically buoyant area of the South-East would look unfavourably on someone who had been unemployed for one or two months, as it suggested work-shyness.

Irrespective of the degree of stereotyping or labelling of the unemployed, employers' recruitment methods may also militate against their gaining access to job opportunities. As pointed out above, this is often the case when informal word of mouth channels are used to solicit applications. Those who are excluded from these information networks are unable to apply. The unemployed are likely to find themselves in this position. It was also found in our research that some job-seekers were denied access to jobs on the basis of the area in which they lived. In many towns and cities the residents of certain housing estates or districts, which have obtained an image of a 'problem area' may be considered as bad risks by employers, at times when there is a ready supply of labour.

The effects of the segmentation of the labour market, as illustrated earlier, coupled with employers' recruitment practices, mean that the jobs available in a local labour market, particularly for those from the aforementioned groups, are restricted, in both number and scope. Thus, simplistic comparisons of the number of unemployed with the number of job vacancies in a locality disguise the true extent of the difficulties faced by groups of unemployed people in finding work. This chapter will now seek to illustrate the potency of some of these issues by referring to the findings of two recent research projects, one which focused on the difficulties experienced by older unemployed job-seekers, and another which addressed the issue of persistently high levels of unemployment in a particular inner city area.

EMPLOYERS' ATTITUDES TOWARDS RECRUITING OLDER WORKERS

For the study of 'Age as a Barrier to Employment', which was funded by the DTI's City Action Team, telephone interviews were carried out with representatives of 152 employing organizations in Leicester, Derby and Nottingham in 1989. Two-thirds of these were manufacturing establishments. The distribution of the sample by establishment size reflected that of firms generally, with over three-quarters of the service industry establishments and two-thirds of the manufacturing industry establishments employing fewer than 250 workers.

Around 60 per cent of all the firms in the sample claimed to be experiencing difficulty in recruiting particular groups of workers at the time of interview (Table 5.1). Over half of these cited skilled manual workers as a problem area (Table 5.2). In terms of numbers recruited recently, however, this occupational group was almost matched in importance by clerical or 'other non-manual' workers (Table 5.3). This points to the latter jobs being less problematic in recruitment terms.

Another significant finding was that 18 per cent of respondents mentioned managerial, professional or supervisory posts. This perhaps reflects shifts in occupational patterns, with increasing proportions of highly qualified workers. It should also be stated that these are not necessarily the types of jobs for which older people, or the long-term unemployed, would be considered. Indeed only three companies (2 per cent of the sample) said that they had recruited older unemployed people for these jobs (Table 5.4). The main points of access for the older unemployed were to manual occupations, 12 per cent of respondents having recruited them for skilled or semi-skilled jobs, and 9 per cent for unskilled jobs. If this can be read as reflecting employers' stereotyping of the capabilities of the older unemployed, the responses to this particular question cannot determine whether or not the stereotyping refers to an individual being old or being unemployed.

Table 5.1 Employers claiming that there were particular groups of workers which they were finding difficulty in recruiting, 1989

	Manufacturing		Service		Total	
	No.	%	No.	%	No.	%
Derby	18	56	10	53	28	55
Leicester	15	50	11	65	26	55
Nottingham	22	67	12	67	34	67
All	56	58	33	60	88	59

Table 5.2 Proportion of employers claiming to have recruitment problems, by occupational group, 1989 Derby, Leicester and Nottingham

Occupational group	%
Managerial/Professional/Supervisory	15
Computer jobs/VDU	8
Non-manual staff, e.g. clerical	16
Personal service, e.g. shop assistant	6
Trainees/apprentices	3
Shiftworkers	1
Skilled/semi-skilled	56
Unskilled	6
Other	19
Base	89

Table 5.3 Occupational type of the last three positions recruited, 1989 Derby, Leicester and Nottingham

Type	Total %	Manufacture %	Services %
Man/Prof/Supv	18	16	21
VDU Op/Computer	3	2	4
Other Non-Manual	25	26	24
Catering/Personal serv.	9	2	22
Appren./trainees	4	5	2
Shiftworkers	1	1	1
Skilled/Semi-skilled	26	34	13
Unskilled manual	9	9	10
Not applicable	4	4	3
Base	152	97	55

Of those who claimed to be experiencing difficulty in recruiting at the time of interview, discounting the 'other' category of which 80 per cent of responses referred to 'advertising', the training of existing staff was the most frequently cited policy response, being mentioned by 39 per cent (see

91

Table 5.5). This was followed by 'taking on people from government training schemes' (15 per cent), and then by 'recruiting older people, that is, over 50 years' (11 per cent). Although the number of establishments seeking to overcome recruitment difficulties by targeting older people was not high, it was in excess of those favouring directing recruitment at female returners to the labour market. This may have been attributable to the types of jobs for which workers were being sought. The sex stereotyping of occupations which is rife in employers' practices may mean that the skilled and semi-skilled manual jobs, which were the biggest single cause of difficulties were regarded as 'male' jobs, and therefore deemed unsuitable for female returners.

Table 5.4 Occupational type of jobs for which older unemployed people had been recruited, 1989 Derby, Leicester and Nottingham

Type	Total %	Manufacture %	Services %
Man/Prof/Supv	2	0	5
VDU Op/Computer	0	0	0
Other Non-manual	4	1	9
Catering/Personal serv.	3	1	7
Appren./trainees	0	0	0
Shiftworkers	1	1	0
Skilled/Semi-skilled	12	14	7
Unskilled manual	9	9	7
Other	1	1	2
Base	152	97	55

Note: Responses are the number of firms mentioning the occupational group etc.

Table 5.5 Measures taken to overcome recruitment problems, 1989 Derby, Leicester and Nottingham

Measure	% of firms claiming difficulties		
	Manufacturing	Service	Total
Training existing staff	43	33	39
Recruiting older people (over 50)	7	16	11
Recruiting retired people	–	1	1
Recruiting long-term unemployed	2	15	7
Taking on people on government training schemes, e.g. YTS, ET	10	30	15
Recruiting mothers returning to the work-force	7	9	8
Taking on part-time workers	2	15	10
Job-sharing	2	6	4
Other	66	52	61
No policy	5	12	8
Base	56	33	88

With regard to attitudes to longer-term unemployed people, fifteen of the twenty-eight respondents who had a specific recruitment policy related to an applicant's age stated that they would employ them. The age of the long-term unemployed did not emerge as a significant issue.

Thirty-two respondents to a question about what they considered to be long-term unemployment provided a spread of responses, from less than six months' (four respondents) to 'over two years' (six), the most frequently mentioned being 'six–eleven months' (eleven) and 'twelve–seventeen months' (nine). Nevertheless, there is a suggestion, albeit from a restricted sample, that anyone whose period of unemployment exceeds six months may be deemed to be less desirable as a prospective employee than those who became unemployed more recently (see also Chapter 3). This clearly has implications for the efficacy of initiatives such as Jobclubs and Restart interviews, access to which may be dependent on being unemployed for a spell of unemployment in excess of six months. Only four respondents stated that they had occupations for which they would only recruit people over 50 years of age, although nineteen claimed to have occupations for which they would tend to recruit older workers. Thirteen of these targeted the 50–54 age group, with smaller numbers favouring the over-55s. The main reasons for preferring older workers were their perceived 'reliability', 'experience' and 'conscientiousness'.

Of concern for the employment prospects of older people was the fact that fifty-nine respondents (39 per cent of the sample), stated that they had jobs for which they would not recruit older people. This again confirms that the labour market is segmented in terms of age. Unsurprisingly, just under 30 per cent of these respondents mentioned traineeships and apprenticeships as areas from which older people were excluded. The same proportion mentioned skilled or semi-skilled manual jobs as areas of exclusion, and a significant number (14) cited unskilled manual jobs. Some possible reasons for precluding older people from consideration for jobs requiring little or no skill will be suggested later. Essentially they relate to stereotyping of older people's capabilities and physical fitness. Suffice it to say at this stage that the responses, in terms of the categories provided, were:

Reason	Number of respondents
Need to be fit	32
Don't have qualifications	3
Don't have experience	1
Older people don't apply	13
Other	18

This clearly points to employers having reservations about older people's physical fitness, although it may also reflect a propensity to consider older people only for those relatively unskilled manual jobs which require physical strength or particular agility.

An analysis of the methods used to recruit workers (Table 5.6) shows local press advertising to be the most used for all types of employee. The Jobcentre scores well for recruitment to manual, clerical and personal service jobs, as do national press advertising for managerial and professional jobs and private employment agencies for managerial, professional and clerical jobs. From previous studies we would have expected 'word-of-mouth' to have been a more significant channel of recruitment. Overall, however, these findings clearly have implications for the advice on job search methods which is given to the unemployed.

Table 5.6 Methods used to recruit workers, 1989 Derby, Leicester and Nottingham

Method	Man./ prof.	VDU comp.	Other non-man.	Pers. service	Appren. trainee	Skilled/ semisk.	Unskilled
Jobcentre	8	4	21	26	4	36	15
Private employment agency	18	3	22	0	1	2	0
National press advert.	22	1	4	0	0	7	0
Local press advert.	46	9	77	27	10	85	17
Advert. on noticeboard	1	0	5	6	0	4	2
Word of mouth	6	1	6	3	0	15	10
Direct application	3	0	7	5	3	12	5
Internal promotion	11	1	11	2	3	10	0
Careers office	4	2	2	1	1	3	0
Trade union	1	0	0	0	1	14	0
Upgrading	0	2	1	0	1	2	0
Back files/personal application	1	0	0	0	0	5	4
Government	0	0	0	1	0	1	0
Other	15	2	12	4	5	12	1

Note: Responses are the number of firms mentioning the method, etc.

When asked to specify which method had been the one used by the successful applicant (Table 5.7), local press advertising remained the most important. However, there were increases in the significance of private employment agencies for clerical posts, and 'word-of-mouth' and 'direct application' for unskilled manual jobs. Conversely, the importance of the Jobcentre was much less than might have been expected from the distribution of methods used. This may be linked to some of the difficulties experienced by older people, by suggesting that employers tend to use other sources of applicants than the agency which places emphasis on assisting the long-term unemployed.

The qualifications required of candidates followed a predictable pattern (Table 5.8), with higher qualifications being significant for managerial and

94

Table 5.7 Methods successful in recruiting workers, 1989 Derby, Leicester and Nottingham

Method	Man./ prof.	VDU comp.	Other non-man.	Pers. service	Appren. trainee	Skilled/ semisk.	Unskilled
Jobcentre	3	1	11	11	0	12	8
Private employment agency	11	2	14	0	0	1	0
National press advert.	10	0	2	0	0	1	0
Local press advert.	32	7	57	23	8	66	14
Advert. on noticeboard	7	0	4	0	0	2	0
Word of mouth	7	1	6	2	0	12	10
Direct application	2	0	5	3	2	8	13
Internal promotion	3	0	4	1	3	3	0
Careers office	1	2	2	1	1	0	0
Trade Union	0	0	0	0	0	11	0
Upgrading	1	0	1	0	0	1	0
Back files/personal application	1	0	1	0	0	2	4
Government	0	0	0	0	0	0	0
Other	10	1	9	2	5	4	0

Note: Responses are the number of firms mentioning methods, etc.

professional jobs, school examinations for 'other non-manual' or clerical jobs, and vocational qualifications for skilled and semi-skilled manual jobs. However, high proportions of respondents claimed that no qualifications were demanded for 'other non-manual', personal service and manual jobs at all skill levels. This points to the lack of qualifications of older people being less of a disadvantage than might be first thought, although it should be remembered that these are the types of jobs which have been declining in numbers over many years.

Table 5.8 Qualifications looked for from candidates in recently filled positions, 1989 Derby, Leicester and Nottingham

Qualification	Man./ prof.	VDU comp.	Other non-man.	Pers. service	Appren. trainee	Skilled/ semisk.	Unskilled
School examinations	8	1	23	5	7	6	2
Vocational qual.	9	0	9	4	2	37	0
Higher qual.	22	4	5	0	1	0	0
Professional qual.	16	3	2	0	0	2	0
Other	11	5	19	13	3	49	1
Can't Say	4	0	2	0	0	5	3
None	17	4	60	27	6	58	36

The most important quality sought by employers in candidates for managerial and professional, computing, 'other non-manual' and skilled and semi-skilled jobs was 'experience' (Table 5.9). The second most important quality was 'reliability'. As will be seen later, these are precisely the qualities which our respondents most frequently mentioned when referring to the attributes of older workers, and points to age being a factor in their inability to gain employment, despite the fine words and expressions of being positive towards their recruitment from employers.

Table 5.9 Qualities sought in candidates, 1989 Derby, Leicester and Nottingham

Quality	Man./ prof.	VDU comp.	Other non-man.	Pers. service	Appren. trainee	Skilled/ semisk.	Unskilled
Experience	61	11	55	17	1	72	6
Reliability	30	4	49	10	7	56	16
Responsibility	21	3	26	8	2	28	6
Smart	13	3	30	26	3	7	7
Pleasant	17	3	42	22	7	11	5
Leadership	16	0	4	1	2	0	0
Internal candidate	14	5	14	8	2	1	0
Language	2	0	0	1	1	0	0
Job skill	15	2	29	7	0	28	0
Other	18	8	46	28	6	34	17
Can't say	6	0	2	3	0	2	3
None	1	0	0	1	3	3	3

Note: Responses are number of firms mentioning the qualifications, etc.

EMPLOYERS' PERCEPTIONS OF OLDER WORKERS

The final question to employers' representatives was 'Are there any other points which you would like to make about older people and your attitude towards their recruitment or anything else we have been discussing?'. This allowed the respondents to make spontaneous comments, which reflected their more general attitudes towards older workers. Some 57 per cent of manufacturing-sector respondents and 64 per cent of service-sector respondents professed a positive attitude towards the recruitment of older people. Only 5 per cent of respondents in manufacturing and 7 per cent from the service sector expressed antipathy towards their recruitment, the remainder being neutral. Indeed, 17 per cent of respondents stated that age was not a factor which was taken into consideration when recruiting.

The positive attributes of older workers mentioned were similar to the responses to the earlier question. Thus, 29 per cent mentioned 'reliability', 22 per cent mentioned 'conscientiousness', 'commitment' or an ability to get on with the job, and 15 per cent pointed to the experience which they possessed. Their perceived stability was also a factor, with a contention that employers would get more years service out of older people, as they were less likely to leave than younger people. With such apparently favourable attitudes towards older workers, it would seem that they would experience little difficulty in gaining employment. However, even when supportive or favourable comments were being made, there were indications of certain qualifications being made which detracted from older people's attractiveness as employees.

Firstly, it was clear that many respondents, while professing a willingness to employ older people, only regarded them as being suitable for a very restricted range of occupations, predominantly at the bottom end of the occupational hierarchy, as in:

> Well, there's only one and he's sweeping up on the factory floor, and I'm very satisfied with him. Firstly, it's a heavy manual job. No other jobs suitable for older people.

> They have to be reliable, honest, hygienic, clean. The last elderly person we employed was a gardener, and we wanted an older person with experience.

> I employed one sweeper, and he's done his job well. For the type of job in my department is set more for younger people. The young ones tend not to like boring jobs where you have to sit a lot for example, older people settle better for those jobs, so I suppose that in the other departments they employ more older people.

Secondly, some respondents stated that older people were reluctant to apply, possibly because they felt they would have little chance of success.

> For an interview, we require quite a high standard. Older people qualify more, because it's very vital for us to know the background of our employees, and older people have got more background. You can get a lot more references from previous employers. I do find when interviewing that older people are more reluctant to apply. They seem to write themselves off. Even though we're desperate for them, it seems difficult to recruit them.

Another drawback was the employers' reluctance to recruit older people for jobs requiring training. The feeling was that, because of their age, they were not regarded as being a sound investment, as in:

> They are all right for jobs that don't need training up, as I don't think it is worth it if they are near retirement.

> In principle, our average age is old at the moment. We would rather take younger people. As we have to train them on new products, we would rather train younger people.

There were also hints that the difficulties of incorporating older people into existing wage structures was used as a reason for their exclusion. A frequently mentioned factor which worked to the disadvantage of older people involved employers' perceptions of their health and physical fitness, particularly where it was related to physically demanding jobs:

> Far more reliable than younger workers in that they stay with us and take little time off. Would like to see more of them, they have a lot to offer but a lot of recruitment is for manual workers and we need young fit people for those jobs.

> Don't have any at all. We are not interested in older people because the job requires a fair amount of lifting and hard work.

> Older people are generally more reliable and conscientious, but unfortunately are not fit enough to do the jobs here.

Thus, there appears to be a considerable mismatch between the attitudes and views articulated by employers about their recruitment of older people, and their behaviour. This may not be due to any conscious attempt to deceive. Rather, it points to inherent stereotyping and discrimination within employing organizations, as exemplified in:

> We do discriminate, I think, as we don't tend to consider anyone of that age. I pulled out an application from someone not too long ago, who was over 50 and very suitably qualified, but had just been put on the 'no interview' pile because of age – I have interviewed that person, and he was just the person for the job.

If this is the case, policy measures need to be aware of the need to influence and educate the gatekeepers to jobs in the labour market about the benefits to be gained from taking older people into consideration for employment.

EMPLOYERS' ATTITUDE TOWARDS EMPLOYING THE INNER CITY UNEMPLOYED

A study conducted by the School for Advanced Urban Studies (1986) contended that employers were prejudiced in their attitudes towards the unemployed and were particularly unwilling to recruit long-term unemployed people. As part of our Employment Service's funded study of urban unemployment in Nottingham, interviews were carried out with local employers to determine the factors which militated against the employment of people from two specific inner city wards. Although at the outset it had been surmised that a lack of qualifications would be a significant factor in explaining the high levels of unemployment in the wards in question, it was found, as it had been in the 'Age as a Barrier to Employment' study, that most jobs for which employers were recruiting were unskilled or semi-skilled, and therefore rarely carried requirements for qualifications.

As far as the issue of discriminating against applicants from certain localities, or 'addressism' was concerned, this was strongly denied by employers. However, when asked about their perceptions of the wards which were the focus of the study, negative images invariably emerged. The reasons they proffered for the continuance of high levels of unemployment in these areas included:

These are socially deprived areas and people who live there do not get the same benefits from education, or the same opportunities;

The housing is cheaper than in other parts of the city and this would tend to attract the unemployed to those areas;

It is a long-standing problem. There has been a loss of jobs from the heavier type of industry from those areas;

These areas have high ethnic population and there is racial discrimination;

A core of the population do not want to work;

A core of the population have unrealistic expectations of pay based on their skill levels;

Some have been discouraged from seeking work by their training experiences which have left them more disillusioned than when they began.

Similarly with regard to the issue of racial discrimination, employers contended that they recruited the most suitable person for the job, irrespective of race. The limitations of the research process need to be remembered here, for it is highly unlikely that employers who are aware of the existence of Race Relations and Equal Opportunities legislation would admit, in response to a postal questionnaire, or telephone or face-to-face interview, that they practised discrimination against any particular group.

In terms of both 'addressism' and 'racism', while not being consciously or overtly discriminatory in their attitudes, the recruitment methods and selection criteria used by employers may operate to the detriment of the unemployed, particularly those from ethnic minority groups, from the inner city. The favoured recruitment methods were through personal recommendation, word of mouth, unsolicited direct applications and internal noticeboards. As stated earlier, these may disadvantage those who do not have access to the information networks involved, and result in the reproduction, racially, of the existing workforce. Although many respondents notified vacancies to the Jobcentre as a matter of course, they were critical of the Jobcentre's inability, or refusal, to undertake the required pre-screening. This highlights a long-standing dilemma of the public employment service, which is often placed in low regard by employers because of its efforts to assist the more disadvantaged job-seekers.

When asked to identify the criteria used in the selection process, those most commonly cited were:

– relevant work experience;
– literacy and numeracy;

- the right attitude to work;
- an assessed ability to do the job;
- personal appearance;
- being fit, healthy and strong;
- willing to do repetitive, boring work;
- willing to work unsocial hours.

On further questioning it was ascertained that a question mark would be placed against anyone who was long-term unemployed, however that was defined.

CONCLUSIONS

The early part of this chapter pointed to the fact that although employers are able to determine which individuals gain access to specific jobs in the labour market, their decisions about recruitment levels are constrained by a variety of factors, some of which are external to the organization. It is also important to stress that the labour market is segmented in occupational terms, but the dynamic element, incorporating the factors such as the relocation of capital to low labour cost countries, the impact of new technology and the intensification of competition through the growth of global product markets, are generating changes in the configuration of the segments. Thus, there have been enormous shifts in the types of occupations which are demanded, in terms of skill level, and in the employment relationship, with the growth of part-time jobs, fixed-term contracts, the use of subcontracting, and so on. Our evidence would suggest, however, that there has been little movement in employers' traditional stereotyping of suitable applicants, by gender, age or length of unemployment. This is despite a growing awareness among employers of the effects of demographic change, and exhortations to re-target their recruitment drives in favour of, for example, older workers and female returners to the labour market.

The attitudes evinced by employers would suggest that devoting greater resources to providing one-to-one guidance and advice to the long-term unemployed would do little to enhance their acceptability in the eyes of employers. It could be argued that the emphasis should be on providing assistance in the early days of individuals' spells of unemployment, in order to prevent them from becoming 'long-term unemployed' and thereby stigmatized. However, this would be difficult to justify on grounds of cost-effectiveness, as undue resources would be expended on those who would have a relatively high probability of experiencing short periods of frictional unemployment, before returning to employment.

Clearly, if employers' attitudes and stereotyping are key factors which work to the disadvantage of certain groups of job-seekers, then some means of effecting a change in employer behaviour needs to be sought. The introduction of the Job Interview Guarantee scheme, with its emphasis on the Employment Service working closely with employers throughout the recruitment process, rather than merely responding to what employers say they want, may be a step forward. Suggestions have been made for the introduction of legislation, such as the implementation of positive action programmes, or contract compliance arrangements, which could be applied in relation to race, gender, disability and long-term unemployment. Legislative intervention in Britain historically, however, as in the cases of the Sex Discrimination Act and the Race Relations Act, has been of a 'weaker' nature and has not on its own significantly affected behaviour. In the absence of more direct and stronger intervention by government in employers' recruitment behaviour, we will have to rely on the emergence of chronic labour shortages, or extreme difficulties in recruiting what have traditionally been deemed to be appropriate job-seekers, both of which seem highly unlikely at a national level in the foreseeable future.

NOTES AND REFERENCES

Notes

1 I would like to thank David Ashton and Martin Hoskins, of the Centre for Labour Market Studies at Leicester University, for their comments and assistance in producing the conference paper from which this chapter was developed, and Richard Jenkins, of the University College of Swansea, and Eithne McLaughlin of the Queen's University, Belfast, for their suggestions of additions and revisions to the original script.
2 The 'Age as a Barrier to Employment' Project was funded by the DTI's City Action Team in 1989. The 'Study of Urban Unemployment in Nottingham' was funded by the Employment Service in 1989.

References

Ashton, D., Maguire, M. and Garland, V. (1982) *Youth in the Labour Market*, Research Paper No. 34, Department of Employment, London.
Ashton, D. and Maguire, M., with Bowden, D., Dellow, P., Kennedy, S., Stanley, G., Woodhead, G. and Jennings, B. (1986) *Young Adults in the Labour Market*, Research Paper No. 55, Department of Employment, London.
Ashton, D., Maguire, M. and Spilsbury, M. (1987) 'Labour Market Segmentation and the Structure of the Youth Labour Market', in P. Brown and D. N. Ashton, (eds), *Education, Unemployment and Labour Markets*, Lewes: Falmer.
—— (1990) *Restructuring the Labour Market: The Implications for Youth*, London: Macmillan.
Bevan, S. and Fryatt, J. (1988) *Employee Selection in the UK*, Brighton: Institute of Manpower Studies.
Crowley-Bainton, T. (1987) 'Unemployed Jobseekers – an underrated talent?', *Personnel Management*, August 1987.
Dex, S. (1985) *The Sexual Divisions of Work*, Brighton: Harvester.
—— (1987) *Women's Occupational Mobility: A Lifetime Perspective*, London: Macmillan.

Fevre, R. (1984) *Cheap Labour and Racial Discrimination*, Cambridge: Gower.

Hakim, C. (1979) 'Occupational Segregation: A Comparative Study of the Degree and Pattern of the Differentiation Between Men and Women's Work in Britain', *The US and Other Countries*, Department of Employment Research Paper, London: Department of Employment.

Jenkins, R. (1986) *Racism and Recruitment: Managers, Organisations and Equal Opportunity in the Labour Market*, Cambridge: Cambridge University Press.

—— (1990) 'Notes on employers role in the labour market', presented to the ES-SPRU Understanding Unemployment Conference, May 1990, York, mimeo.

Jewson, N. and Mason, D. (1986) 'Modes of Discrimination in the Recruitment Process: Formalisation, Fairness and Efficiency', *Sociology*, 20: 43–63.

Jewson, N., Mason, D., Waters, S., and Harvey, J. (1990) *Ethnic Minorities and Employment Practice*, Research Paper No. 76, London: Department of Employment.

Lee, G. and Wrench, J. (1987) 'Race and Gender Dimensions of the Youth Labour Market: from Apprenticeship to YTS', in G. Lee and R. Loveridge (eds), *The Manufacture of Disadvantage*, Milton Keynes: Open University Press.

Martin, J. and Roberts, C. (1984) *Women and Employment: A Lifetime Perspective*, Department of Employment/OPCS, London: HMSO.

Meager, N. and Metcalf, H. (1987) *Recruitment of the Long-Term Unemployed*, Brighton: Institute of Manpower Studies.

School for Advanced Urban Studies (1986) *Shutting Out the Inner City Worker*, SAUS Occasional Paper 23, University of Bristol.

Turbin, J. (1987) 'State Intervention into the Labour Market for Youth: The Implementation of the Youth Training Scheme in Three Local Labour Markets', Unpub. Ph.D. Thesis, University of Leicester.

Walby S. and Bagguley, P. (1990) 'Sex Segregation in Local Labour Markets', *Work Employment and Society*, 4, 1: 59–81.

Wood, S. and Manwaring, T. (1988) 'External Recruitment and the Recession', in P. Windolf and S. Wood (eds), *Recruitment and Selection in the Labour Market*, Cambridge: Gower.

6

PSYCHOLOGICAL OR MATERIAL DEPRIVATION: WHY DOES UNEMPLOYMENT HAVE MENTAL HEALTH CONSEQUENCES?

David Fryer[1]

INTRODUCTION

It is increasingly accepted that the mental health of the majority of unemployed people suffers. Inferences about the importance of employment as a major social institution through which many people, in contemporary industrialized nations such as our own, meet fundamental psychological needs are frequently drawn. Research from the 1930s to the present day has demonstrated that the psychological consequences of unemployment include impaired psychological well-being, anxiety, depression, reduced self-confidence, social isolation and reduced levels of activity. Some interpreters of this literature appear to have reached the conclusion, actually unsupported by empirical evidence (see below), that unemployment significantly reduces people's will to rejoin the world of paid work. In particular, during the 1980s UK government concern about unemployment, and the measures appropriate to deal with it, appears to have been heavily oriented towards remotivation programmes combined with increasingly harsh benefit regimes (see Oppenheim 1990: 66). The apparent assumption is that long-term unemployment is primarily a problem of discouraged, demotivated, quasi-voluntarily, unemployed workers with overambitious expectations of their labour market opportunities.

It is the purpose of this chapter to review the evidence relating to the psychological consequences of unemployment and in particular to critically address the question: are the documented mental health and behaviourial effects of unemployment primarily due to psychological deprivation (that is removal of psychologically supportive aspects of the social relationship of employment) or are they primarily due to material deprivation (that is relative poverty and its social psychological sequelae). If, as is argued below, much of the psychological ill-health of unemployed people and their families is caused by income-related factors rather than by, or even as

103

well as, the absence of employment itself, there follow profound policy implications. In particular, the appropriateness of recent policy initiatives, which have combined remotivation programmes with punitive assaults on benefit levels and entitlements, could be called into question.

In the first section of this chapter I summarize psychological research evidence from the 1930s and in the second, evidence from the 1980s. In the third part I examine in some detail the explanations which psychologists have offered for the personal and social impacts of unemployment. The fourth section offers some conclusions.

FINDINGS IN THE 1930s

In 1930 a group of young researchers committed themselves to leaving the laboratory of the Psychological Institute of the University of Vienna to investigate contemporary social problems in the field from a psychological perspective. In 1929 the textile industry, which had provided employment for the majority of the population of a village just outside Vienna, had collapsed and by February 1930 the only paid jobs in the textile plant were for a few demolition workers. Some 77 per cent of the families in the village (Marienthal) did not have a single employed member at that time. In the autumn of 1931, a team of fourteen researchers, led by Marie Jahoda and Paul Lazarsfeld, went into the village to systematically and painstakingly uncover the social psychological fabric of the life of the unemployed community (Jahoda *et al.* 1933; English translation published 1972; see also Fryer 1987: 74–93 for further discussion). The earliest published summary of the findings of this research on the unemployed community of Marienthal states that: 'their psychic life has contracted; a narrowing of the psychological sphere of wants occurs . . . we defined this psychic attitude as resignation' (Lazarsfeld 1932: 149). Resignation was characterized by 'no plans, no relation to the future, no hopes, extreme restriction of all needs beyond the bare necessities, yet at the same time maintenance of the household, care of the children, and an overall feeling of relative well-being' (Jahoda *et al.* 1933: 53). However this was only one aspect of psychological well-being claimed by the investigators to be part of the experience of unemployment. Decreasing levels of activity and disintegration of sense of time were reported to be widespread. Some – a minority of families – escaped unscathed, but family disharmony, demoralization, depression, despair, apathy and complete passivity were said to be demonstrated as consequences of unemployment for many (Eisenberg and Lazarsfeld 1938; Jahoda 1979).

Although the single most impressive investigation into psychological effects in the 1930s, and certainly the most celebrated and cited, the Marienthal research was by no means the only important research carried out during that decade. Bakke was also responsible for two major field studies in the 1930s. In 1931 in Greenwich, London, he used participant observation, interviews, time budget analyses and public document analysis (Bakke 1933). From 1932 in New Haven, USA, he used family interviews, questionnaires and document analysis, cross checking his material with accounts of social workers, ministers of religion, public health officials and employers (Bakke 1940a and 1940b). Taken as a whole, Bakke's research again revealed widespread psychological debilitation, economic insecurity, exhaustion, declining social contact, dented self-confidence and despondency amongst unemployed people. However, he did also emphasize the resilience of families and individuals, the heterogeneity of unemployment experience and, in Greenwich, a basic sense of security even amongst the unemployed. Bakke attributed this security to the existence of unemployment insurance.

These, and many other studies, of which Eisenberg and Lazarsfeld reviewed 112 in 1938, had conclusions which converged on a number of themes. Unemployment was reported as associated with: hopelessness regarding the future (Israeli 1935); low self-esteem (Kardiner 1936); low self-confidence (Carnegie Trust 1943); social isolation (Beales and Lambert 1934; Pilgrim Trust 1938); anxiety (Beales and Lambert 1934; Lewis 1935; Newman 1932; Pilgrim Trust 1938;) depression (Israeli 1935; Pilgrim Trust 1938) and impaired physical health (Pilgrim Trust 1938).

One frequently overlooked feature of the literature of the 1930s was the recognition that the psychological impact of unemployment was by no means homogenous. Eisenberg and Lazarsfeld (1938: 371) wrote that 'it is quite apparent that the same situation will not produce the same consequences, simply because we are dealing with individuals'. They identified social status, age, gender, personality, economic resources and length of unemployment as factors, each of which is weighted in some way, to bring about, in differing combinations, differing effects of unemployment.

While the majority of 1930s research addressed the negative effects of unemployment upon white working class males in their middle years, many exceptions to this preoccupation can be found in the 1930s literature. The effects of unemployment upon redundant women were addressed, despite the title *Men without Work*, by Pilgrim Trust (1938). The researchers concluded that job loss was a blow to women on both social and financial grounds. The effects of unemployment upon women who were not themselves unemployed but were affected by men's redundancy were also emphasized in the 1930s by the Pilgrim Trust (1938). They reported on their research in Liverpool commenting that 'the analysis brings out clearly how the wives bear the brunt of unemployment' (Pilgrim Trust 1938: 126). In one third of these families, the mother was suffering from anaemia and/ or nervous debilitation. They concluded that their research supported claims made by a certain Dr Gillespie in a paper presented to the British Association in 1936: 'My experience is that among the working classes unemployment is more apt to affect the nervous condition of the mother of the family than that of the breadwinner himself' (Gillespie quoted in Pilgrim Trust 1938: 139). Pilgrim Trust pinpointed 'undernourishment, combined with the strain of 'managing' on very limited resources and dealing with the domestic crises which almost inevitably crop up from time to time during a long spell of unemployment' as making 'heavy demands on the physical and psychic resources of mothers of families' (Pilgrim Trust 1938: 139).

Much of the 1930s research attention was however directed at the family in general rather than the mother in particular. Komarovsky (1940), directed by Lazarsfeld, and Bakke (1940a and 1940b) both independently concluded that unemployment exacerbated pre-unemployment problems rather than causing them (see also Cavan and Ranke 1938). The psychological impact of unemployment upon children was reported in the 1930s by Eisenberg and Lazarsfeld (1938) and Save the Children International Union (1933). Examples of sub-headings from Elderton's (1931) summary of 150 case studies of unemployed families across the USA gives a depressing impression of the reported impact of unemployment upon children: 'cruelty towards wife and children'; 'anxious attitude of children'; 'delinquency'; 'children put in homes'.

FINDINGS IN THE 1980s

The findings of psychological research on unemployment in the 1980s mirror those of the 1930s extraordinarily closely. Again the emphasis has been on psychological well-being. The following have all recently been shown to be associated with unemployment in directions indicating poor psychological health: positively and negatively experienced emotional states (Warr 1987); happiness (Bradburn 1969); present life satisfaction (Hepworth 1980); experience of pleasure and of strain (Warr and Payne 1982); hopelessness regarding the future (Fryer and McKenna 1989). Unemployed people are again found to have relatively low levels of daily activity (Fagin and Little 1984) and this is of special concern given the demonstrated negative association between passive behaviour and psychological well-being (Warr and Payne 1983; Kilpatrick and Trew 1985) and the finding that activity moderates psychological distress (Feather and Bond 1983; Hepworth 1980). Unemployed people are again shown to be socially isolated (Henwood and Miles 1987). As regards self-esteem, research has been less definitive. Some researchers claim that unemployment has an impact (Donovan and Oddy 1982; Gurney 1980), others that it has no impact (Cobb and Kasl 1977; Hartley 1980). Warr and Jackson (1983) clarified the issue by showing that a scale of positive self-esteem was affected by unemployment but a scale of negative self-esteem was not.

Research in the 1980s has been dominated by survey style methods using reliable well-validated measures such as the General Health Questionnaire. Cross-sectional studies using such measures of psychological well-being have shown groups of unemployed people to have poorer mental health than matched groups of employed people (Banks and Jackson 1982; Payne 1988; Warr and Jackson 1985). The General Health Questionnaire twelve-item version, which is highly correlated with the anxiety sub-scale of a longer version with sub-components, is widely regarded as an acceptable index of general anxiety. Depression, too, as measured by well-validated, reliable inventories, has been demonstrated to be higher in groups of unemployed people than in matched groups of employed people (Feather 1990; Tiggemann and Winefield 1980; Warr 1987). Physical health has been more frequently researched in the 1980s than in the 1930s. Although the issue is methodologically complex, there is an emerging consensus that the health of unemployed people is generally poorer than that of employed people and that unemployment is a major causal factor (Beale and Nethercott 1986; King 1989; Westin, Schlesselman and Korper 1989; Yuen and Balarajan 1989).

Again, one of the features of the literature in the 1980s has been the recognition that the psychological impact of unemployment is by no means homogenous. As before, the majority of research has addressed the negative effects of unemployment upon white, working class, males in their middle years (Griffin 1986), but as before exceptions to this preoccupation can be found. The crucial factor regarding the negative effect of unemployment on psychological well-being appears to be not gender but whether or not the unemployed person is a principal wage earner. A meta-review of the effects of unemployment upon redundant women led Warr and Parry (1982) to conclude that unemployment is associated with high levels of psychological distress for both single and married childless women but they could find no evidence for an association between unemployment and well-being for mothers unless living in very deprived home environments. Similar evidence exists for satisfaction with self (Cohn 1978) and emotional strain (Warr and Payne 1982). Popay (1990), however, points out that women at home with young children (women who frequently perceive themselves as non-employed rather than unemployed) have many mental health stressors in common with unemployed people (lack of power, control, income, social status, etc.). There is some empirical evidence bearing on this issue. Henwood and Miles (1987) compared the experience of housewives with employed and unemployed women and found that the housewives scored as low as unemployed women on measures of social contact and activity and both were significantly lower than employed women on these variables. However, the housewives resembled full time employed women in their scores on status and time structure and both scored significantly higher than unemployed women on these variables. As regards young women, groups of unemployed female school leavers show more distress than matched groups of young employed women (Banks and Jackson 1982; Warr *et al.* 1985). Longitudinally, significant differences in scores of well-being of employed and unemployed young women are found, even though no such differences could be found between the groups' scores when at school (Banks and Jackson 1982; see also Hall and Johnson 1988; Henwood and Miles 1987).

The effects of unemployment upon women as wives and mothers of unemployed men have again been investigated in the 1980s (Allatt and Yeandle 1986; Binns and Mars 1984; Fagin and Little 1984; Farran and Margolis 1987; Hutson and Jenkins 1989; Jackson and Walsh 1987; Liem and Liem 1988; McKee and Bell 1986; Bromet and Dew 1988). In general these studies emphasize family strain.

Callendar has argued that 'prevailing ideas surrounding employment and unemployment are male dominated and . . . inappropriate for understanding the position of women in the labour market' (Callendar 1987: 23; see also Popay 1990). There is justice to this claim. The 'principal wage earner' approach takes women's unemployment seriously only to the extent that women mimic the stereotypical male in benefit and job search behaviour. Yet many women see themselves as neither employed nor unemployed (Cragg and Dawson 1984), do not appear to believe they have a legitimate right to a job in terms of a queue of 'priority' candidates (Martin and Wallace 1984), yet have an experience of unemployment which calls out legitimately for research attention. Certainly, the issues surrounding women, employment, unemployment and non-employment, need stronger conceptualization and a fresh research initiative.

The psychological impact of unemployment on children is one area more investigated in the 1930s than in the 1980s, although a number of contemporary researchers have drawn attention to the issue (Madge 1983; Steinberg, Catalano and Dooley 1981). It is likely that many children with unemployed parents suffer not only materially and economically but also socially, educationally and psychologically compared with peers of employed parents. Given that in 1987, for example, there were over one and a quarter million dependent children in households with an unemployed head, of whom over half a million had experienced more than two years of unemployment (Popay 1990), this is a cause for grave concern.

Research in the 1980s has also focused upon other apparent moderators of the impact of unemployment. These include: belonging to an ethnic minority (Ullah 1987; Warr *et al.* 1985); taking part in interventions such as Government-funded job-creation schemes (Branthwaite and Garcia 1985; Cassell *et al.* 1988; Stafford 1982); social class (Fineman 1979; Hartley 1980; Kaufmann 1982; Payne *et al.* 1984; Schaufeli 1988); age (Daniel 1974; Feather 1990; Hepworth 1980; Jackson and Warr 1984); hardiness (Kobasa *et al.* 1982) and neuroticism (Payne 1988).

With regard to the policy implications relevant to the theme of this volume, one of the most interesting of these moderators is employment commitment (Jackson *et al.* 1983; Warr *et al.* 1985). Studies using a number of measures of this (essentially attempts to translate the (secularized) work ethic into brief survey questions or scales) have been reported in the last decade. In brief those unemployed people with the highest levels of employment commitment tend to have the worst mental health scores. The most striking feature of this research however is that almost everybody scores high on employment commitment measures. For example, Warr (1982) asked random samples of over 2,000 men and over 1,000 women if they would want paid work if they were to get enough money to live on for the rest of their life from some other source. Some 62 per cent of unemployed men and 69 per cent of employed men said they would want jobs even if they were not financially necessary! Banks and Ullah studied a large national cohort of 16–19 year-olds and reported high levels of employment commitment. For example, even after a year of unemployment over three quarters of the same agreed that 'Even if I won a great deal of money, I would still want to have a job'. The researchers pointed out that 'these results provide little support for the "workshy" hypothesis' (Banks and Ullah 1988: 75).

To summarize, in the last decade well-designed, longitudinal, studies utilizing well validated measures with large samples and making comparisons with matched comparison groups have been carried out. They provide compelling evidence that groups which become unemployed during the course of the studies exhibit mean score changes which indicate psychological deterioration compared with continuously employed groups. Groups which become employed during the course of the studies exhibit mean score changes which indicate psychological improvement compared with continuously unemployed groups with respect to happiness, present life satisfaction, experience of pleasure and of strain, satisfaction with self, negative self-esteem, anxiety, depression and physical health.

EXPLANATIONS OF THE PSYCHOLOGICAL EFFECTS

Given the similarity in foci of empirical attention and convergence of findings of the research of the 1930s and the 1980s, it is especially striking that explanation of those findings is treated very differently in the two periods. It is argued below that in the earlier period the explanatory role of poverty was emphasized whereas in the later period the explanatory role of poverty has been minimized. Very different policy approaches are implicit in the adoption of one explanatory model rather than the other.

Explanations in the 1930s

In the 1930s the explanation of the psychological effects of unemployment was overwhelmingly provided in terms of poverty. Whilst it is widely appreciated that Jahoda *et al.* (1933/1972) assigned each of the families studied in Marienthal to one of four psychological categories (unbroken; resigned; apathetic; in despair), it is less frequently appreciated that there was such a clear connection 'between a family's attitude and its economic situation' that the investigators were able to predict 'at approximately what point the deterioration of income will push a family into the next category' (Jahoda *et al.* 1972: 81). The investigators commented that despair and apathy are 'probably but two different stages of a process of psychological deterioration that runs parallel to the narrowing of economic resources and the wear and tear on personal belongings. At the end of this process lies ruin and despair' (Jahoda *et al.* 1972: 87). Indeed, the Marienthal monograph emphasizes 'the connection between powers of resistance, income and previous life history' (Jahoda *et al.* 1972: 9). 'Economic deterioration carries with it an almost calculable change in the prevailing mood. This fact is intensified by the concomitant decline in health' (Jahoda *et al.* 1972: 82).

Likewise, the Marienthal study is remembered for its demonstration of a general decline in activity with unemployment. For example, the unemployed people generally reduced their attendance of clubs and use of the library (Jahoda 1982: 25). Again however, it is less often remembered that this was largely a consequence of poverty: 'as privation increases organization membership becomes less a matter of conviction and more a matter of financial interest' (Jahoda *et al.* 1972: 42). Careful reading of the Marienthal monograph reveals that the membership of a cycling club which helped with legally required cycle insurance remained unchanged, whilst a Catholic organization which ran a nursery school grew considerably in size and a cremation society, which subsidized funeral costs, actually grew by 11 per cent.

Both principal researchers from Marienthal were active in other studies during 1930s. Lazarsfeld was responsible for an influential six-stage account of unemployment effects based on personal document analysis. Like the categories in the Marienthal study these stages were very much anchored to income. The final stage, for example, was described as fluctuating according to momentary changes in the material situation (Zawadski and Lazarsfeld 1935). O'Brien described this study as demonstrating that 'negative feelings were not associated with the loss of a job *per se* but rather the state of poverty' (O'Brien 1986: 187). Lazarsfeld was also responsible for probably the most influential review in the field. This, too, emphasized the role of poverty in the psychological distress of unemployment citing studies showing that those who are not as hard hit by poverty do not suffer as much in unemployment (Eisenberg and Lazarsfeld 1938: 376), and claiming that economic deprivation is a factor in the production of emotional instability, at least in unemployed transients (Eisenberg and Lazarsfeld 1938: 362). The authors were led to conclude that 'just having a job in itself is not as important as having a feeling of economic security. Those who are economically insecure, employed or unemployed, have a low morale' (Eisenberg and Lazarsfeld 1938: 361).

Jahoda conducted a second major unemployment field study in the 1930s, this time in Wales (Jahoda 1938, first published in 1987). Here too 'the normal attitude amongst the unemployed was one of resignation'. However 'nothing worse than resignation was found' (Jahoda 1987: 13) unlike in Marienthal. Jahoda suggests that the absence of the more extreme conditions of despair and apathy in the Welsh sample 'may have been mainly because of the size and permanence of the unemployment allowance in Wales' (Jahoda 1987: 13). The unemployed men Jahoda was studying were also financially buffered since they were members of a co-operative from which they could purchase with their unemployment allowance more and better quality goods than could non-members.

Bakke, too, emphasized poverty as the major factor in explaining the effects of unemployment which he documented, although he also emphasized the social and cultural inheritance of the individual. For example, in connection with reduced leisure activity, he writes 'the plain fact is that the decline in recreation results from a decline in income and only an increased income will make it possible for the unemployed to use their ordinary experience and habits in restoring that leisure-time life to which they have become accustomed' (Bakke 1933: 17).

O'Brien, who has closely studied the 1930s literature and Bakke's contribution in particular, has asserted that the depression literature 'seems to identify the major stressor as economic deprivation' (O'Brien 1986: 201) but that 'the importance of economic factors for the understanding of unemployment effects . . . appears to have been underrated by psychological interpreters' (O'Brien 1986: 196). This is true in the sense that later generations of psychological researchers have paid less explanatory heed to the importance of economic factors than those in the 1930s. However, even in the 1980s, although they have not in general placed explanatory emphasis upon it, psychological researchers have continued to describe poverty related distress among unemployed people, albeit sometimes in passing. O'Brien's observation is true also in the sense that those who consult, or should consult, the psychological literature on unemployment (for example, policy-makers) seem to have ignored what psychologists of all generations have been discovering about the intricate intertwining of material deprivation and the psychological experience of unemployment.

Explanations in the 1980s

There are currently three major frameworks for explaining the psychological consequences of unemployment: social cognitive, social environmental and agency restriction approaches. The former has been influential in a series of important studies of youth unemployment in South Australia. However, the European field has been almost totally dominated in the last decade by the social environmental approach associated with Marie Jahoda and, more recently, Peter Warr. Both of these approaches have been stimulating and productive generators of research hypotheses but both marginalize poverty and material deprivation as factors in the explanation of the psychological consequences of unemployment. A third approach, agency restriction, which rehabilitates the importance of material deprivation recognized in the 1930s research, has recently emerged.

Social Cognitive Approaches

Feather (1990) and O'Brien (1986), working in South Australia, and predominantly on youth unemployment, approach the explanation of the psychological impact of unemployment via traditional social psychological concepts. Feather draws upon attribution theory and learned helplessness theory (two accounts which relate emotionality and behaviour to expectations and causal beliefs) but Feather particularly favours the extension of expectancy-value theory to the explanation of psychological aspects of unemployment. This theory, with which Feather has been closely associated for over thirty years, attempts to explain a person's actions in terms of the perceived attractiveness or aversiveness to that person of certain expected outcomes. In brief, 'whether or not a person has a tendency to act in a particular direction will depend on that person's expectation about whether he or she can perform the action to the required standard, thereby achieving a successful outcome, on a further set of expectations about the possible consequences of the outcome, and on the valence (or subjective value) associated with the action outcome' (Feather 1990: 63).

Expectancy value theory has evident applications with respect to job-seeking behaviour. Persons would be predicted to cease job search, for example, if they believed that they were not capable of performing at interview well enough to be offered a job. Here interview skill training might be useful. They would also be predicted to cease job search, however, if they had no expectation that they would get a job no matter how talented an interview performer they were, because, for example, there were simply not enough jobs. However, the approach provides at best a partial account of findings more generally: that is why the mental health of unemployed people suffers. Moreover, it is essentially a process theory of motivation in general and is not designed for the particular case of employment and unemployment with their compelling behaviourial norms. Strictly speaking the account is neutral to particular content and whilst it makes no specific reference to poverty or income, it does not exclude them being instantiated in particular substantive accounts of the approach. However, in the light of the tradition of explanation in this field outlined above it is striking that the approach does not emphasize the explanatory role of income related factors.

O'Brien, who has worked and published with Feather, has been prominent in driving home the point that the negative psychological states reported in 1930s studies of unemployed people were due largely to poverty, and interprets these as the effects of poverty rather than effects of unemployment. For O'Brien, explanation of the psychological as opposed to economic effects of unemployment remains to be provided.

Social environmental approaches

In addition to her seminal fieldwork in the 1930s and the explanation implicit in then contemporary reports of the work, Jahoda has developed a second explanatory line in terms of the manifest and latent consequences of employment of which the unemployed person is said to be deprived (Jahoda 1979; 1982; Jahoda and Rush 1980). Jahoda's account has been extremely influential, widely quoted as a source and resonates within the work of some of the most influential figures in the field (Hartley 1980; Henwood and Miles 1987; O'Brien 1986; and Warr 1987). Jahoda's account has been commended elsewhere for its valuable integrative, predictive and policy relevant features but also criticized on pragmatic, methodological, empirical, theoretical and ideological grounds (Fryer 1986). What is of particular interest here, however, is Jahoda's shift from explanatory emphasis on poverty in the 1930s to the peripheral explanatory role she gives poverty in her account of the 1980s.

Jahoda argues that employment is a social institution which has both manifest, or intended, consequences and latent, or unintended, consequences. Earning a living is taken for granted as the manifest consequence of employment and thereafter little discussed. Social contact, activity, status, purposefulness, time structure and being controlled, each of which are said to be imposed or enforced by employment, are said to be the latent consequences of employment (for example, Jahoda 1986). Crucially, unemployment is said to be psychologically destructive because of the absence of the unintended latent consequences of employment which normally function as psychological supports.

Warr has developed a model in many respects very similar to Jahoda's. Warr's model has nine environmental features responsible for psychological well-being. These mirror Jahoda's six consequences with slight variations. The nine features are: opportunity for control; skill use; interpersonal

113

contact; external goal and task demands; variety; environmental clarity; availability of money; physical security; and valued social position (Warr 1987). Both Jahoda and Warr emphasize deprivation or decrement as a process, although Warr also admits one can have too much of at least some environmental features. The most striking similarity, however, is the marginalization of poverty as a factor in both explanations of the psychological impact of unemployment.

The shift of social psychological emphasis away from poverty must have been a convenient coincidence for policy-makers in the late 1970s and 1980s. The earlier emphasis was on redundant workers who were desperate to escape unemployment and whose mental health was suffering from the associated poverty and was consistent with unemployment perceived politically as a problem of lack of demand in the economy resulting in enforced redundancy. The reduction in emphasis on poverty was subsequently more in line with the rhetoric adopted by policy-makers of unemployment as largely a result of the 'weak' supply of labour by unemployed people who were represented as too financially cossetted by over-generous state benefits to compete seriously for jobs.

Agency restriction approaches

This approach arose out of close critical attention to Jahoda's work and attempts to reinstate material deprivation, so central in 1930s explanations but marginalized in contemporary social cognitive and social environmental approaches.

Fryer (for example, 1986, 1988), and Fryer and Payne (1986), claim that in addition to pragmatic, methodological and empirical criticisms, the dominant approach has implicit within it a model of the unemployed person as passive, dependent, retrospectively orientated and reactive; and a model of that which is alleged to be primarily responsible for the unemployed person's plight – the social institution of employment – as overly supportive and benevolent psychologically.

The agency restriction approach rests on a model of the unemployed, and indeed any other, person as an active, initiating, future-oriented agent, striving to make sense of and influence events. It also rests upon an implicit model of that which is primarily responsible for the unemployed person's plight – the social institution of unemployment – as impoverishing, restricting, baffling, discouraging and disenabling (see Fryer 1986 for further details).

Of course, this is something of a caricature of both approaches and eventually both approaches are likely to be incorporated (with others) in a satisfactory account. People are neither puppets on strings pulled by the psychologically benevolent features of employment nor proactive super-beings immobilized by the straitjacket of unemployment. However, the caricature perhaps captures something of the differences in starting assumptions of the two approaches about the person and social context and their relative emphasis and has been encouraged informally by both Jahoda and Fryer as a way of encouraging debate.

It is not suggested that the typical unemployed person is an exemplar of proactive behaviour: the restrictive and debilitating context of unemployment sees to that. However, some cope with unemployment effectively and some very well indeed (Fryer and Payne 1984) just as some agents find themselves distressed and others overwhelmed by the demands of both employment and unemployment as they are socially constructed. Nor is it argued that to emphasize that the person is not a passive object but an active agent is new and original in psychology but rather that it fits uneasily with the currently dominant account in the unemployment field.

The agency restriction account is none the less congruent with the positions of some researchers not generally regarded as agency proponents. O'Brien observes that in his 1940 publications Bakke maintained 'that it is inaccurate to depict the unemployed as fatalistic, dependent, inactive and lacking self reliance. Within the severe external restrictions imposed upon them the unemployed tried to control their own affairs. They showed high self-reliance in job-hunting, stretching their income, obtaining relief, developing a new domestic economy and appraising job opportunities (O'Brien 1986: 195). For unemployed people 'the main feature of their behaviour was not apathy, fatalism or other psychiatric disturbance, but rather resilience in an impoverished environment' (O'Brien 1986: 201). Robb also exemplified agency restriction assumptions when he wrote: 'When a man is unemployed, there is no external outlet for his energies. He becomes aware that he is not a free agent. He is impelled to receive a meagre allowance from others – relatives, friends, usually the state . . .' (cited in Beales and Lambert 1934: 274–5).

The agency restriction approach is not only congruent with the research findings of, and explanations offered during, the 1930s but it is also increasingly being accommodated to by contemporary researchers. Feather, for example, adopts an 'interactional forms of analysis' which 'sees the person as an active agent and not as passive point of contact of situational forces' (Feather 1990: 6). The approach also makes sense of many findings puzzling within the dominant approach. It is consistent with a vast number of findings whose importance is under-recognized and underemphasized. In other words the supportive evidence and other relevant considerations are considerably greater in number and persuasive power than the research generated directly by the account in the short time since its proposal.

Nevertheless, agency restriction assumptions have been used to focus research on three particular aspects of the experience of unemployed people: future orientation (Fryer and McKenna 1987, 1989; McKenna and Fryer 1984), manifestations of extreme agency or proactivity (Fryer and

115

Payne 1984); and agency restriction by poverty (Fryer 1988; Fryer and Payne 1986; Hartley and Fryer 1984; McGhee and Fryer 1989). Only agency restriction by poverty will be pursued below.

Restriction of unemployed persons' agency by poverty

It seems that almost everyone involved with unemployed people has been struck by the role of poverty in their distress. This includes social anthropologists (for example, Bostyn and Wight 1987), Government social researchers (for example, Moylan, Millar and Davies 1984), leisure scholars (for example, Glyptis 1989), social ecologists (for example, Brenner 1984; Bruce *et al.* 1991; Dooley and Catalano 1988; Rodgers 1991), sociologists (for example, Coates and Silburn 1970) and social commentators (for example, Campbell 1984; Mack and Lansley 1985; Pilger 1989; Seabrook 1982). Moreover, when unemployed people are given the opportunity, they say loudly and clearly what they themselves perceive as their greatest problem: 'studies of unemployed people consistently indicate that shortage of money is viewed as the greatest source of personal and family problems' (Warr 1987: 217). This is not surprising since we know that unemployment generally brings with it a drastic drop in living standards (Cooke 1987). Davies *et al.* (1982) found that nearly 50 per cent of their respondents were receiving less than half in state benefits than previously in wages. Only 6 per cent were receiving more in benefit than they had in wages. Warr and Jackson (1984) found that 66 per cent of their unemployed respondents reported a household income of 33–50 per cent of their household income when employed. Debt is also a common feature of unemployment (Smith 1980). Finlay Jones and Eckhardt (1984) found two-thirds of their sample were in debt after ten months of unemployment. Community credit unions, functioning essentially as community banks, number many unemployed people among their users. McArthur and McGregor (1988) found that more than half of the users of community credit unions whom they interviewed were not employed.

There is a well-documented decline in activities requiring money with unemployment (Miles 1983; Warr and Payne 1983). Even black economic activity is low amongst unemployed people (Bostyn and Wight 1987; Hakim in this volume; Wallace and Pahl 1986), in part perhaps because unemployed people cannot even afford the wherewithal to participate: most moonlighters have access to the tools, materials and equipment of their day jobs.

Psychological distress is known to vary inversely with level of income: the greater the income, the less the distress. Psychologists have tried to operationalize experienced financial difficulties and look at its association with well-being but this has proved very hard to do, perhaps because the complexity and nature of the subject make it unsuitable for brief questionnaires. Certainly, measures of self-reported financial strain have so far been found to be only modestly associated with General Health Questionnaire scores (Warr and Payne 1983). However, Jackson and Warr (1984) found the proportion of family income change predicted GHQ assessed distress. Feather operationalized both financial strain and financial stress in a programme of research from which he concluded: 'it is those people who suffer financial hardship and who feel that their lives have no purpose and structure who seem to be most affected by unemployment . . . these two factors seem to play a central role in regard of psychological distress' (Feather 1990: 49). Little (1976) found professional workers in worse financial circumstances reported job loss as more negative than those in relatively better ones (see also Estes and Wilensky 1978; Kessler, Turner and House 1988; Pearlin, Lieberman, Managhan and Mullan 1981).

Whilst the above studies indicate the necessity for systematic investigation of income in relation to unemployment distress they rather seem to circle around the core of the issue. The actual measures themselves were designed to be used in survey style research – that is to be brief, unambiguous, close-ended and easily quantifiable and by survey criteria are acceptable. At the same time they miss much of the detail and texture of the experience of unemployed poverty: which aspects and why are psychologically corrosive.

Some insights are available in this regard from qualitative, ethnographic and other studies from both the 1930s and the 1980s. Cameron, Lush and Mears (1942: 5) pinpointed a social psychological aspect of poverty in their study of unemployed young adults, when they emphasized the importance of 'money earned by their own effort. One young wife put it this: "Somehow when it's money that your man has worked for, it goes further." '

Receipt of unemployment and social security benefits are frequently reported to impart stigma to the recipients. Bakke (1940a and 1940b) found 40 per cent of his New Haven sample of unemployed men waited more than two years before applying for relief (see also Ginsburg 1942). Unemployed people still have grounds to complain about the ignominy of poor conditions, seat-shuffling, queueing and long waits (Kay 1984). In Kay's study, 12 per cent of the informants reported waits of between one and three hours. People also complained of dirty, litter-strewn, smoky, smelly conditions. Some 60 per cent said there was insufficient privacy at the counter and many found means testing demeaning. People frequently felt passively processed by the clerical staff in an over-speedy and dismissive fashion. The whole interaction was often regarded with incomprehension and distrust. Kelvin (1984) has remarked that receipt of unemployment benefit implies the illegitimate role of the inadequate and Liem (1983) has suggested that unemployed people do not seek help from formal agencies in order to maintain a sense of dignity: 'when help receiving is actually stigmatized, resistance to seeking this help is a positive assertion of one's humanity'. Moreover, income maintenance appears to carry stressors in its own right (Thoits and Hannan 1979).

The role of consumer is largely unavailable to the unemployed person (Seabrook 1982) yet conspicuous consumption is an important part of the culture of many unemployed people (Bostyn and Wight 1987). Moreover, the socially constructed role of unemployed person demands that unemployed people (apart from those with independent means) are expected to exhibit a frugal life style, diligent job search, gratitude, humility, etc. as well as self blame (Breakwell 1985; Furnham 1983).

McGhee and Fryer's (1989) exploratory study of social psychological dimensions of unemployed poverty suggested that symbolic consumption, perceived entitlements to consume, others' perceived expectations of one's income-related behaviour, implications of the source of income, the way income is delivered, family income-coping strategies and the family division of poverty-coping behaviour, were all vital aspects of the experience of unemployed poverty.

CONCLUSIONS

Although the research has taken place in a variety of countries and cultures, from within differing institutional settings, by investigators from differing ideological backgrounds, using the whole gamut of available social psychological methods over a period of sixty years of major social change, the research findings are remarkably consistent. They indicate the important role of material deprivation in intensifying or even bringing about the documented psychological consequences of unemployment. However, whilst the dominant explanatory framework of the 1930s was in terms of poverty and material deprivation, in the 1980s the dominant explanatory frameworks for very much the same phenomena have marginalized poverty.

Some contemporary researchers have bemoaned the fact that psychologists have neglected poverty both generally (Connolly 1982) and with respect to its role in the psychological distress of unemployment in particular (Gurney and Taylor 1981; Hartley and Fryer 1984). Why this neglect occurs, however, has received less attention.

For some, disciplinary boundaries and specialist area protectionism may have played a part. Some appear only willing to allow economic consequences parallel to, but separate from, psychological consequences: these can conveniently then be deemed outside the remit of psychological research but rather in the province of economics. For others, the move away from poverty may have been encouraged by a mistaken belief that poverty was a thing of the past due to improved welfare provisions, a realization that the psychological distress of unemployment has persisted, and fallacious inference. For still others, evidence that unemployment could

118

be psychologically distressing for relatively well-heeled middle class unemployed people could have been taken to suggest that employment deprivation rather than financial deprivation was crucial. Such beliefs rely upon a rather crude notion of absolute rather than relative poverty (Townsend 1979) and a refusal to admit that poverty is a social psychological as well as an economic state. For still others, the ethical and methodological difficulties of investigating such a notoriously private sphere as experienced poverty, especially in an already intruded upon and emotionally bruised group such as unemployed people, may have seemed insurmountable.

In this chapter I have argued that it is vital for researchers to bring the poverty, which is so central and corrosive a feature of unemployment for so many people, back into focus. It is vital for descriptive purposes, if our accounts are to be full and accurate. It is vital for theoretical purposes, if our explanations are to be extensive and powerful. It is vital for policy purposes, if policy is to be both humane and effective.

The research evidence reviewed provides little support for many ideas popular in some political, policy-making and media circles. Unemployed people are not work-shy; the vast majority are highly committed to paid employment. There is poverty in Western industrialized nations today: between 1975 and 1985 poverty in the UK increased more rapidly than in any country in the EEC. Over 10 million people, a fifth of the population, lived in poverty in 1987 (Oppenheim 1990). Moreover, poverty is particularly concentrated amongst unemployed people. In addition, previously unemployed people when in employment are disproportionately likely to be located in disadvantaged sectors of the labour market with their own associated psychological, social and material hazards: they therefore suffer cumulative labour market disadvantage which may exacerbate the impact of unemployment (Popay 1990). Unemployed people do not live 'comfortably enough' on benefits. Rather than benefit levels needing to be reduced still further to maintain incentives for paid employment, as some believe, they clearly need to be increased in the interests of better mental health. If much of the psychological distress of unemployment, diminished self-confidence, reduced activity levels and physical health costs of unemployment are due to inadequate, stigmatized and social psychologically corrosive incomes, then 'counselling' approaches such as Restart/ Claimant Adviser Interviews and the like (Finn and Ball 1991: 98–109), combined with the threat of loss of benefit for non-attendance, and policies which are intended to reduce unemployed people's incomes, cannot possibly succeed: one arm of policy is undoing what another arm of policy is trying to achieve.

NOTE AND REFERENCES

Note

1 Thanks to Jennie Popay and Eithne McLaughlin for their valuable comments on a draft of this chapter.

References

Allatt, P. and Yeandle, S. (1986) 'It's not fair is it?: youth unemployment, family relations and the social contract', in S. Allen, A. Waton, K. Purcell and S. Wood (eds), *The Experience of Unemployment*, Basingstoke: Macmillan.

Bakke, E.W. (1933) *The Unemployed Man*, London: Nisbet.

—— (1940a) *Citizens without Work*, New Haven: Yale University Press.

—— (1940b) *The Unemployed Worker: A Study of the Task of Making a Living Without a Job*, New Haven: Yale University Press.

Banks, M.H. and Jackson, P.R. (1982) 'Unemployment and risk of minor psychiatric disorder in young people: cross-sectional and longitudinal evidence', *Psychological Medicine*, 12: 789–98.

Banks, M.H. and Ullah, P. (1988) *Youth Unemployment in the 1980s: Its Psychological Effects*, London: Croom Helm.

Beale, N. and Nethercott, S. (1986) 'Job-loss and health – the influence of age and previous morbidity', *Journal of the Royal College of General Practitioners*, 36: 261–4.

Beales, H.L. and Lambert, R.S. (1934) *Memoirs of the Unemployed*, Wakefield: E.P. Publishing.

Binns, D. and Mars, G. (1984) 'Family, community and unemployment: a study in change', *The Sociological Review*, 32, 4: 662–95.

Bostyn, A.M. and Wight, D. (1987) 'Inside a community: values associated with money and time', in S. Fineman (ed.), *Unemployment: Personal and Social Consequences*, London: Tavistock.

Bradburn, N.M. (1969) *The Structure of Psychological Well-Being*, Chicago: Aldine.

Branthwaite, A. and Garcia, S. (1985) 'Depression in the young unemployed and those on Youth Opportunities Schemes', *British Journal of Medical Psychology*, 58: 67–74.

Breakwell, G.M. (1985) 'Abusing the unemployed: an invisible justice', *Journal of Moral Education*, 14, 1: 56–62.

Brenner, M.H. (1984) *Estimating effects of economic change on national health and social well-being*, study prepared for the Joint Economic Committee of Congress, Washington: US Government Printing Office.

Bruce, M.L., Takeuchi, D.T. and Leaf, P.L. (1991) 'Poverty and psychiatric status: longitudinal evidence from the New Haven epidemiologic catchment area study', *Archives of General Psychiatry*, 48: 470–4.

Callendar, C. (1987) 'Women seeking work', in S. Fineman (ed.), *Unemployment: Personal and Social Consequences*, London: Tavistock.

Cameron, C., Lush, A. and Mears, G. (1942) *Disinherited Youth: A report on the 18 plus Age Group*, Edinburgh: T. & A. Constable.

Campbell, B. (1984) *Wigan Pier Revisited*, London: Virago Press.

Carnegie UK Trust (1943) *Disinherited Youth: A Survey 1936–39*, London: Constable.

Cassell, C., Fitter, M., Fryer, D. and Smith, L. (1988) 'The development of computer applications by unemployed people in community settings', *Journal of Occupational Psychology*, 61: 89–102.

Cavan, R.S. and Ranke, K.H. (1938) *The Family and the Depression*, Chicago: University of Chicago Press.

Coates, K. and Silburn, R. (1970) *Poverty: The Forgotten Englishmen*, Harmondsworth: Penguin Books.

Cobb, S. and Kasl, S.V. (1977) *Termination: The Consequences of Job Loss*, Cincinatti: US Department of Health, Education and Welfare.

Cohn, R.M. (1978) 'The effect of employment status change on self attitudes', *Social Psychology*, 41: 81–93.

Connolly, K. (1982) 'Psychology and poverty', *Bulletin of the British Psychological Society*, 35: 1–9.

Cooke, K. (1987) 'The living standards of unemployed people', in D.M. Fryer and P. Ullah (eds), *Unemployed People: Social and Psychological Perspectives*, Milton Keynes: Open University Press.

Cragg, A. and Dawson, T. (1984) *Unemployed women: a study of attitudes and experiences*, Research Paper No. 47, London: Department of Employment.

Daniel, W.W. (1974) *A National Survey of the Unemployed*, London: Political and Economic Planning Institute.

Davies, R., Hamill, L., Moylan, S. and Smee, C.H. (1982) 'Incomes in and out of work', *Employment Gazette*, 90: 237–43.

Donovan, A. and Oddy, M. (1982) 'Psychological aspects of unemployment: an investigation into the emotional and social adjustment of school leavers', *Journal of Adolescence*, 5: 15–30.

Dooley, D. and Catalano, R. (1988) 'Recent research on the psychological effects of unemployment', *Journal of Social Issues*, 44: 4, 1–13.

Eisenberg, P. and Lazarsfeld, P.F. (1938) 'The psychological effects of unemployment', *Psychological Bulletin*, 35: 258–390.

Elderton, M. (1931) *Case Studies of Unemployment*, Philadelphia: University of Philadelphia Press.

Estes, R.J. and Wilensky, H.L. (1978) 'Life cycle squeeze and the morale curve', *Social Problems*, 25: 277–92.

Fagin, L. and Little, M. (1984) *The Forsaken Families*, Harmondsworth: Penguin.

Farran, D.C. and Margolis, L.H. (1987) 'The family economic environment as a context for children's development', *New Directions for Child Development*, 35 (Spring): 69–87.

Feather, N.T. (1990) *The Psychological Impact of Unemployment*, New York: Springer-Verlag.

Feather, N.T. and Bond, M.J. (1983) 'Time structure and purposeful activity among employed and unemployed university graduates', *Journal of Occupational Psychology*, 56: 241–54.

Fineman, S. (1979) 'A psychosocial model of stress and its application to managerial unemployment', *Human Relations*, 32: 323–45.

Finlay-Jones, R.A. and Eckhardt, B. (1984) 'A social and psychiatric survey of unemployment among young people', *Australian and New Zealand Journal of Psychiatry*, 18: 135–43.

Finn, D. and Ball, L. (1991) *Unemployment and Training Rights Handbook*, London: The Unemployment Unit.

Fryer, D. (1986) 'Employment deprivation and personal agency during unemployment', *Social Behaviour*, 1, 1: 3–23.

—— (1987) 'Monmouthshire and Marienthal: sociographies of two unemployed communities', in D. Fryer and P. Ullah (eds), *Unemployed People: Social and Psychological Perspectives*, Milton Keynes: Open University Press.

Fryer, D. (1988) 'The experience of unemployment in social context', in S. Fisher and J. Reason (eds), *Handbook of Life Stress, Cognition and Health*, Chichester: Wiley.

—— (1990) 'The mental health costs of unemployment: towards a social psychology of poverty', *British Journal of Clinical and Social Psychiatry*, 7, 4: 164–76.

Fryer, D. and McKenna, S. (1987) 'The laying off of hands: unemployment and the experience of time', in S. Fineman (ed.), *Unemployment: Personal and Social Consequences*, Tavistock: London.

—— (1989) 'Redundant skills: temporary unemployment and mental health', in M. Patrickson (ed.), *Readings in Organisational Behaviour*, New South Wales: Harper & Row.

Fryer, D. and Payne, R.L. (1984) 'Proactivity in unemployment: findings and implications', *Leisure Studies*, 3: 273–95.

—— (1986) 'Being unemployed: a review of the literature on the psychological experience of unemployment', in C.L. Cooper and I. Robertson (eds), *International Review of Industrial and Organisational Psychology 1986*, Chichester: Wiley.

Fryer, D. and Ullah, P. (1987) *Unemployed People: Social and Psychological Perspectives*, Milton Keynes: Open University Press.

Furnham, A. (1983) 'Attitudes towards the unemployed receiving social security benefits', *Human Relations*, 36, 2: 135–50.

Ginsburg, S.A. (1942) 'What unemployment does to people', *American Journal of Psychiatry*, 99: 439–46.

Glyptis, S. (1989) *Leisure and Unemployment*, Milton Keynes: Open University Press.

Griffin, C. (1986) 'It's different for girls: the use of qualitative methods in a study of young women's lives', in H. Beloff (ed.), *Getting into Life*, London: Methuen.

Gurney, R.M. (1980) 'Does unemployment affect the self-esteem of school leavers?', *Australian Journal of Psychology*, 32: 175–82.

Gurney, R.M. and Taylor, K. (1981) 'Research on unemployment: defects, neglect and prospects', *Bulletin of the British Psychological Society*, 34: 349–52.

Hall, E.M. and Johnson, J.V. (1988) 'Depression in unemployed Swedish Women', *Social Science and Medicine*, 27, 12: 1349–55.

Hartley, J.F. (1980) 'The impact of unemployment upon self-esteem of managers', *Journal of Occupational Psychology*, 53: 247–55.

Hartley, J.F. and Fryer, D. (1984) 'The psychology of unemployment: a critical appraisal', in G.M. Stephenson and J.H. Davis (eds), *Progress in Applied Social Psychology*, Chichester: Wiley.

Henwood, F. and Miles, I. (1987) 'The experience of unemployment and the sexual division of labour', in D. Fryer and P. Ullah (eds), *Unemployed People: Social and Psychological Perspectives*, Milton Keynes: Open University Press.

Hepworth, S.J. (1980) 'Moderating factors of the psychological impact of unemployment', *Journal of Occupational Psychology*, 53: 139–45.

Hutson, S. and Jenkins, R. (1989) *Taking the Strain: Families, Unemployment and the Transition to Adulthood*, Milton Keynes: Open University Press.

Israeli, N. (1935) 'Distress in the outlook of Lancashire and Scottish unemployed', *Journal of Applied Psychology*, 19: 67–8.

Jackson, P.R. and Walsh, S. (1987) 'Unemployment and the family', in D. Fryer and P. Ullah (eds) *Unemployed People: Social and Psychological Perspectives*, Milton Keynes: Open University Press.

Jackson, P.R. and Warr, P.B. (1984) 'Unemployment and psychological ill-health: the moderating role of duration and age', *Psychological Medicine*, 14: 605–14.

Jackson, P.R., Stafford, E.M., Banks, M.H. and Warr, P.B. (1983) 'Unemployment and psychological distress in young people: the moderating role of employment commitment', *Journal of Applied Psychology*, 68: 525–35.

Jahoda, M. (1938/1987) 'Unemployed men at Work', in D. Fryer and P. Ullah (eds), *Unemployed People: Social and Psychological Perspectives*, Milton Keynes: Open University Press.

—— (1979) 'The impact of unemployment in the 1930s and the 1970s', *Bulletin of the British Psychological Society*, 32: 309–14.

—— (1982) *Employment and Unemployment*, Cambridge: Cambridge University Press.

—— (1986) 'The social psychology of the invisible: an interview with Marie Jahoda by David Fryer', *New Ideas in Psychology*, 4, 1: 107–18.

Jahoda, M. and Rush, H. (1980) *Work, Employment and Unemployment*, Occasional paper series, No. 12, Sussex: Science Policy Research Unit, University of Sussex.

Jahoda, M., Lazarsfeld, P.F. and Zeisel, H. (1933/1972) *Marienthal: The Sociography of an Unemployed Community*, New York: Aldine-Atherton.

Kardiner, E. (1936) 'The role of economic security in the adaptation of the individual', *The Family*, 17: 187–97.

Kaufman, H.G. (1982) *Professionals in Search of Work*, New York: Wiley.

Kay, D. (1984) *Counter benefits: making contact with the DHSS*, Scottish Consumer Council Working Paper 7, Glasgow: Scottish Consumer Council.

Kelvin, P. (1984) 'The historical dimensions of social psychology: the case of unemployment', in H. Tajfel (ed.), *The Social Dimension*, Cambridge: Cambridge University Press.

Kelvin, P. and Jarrett, J.E. (1985) *Unemployment: Its Social Psychological Effects*, Cambridge: Cambridge University Press.

Kessler, R.C., Turner, J.B. and House, J.S. (1988) 'Effects of unemployment on health in a community survey: main, modifying and mediating effects', *Journal of Social Issues*, 44, 4: 69–85.

Kilpatrick, R. and Trew, K. (1985) 'Life styles and psychological well-being among unemployed men in Northern Ireland', *Journal of Occupational Psychology*, 58: 207–16.

King, S.S. (1989) 'Developmental trajectories: an investigation of the differential psychological effects of employment, unemployment, YTS and further education for the school leaver', University of Aberdeen: Unpublished Ph.D thesis.

Kobasa, S.C., Maddi, S.R. and Kahn, S. (1982) 'Hardiness and health: a prospective study', *Journal of Personality and Social Psychology*, 42: 168–77.

Komarovsky, M. (1940) *The Unemployed Man and His Family*, New York: Dryden.

Lazarsfeld, P.F. (1932) 'An unemployed village', *Character and Personality*, 1: 147–51.

Lewis, A. (1935) 'Neurosis and unemployment', *The Lancet*, 2: 293–7.

Liem, R. (1983) 'Reconsidering the concept of social victim: the case of the unemployed', paper presented to the Annual Meeting of the American Psychological Association, Anaheim, California, mimeo.

Liem, R. and Liem, J.H. (1988) 'Psychological effects of unemployment on workers and their families', *Journal of Social Issues*, 44, 4: 87–105.

Little, C.B. (1976) 'Technical-professional unemployment: middle-class adaptability to personal crisis', *The Sociological Quarterly*, 17: 262–74.

McArthur, A.A. and McGregor, A. (1988) 'Community Credit Unions: Effects on People', Unpublished report, Training and Employment Research Unit, Glasgow: University of Glasgow.

McGhee, J. and Fryer, D. (1989) 'Unemployment, income and the family: an action research approach', *Social Behaviour*, 4: 237–52.

Mack, J. and Lansley, S. (1985) *Poor Britain*, London: George Allen & Unwin.

McKee, L. and Bell, C. (1986) 'His unemployment, her problem: the domestic and marital consequences of male unemployment', in S. Allen, A. Waton, K.

Purcell and S. Wood (eds), *The Experience of Unemployment*, Basingstoke: Macmillan.

McKenna, S.P. and Fryer, D. (1984) 'Perceived health during lay-off and early unemployment', *Occupational Health*, 36: 201–6.

Madge, N. (1983) 'Unemployment and its effects on children', *Journal of Child Psychology and Psychiatry*, 24: 311–19.

Martin, R. and Wallace, J. (1984) *Working Women in Recession: Employment, Redundancy and Unemployment*, Oxford: Oxford University Press.

Miles, I. (1983) *Adaptation to unemployment*, Science Policy Research Unit Technical Report, University of Sussex.

Moylan, S., Millar, J. and Davies, R. (1984) *For richer for poorer? DHSS cohort study of unemployed men*, DHSS Social Research Branch Research Report No. 11, London: HMSO.

Newman, G. (1932) *On the State of Public Health. Annual Report of the Chief Medical Officer of the Ministry of Health*, London: HMSO.

O'Brien, G.E. (1986) *Psychology of Work and Unemployment*, Chichester: John Wiley and Sons.

Oppenheim, C. (1990) *Poverty: The Facts*, London: Child Poverty Action Group.

Payne, R.L. (1988) 'A longitudinal study of the psychological well-being of unemployed men and the mediating effect of neuroticism', *Human Relations*, 41, 2: 119–38.

Payne, R.L., Warr, P.B., and Hartley, J. (1984) 'Social class and the experience of unemployment', *Sociology of Health and Illness*, 6: 152–74.

Pearlin, L.I., Lieberman, M.A., Managhan, E.G. and Mullan, J.T. (1981) 'The stress process', *Journal of Health and Social Behaviour*, 22: 337–56.

Penkower, L., Bromet, E.J. and Dew, M.A. (1988) 'Husband's layoff and wives' mental health', *Archives of General Psychiatry*, 45, 11: 994–1000.

Pilger, J. (1989) *A Secret Country*, London: Jonathan Cape.

Pilgrim Trust (1938) *Men Without Work*, Cambridge: Cambridge University Press.

Popay, J. (1990) 'Notes on the impact of unemployment on the individual and the family', presented to the ES-SPRU Understanding Unemployment Conference, May 1990, York, mimeo.

Rodgers, B. (1991) 'Socio-economic status, employment and neurosis', *Social Psychiatric Epidemiology*, 26, 3: 104–14.

Save the Children International Union (1933) *Children, young people and unemployment: a series of enquiries into the effects of unemployment on children and young people*, Geneva: SCIU.

Schaufeli, W. (1988) 'Unemployment and Psychological Health: An Investigation among Dutch Professionals', Unpublished Ph.D. Thesis: Rijksuniversiteit Groningen, The Netherlands.

Schlozman, K.L. and Verba, S. (1979) *Injury to Insult: Class and Political Response*, Cambridge, MA: Harvard University Press.

Seabrook, J. (1982) *Unemployment*, London: Quartet Books.

Smith, D.J. (1980) 'How unemployment makes the poor poorer', *Policy Studies*, 1: 20–6.

Stafford, E.M. (1982) 'The impact of the Youth Opportunities Programme on young people's employment prospects and psychological well-being', *British Journal of Guidance and Counselling*, 10, 1: 12–21.

Steinberg, L.D., Catalano, R. and Dooley, D. (1981) 'Economic antecedents of child abuse', *Child Development*, 52: 975–85.

Thoits, P. and Hannan, M. (1979) 'Income and psychological distress: the impact of an income maintenance experiment', *Journal of Health and Social Behaviour*, 20: 120–38.

Tiggemann, M. and Winefield, A.H. (1980) 'Some psychological effects of unemployment in school leavers', *Australian Journal of Social Issues*, 15: 269–76.

Townsend, P. (1979) *Poverty in the UK*, Harmondsworth: Penguin.

Ullah, P. (1987) 'Unemployed black youth in a northern city', in D. Fryer and P. Ullah (eds), *Unemployed People*, Milton Keynes: Open University Press.

Wallace, C. and Pahl, R. (1986) 'Polarisation, unemployment and all forms of work', in S. Allen, A Waton, K. Purcell and S. Wood (eds), *The Experience of Unemployment*, Basingstoke: Macmillan.

Warr, P.B. (1982) 'A national study of non-financial employment commitment', *Journal of Occupational Psychology*, 55: 297–312.

—— (1987) *Work Unemployment and Mental Health*, Oxford: Clarendon Press.

Warr, P.B. and Jackson, P.R. (1983) 'Self esteem and unemployment among young workers', *Le Travail Humain*, 46: 335–66.

—— (1984) 'Men without jobs; some correlates of age and length of unemployment', *Journal of Occupational Psychology*, 57: 77–85.

—— (1985) 'Factors influencing the psychological impact of prolonged unemployment and re-employment', *Psychological Medicine*, 15: 795–807.

Warr, P.B. and Parry, G. (1982) 'Paid employment and women's psychological well-being', *Psychological Bulletin*, 9: 498–516.

Warr, P.B. and Payne, R.L. (1982) 'Experience of strain and pleasure amongst British adults', *Social Science and Medicine*, 16: 1691–7.

—— (1983) 'Social class and reported changes after job loss', *Journal of Applied Social Psychology*, 13: 206–22.

Warr, P.B., Banks, M.H. and Ullah, P. (1985) 'The experience of unemployment among black and white urban teenagers', *British Journal of Psychology*, 76: 75–87.

Westin, S., Schlesselman, J.J. and Korper, M. (1989) 'Long-term effects of a factory closure: unemployment and disability during ten years' follow-up', *Journal of Clinical Epidemiology*, 42, 5: 435–41.

Yuen, P. and Balarajan, R. (1989) 'Unemployment and patterns of consultation with the general practitioner', *British Medical Journal*, 298: 1212–14.

Zawadski, B. and Lazarsfeld, P.F. (1935) 'The psychological consequences of unemployment', *Journal of Social Psychology*, 6: 224–51.

7

SOCIAL SECURITY AND LABOUR MARKET POLICY

Andrew Dilnot[1]

INTRODUCTION

Throughout the 1980s much was heard about the impact of social security benefits on the level of unemployment. On the one hand were those who saw the unemployed as living a life of indolent luxury as parasites on the rest of society, on the other were those who saw the unemployed living at or below the breadline, unable to find a job at any wage. These extreme views are obvious caricatures, but interest in the issues was, and still is, very great.

The second part of this chapter outlines briefly some of the sorts of questions that might be asked about the impact of benefits on the labour market, and some of the sorts of data which can be appealed to for answers. The third part attempts to summarize empirical evidence on the most common question, which is the impact of unemployment benefits on unemployment durations of men, but also suggests a number of problems and shortcomings with much of this work. Two examples of analysis of rather different groups are presented in the fourth part of the chapter, and some reasons for their apparently greater sensitivity to the social security system discussed. In the fifth part, some attempt is made to assess the direction of current government policy on social security and incentives to work.

EVIDENCE AND QUESTIONS

There are many different questions that might be, and are, asked about the impact of the tax and benefit system on unemployment. There are correspondingly many sources of information which might be used to attempt to answer these questions. This section outlines briefly some of the questions and some of the sources of data.

Potential questions

What impact does the social security system have on levels of unemployment?

This is in fact a rather unclear question, related to two clearer ones. First, what impact does the tax and social security system have on the rate at which individuals leave unemployment and thus the duration of unemployment. Second, what impact does the system have on the rate at which individuals flow on to the unemployment register? Much the greater amount of work has been done on the question of duration, typically in the context of job search models, where increases in unemployment compensation increase the 'reservation wage' which is required before a job offer is accepted, and thus lengthen the duration of unemployment. (See Atkinson and Micklewright 1989, for a discussion of these models.)

Does the social security system discourage participation in the labour market altogether?

Most social security systems provide different benefits to those actively seeking work and those who are unoccupied, and are not searching for work. Does the relative level of benefits for these two groups encourage individuals to leave the labour market and opt to be economically inactive?

Does the social security system encourage early retirement?

The way in which social security systems treat the early retired might have significant implications for labour supply. Issues such as whether or not the early retired have to pass a work test to be eligible for certain benefits might dramatically affect the size of the potential labour force. Similarly, the treatment of income from part-time jobs in assessing post-retirement benefits may be an important element in the labour supply decisions of the retired (see Barton, Pissarides and Zabalza 1980).

Does the social security system increase the number of individuals registered as sick?

If the social security system pays more generous levels of benefit to certain categories of those not in work, such as the long-term sick (who, in the UK, may be entitled to invalidity benefit, paid at a higher level than unemployment benefit, or Severe Disablement Allowance, paid at a lower level), there may be an incentive for the unemployed to register as sick. Perhaps more likely, in periods of high unemployment, individuals who have been sick and receiving invalidity benefit may remain registered as sick rather than rejoin the labour force only to find themselves unable to

127

find a job, and therefore dependent on the less generous unemployment benefits (see Disney and Webb 1990 for a discussion in the UK context).

Data sources

Faced with these, and other questions, a wide range of different sources of data has been used.

Anecdote

'I met this man in the Pub, and he knew someone who had met a man in the Pub last Friday. He had a wife and seventeen children. They were living in a council provided mansion, and he drove an Alfa-Romeo, G-reg. He hadn't worked for eight years, and said he couldn't afford to because he was better off on the dole. And it paid him to have more children, because the DSS paid for a home help if they did. No wonder we've got such high unemployment.' Second to the informal economy (tax evasion), benefit scroungers appear to be the richest available seam of anecdotal evidence in the UK (see also Chapter 8). Contrary to the apparent belief of many speech writers, this form of evidence is almost worthless.

Hypothetical/individual households

The use of individual examples of real or hypothetical families or house-holds has an important and valuable role in helping us to understand and explain the structure of social security systems. Such examples cannot however convey the true significance of any features which they demon-strate, since to understand that we must know how many such families are likely to exist. It might be argued that a sufficiently large and diverse group of hypothetical families, chosen to match the population, would deal with this objection. While this is to some extent true, the number of families required would be so great that there can be little point in using invented rather than real data.

Aggregate time series data

In most developed countries, including the UK, there is ready access to aggregate data on the level of unemployment. This can be combined with summary information on changes in the tax and social security system in an attempt to identify the impact of changes in income support on the level of unemployment, or its duration (see Layard and Nickell 1986, and Maki and Spindler 1975, for example). The main shortcoming of this approach is its inability to take adequate account of the enormous variation in actual and potential individual circumstances. In particular, it is very difficult to find an adequate summary measure of the impact of the tax and social security system on incomes in an out of work.

Large cross-section datasets

Cross-section data, such as the Family Expenditure Survey (FES) or General Household Survey (GHS) can help in providing detailed information about a wide range of individuals and families, thus allowing fuller modelling of the tax and social security system and the impact of unemployment. Unfortunately, all of the information required is rarely available. More significantly, since cross-section data provide only a 'snapshot' of individual circumstances, it is difficult to estimate what the individual's or family's circumstances would be if, for example, unemployment was replaced by employment. (See Atkinson and Micklewright 1985, for a detailed discussion of the use of cross-section data in this type of work.)

Panel data

Panel data such as the DHSS cohort study of the unemployed (Moylan *et al.* 1984) is of enormous value in this area, allowing individuals' experiences to be traced over time, and thus avoiding some of the problems caused by use of cross section data. However, it is expensive to collect, and consequently rather rare. (See Garcia *et al.* 1989 for further discussion of the DHSS 1978 cohort study of the unemployed and Garman and Redmond 1990 for a discussion of the subsequent 1987 DHSS cohort study of the unemployed. The new ESRC-funded panel survey at Essex will add greatly to our knowledge in this area.)

Small-scale interview studies

To understand better the impact of income maintenance systems on decision-making and implications for policy, detailed studies of the position and views of small numbers of families can often prove very useful. Millar (1990) has pointed out that the importance of uncertainty and risk has become clearer as a result of collection and analysis of this type of data (see McLaughlin, Millar and Cooke 1989).

EMPIRICAL EVIDENCE TO DATE

The previous section described some of the questions we might want to ask and some of the data sources which might be used. This section begins by sketching the conclusions of the very substantial amount of work on the effect of social security benefits on levels of unemployment. I then move on to consider the many problems and omissions inherent in much of this work, and in the next section look at evidence of benefit induced distortions of the labour market in two rather specific cases.

This chapter makes no attempt to provide a complete analysis of work done in the UK and elsewhere on the effects of benefits on unemployment, rather to give a brief summary of conclusions. (For a detailed account see Atkinson and Micklewright 1985 and 1989.) As will be noted at greater length below, the bulk of work done to date has concentrated on men, and has assumed a fairly straightforward choice between employment and unemployment.

To the extent that any form of consensus has been reached, it relates to the impact of unemployment benefits on the duration of unemployment; this is true in the US and the UK. Lancaster and Nickell (1980), for example, summarizing their work, reported that this effect was 'a rather firmly established parameter'. This parameter, the elasticity of duration of unemployment with respect to out of work benefit level, was about 0.6 – a 10 per cent cut in unemployment benefits would lead to a 6 per cent cut in average unemployment duration. Narandrenathan *et al.* (1985), using the DHSS cohort data, found an even smaller elasticity, of around 0.3. The results of these studies are broadly representative of the literature, although it is worth noting that there are dissenting voices such as Minford (1983).

A great deal of work has been done, the conclusion of which is that the level of unemployment benefit does have some impact on the duration of individuals' unemployment spells, but the effect is a rather small one. To have a dramatic impact on the level of unemployment, massive cuts in unemployment benefit levels would appear to be required. And such cuts would create a regime so different from the regime under which the estimates of elasticities were derived that their predictive usefulness must be at best doubtful. Furthermore, as Atkinson *et al.* (1984) show, the results can be very sensitive to changes in the way benefit systems are modelled. The limited conclusion that has been reached is important, but it seems sensible to ask whether other questions should have been asked, or at least should be asked now.

Problems and shortcomings

There are many ways in which the work outlined above could be extended, and it is hard to summarize the direction of greatest importance. Perhaps the most obvious problem has been too simple and homogeneous a view of both the labour market and the social security and tax systems. This rather simple view has led to certain rather important features of both the labour market and the social security system receiving too little attention.

One clear example of this failing has been the concentration on men, of which I have myself been guilty (see, for example, Dilnot and Morris

1983). There are many reasons why such an imbalance has existed, but it seems clear that, if anything, the weight of work should shift the other way. Women appear in most studies of labour supply issues to be far more sensitive to changes in tax and benefit systems than do men (see Killingsworth and MacCurdy 1986). Women's participation in the labour force continues to rise, and there seem to be few reasons for believing them to be less likely to become either unemployed or re-employed than men, quite possibly the reverse. (See Chapter 4 for a discussion of gender and unemployment risks.)

A somewhat related point is that many studies view the choice facing the unemployed as a simple one of remaining unemployed or becoming employed. This seems an excessive simplification of the labour market, where other options such as taking up the opportunity of training, leaving the labour force altogether and becoming unoccupied, becoming self-employed, or choosing between temporary and permanent or part-time and full-time jobs are also available. The 1985 Labour Force Survey shows that in the UK, of those unemployed twelve months earlier, 51 per cent remained unemployed, 29 per cent had become employed, and 20 per cent had left the labour force. Given the dramatic growth in part-time work and self-employment, and the rapid change in the structure of the UK labour force, a simple view of the labour market choices facing an individual is likely to be misleading.

Just as too simple a view of the labour market can be misleading, too simple a view of the social security system presents problems. One difficulty can arise if the structure of the system itself is difficult to model using available data. A good example of this is the Earnings Related Supplement to Unemployment Benefit, which existed until 1982. Since this was based on past earnings, it was difficult to estimate from cross-section data, and yet could be a very significant element of the benefits received by an unemployed person (see Micklewright 1985 for details). More worrying still are changes which simply do not fit into this framework. As we have already noted, the consensus, if there is one, is that enormous cuts in unemployment benefits would be required to have a significant effect on the level of unemployment. No such cuts have occurred, but unemployment in the UK fell dramatically from 1987, only to rise again from 1989. Much of the fall may have been the result of demand side changes, which we will discuss next, but some may have been the result of changes in the administration of the benefit systems. There has been much talk of tightening of availability of work tests, and of programmes such as Restart (see Chapter 3). These are hard to fit into the standard calculation of a replacement ratio, the ratio of out-of-work income to in-work, and yet may well have effects on measured and actual unemployment.

Thus far, we have considered only the 'supply' side, but we must also mention the demand side. Few would argue with the statement that much of the fluctuation in unemployment over the last decade has been the result of changes in the level of aggregate demand in the economy. Given this, we must take great care when analysing individual 'choices' over labour market states. With up to 3 million unemployed people in Britain today, it makes little sense to assume that each unemployed individual is 'voluntarily' unemployed. Most models have implicitly assumed that individuals fall into two groups; either wanting to work at the going wage, and therefore working, or not wanting to, and therefore unemployed. A more sensible view might be to split those who were not working into those who did not want to work at the going wage, and those who did, but could not find any job offers. This 'double hurdle' approach seems far more consistent with the UK labour market of the 1980s (see Blundell, Ham and Meghir 1988). As Millar (1990) and McLaughlin, Millar and Cooke (1989) have emphasized, care needs to be taken over the theoretical underpinnings of analysis of individual choice and decision-making.

Finally, most work to date has not dealt with uncertainty and problems of low take-up. Uncertainty about the provision of benefits to the low paid in work, or about the impact of the tax system, may prevent individuals from taking the risk of leaving unemployment, where incomes are stable although low, for a job which will leave them with a net income after tax and benefits which they find hard to assess (see Jenkins and Millar 1989 and McLaughlin, Millar and Cooke 1989). This point ties in with the more general problem of trying to estimate the probability that individuals will take-up benefits to which they are entitled (see Blundell *et al.* 1988 and Fry and Stark 1987). Most work has assumed that all individuals receive all benefits to which they are entitled, whether in or out of work. Since only 70–80 per cent of those entitled to Housing Benefit and Supplementary Benefit/Income Support take up their entitlement, and only 50 per cent of those entitled to Family Income Supplement/Family Credit, this is clearly misleading, and can have dramatic implications for the results obtained.

This has been a rather long list of problems, but one which leaves many avenues open for further research. The next section draws on some of these lessons to consider two specific groups of people, where we can see quite clearly an impact on labour market behaviour.

TWO EXAMPLES

1 Women married to unemployed men

One of the problems noted earlier was that most work in this area had concentrated on men. A group of women who are subject to particularly severe potential disincentives because of the tax and social security system are those married to unemployed men. The three main benefits to which such families are entitled are Unemployment Benefit, Income Support, and Housing Benefit. All three are subject to withdrawal if the wife of an unemployed man goes to work, as of course is also the case where the husband of an unemployed woman goes to work: the dependents addition to unemployment benefits is lost when the partner's earnings exceed the level of the addition; Income Support is withdrawn pound for pound once earnings exceed the disregard of £5 a week (or £15 if unemployed more than two years); Housing Benefit is also income related with a slightly less rapid rate of withdrawal than Income Support.

Table 7.1 illustrates for a hypothetical family with two children aged 11–15 paying £20 a week rent and £5 a week rates, the gain in net income from the wife working on different assumptions. The first assumption is that the husband is employed, and there is not entitlement to means-tested benefits; the second is that the husband is unemployed, but entitled to contributory National Insurance Unemployment Benefit; the third is that the husband is unemployed and has not entitlement to Unemployment Benefit, either because of an inadequate contribution record or a lengthy spell of unemployment. The figures are as at April 1987, so show Supplementary Benefit rather than Income Support. The hourly wage for the wife is assumed to be £2.50.

Table 7.1 Additional net income (£/week) at different hours worked by wife, April 1987 system

Wife's hours	0	10	20	30	40	50
Husband in work	–	25.00	46.59	62.09	76.59	92.59
Husband unemployed. Unemployment Benefit	–	8.57	22.80	27.84	35.16	51.16
Husband unemployed. Supplementary Benefit	–	4.00	4.00	4.00	6.55	7.09

The gain from part-time work is shown to be relatively small for the wife of the man entitled to unemployment benefit both because of the withdrawal of housing benefit and the loss of the whole of the dependent adult allowance (£19.40 a week) as soon as the wife's income exceeds that amount. We would therefore not expect many wives of unemployed men receiving unemployment benefit to work part-time, but might expect the low level of family income to encourage a number to work full-time, escaping from the most severe area of benefit withdrawal, and boosting family income. By contrast, we would expect to find very few women married to unemployed men receiving supplementary benefit (now income

133

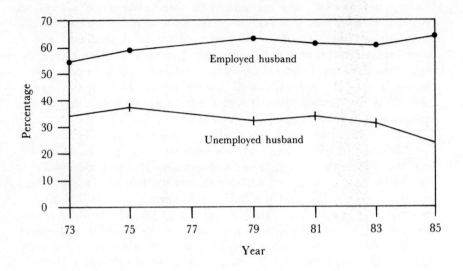

Figure 7.1 Participation rate of women married to employed and unemployed
men
Source: GHS, 1985

support) working at all. Overall, we would expect lower rates of labour
force participation for the wives of unemployed men than of employed
men, as a result of the operation of the benefit system, although we should
stress that many other factors might be important.

Figure 7.1 compares the participation rates of married women where the
household head is unemployed and employed, over the period 1973 to 1984.
The participation rate for the wives of unemployed men is consistently and
significantly lower than that for that of the wives of employed men. Figures
7.2 and 7.3, drawn from the 1984 FES, compares the labour market
characteristics of the wives of employed men first with that of the wives
of unemployed men receiving Unemployment Benefit, and second with
that of the wives of unemployed men receiving Supplementary Benefit.

Figure 7.2 shows that while the wives of husbands on unemployment
benefit are slightly less likely to work at all than the wives of employed
men, they are far more likely to work full-time, and far less likely to work
part-time. This is consistent with the impact of the benefit system. Figure
7.3 shows that receipt of supplementary benefit in almost all cases coincides
with the wife not working, which is again consistent with what we would
expect given the benefit system.

These data can only be indicative but further work (Kell and Wright
1990) has found strong and statistically robust evidence of these effects

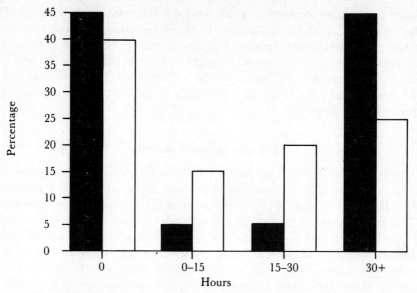

Key: □ Participation rates of women married to employed men
      ■ Men receiving unemployment benefit

Figure 7.2 Participation rates of women married to employed men and receiving
unemployment benefit

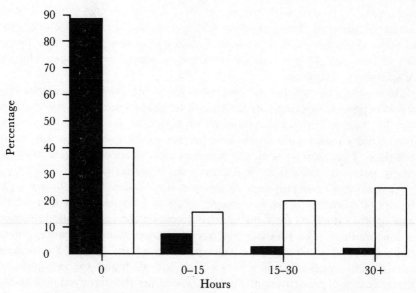

Key: □ Participation rates of women married to employed men
      ■ Men receiving unemployment benefit

Figure 7.3 Participation rate of women married to employed men on
supplementary benefit

135

using econometric techniques to analyse the same data (see Garcia 1989 for somewhat similar conclusions). It would be wrong to claim that the whole of the difference between the labour market behaviour of women married to employed and unemployed men can be explained by the benefit system, but a significant impact can be identified which is consistent with what we would expect. In the last section of this chapter possible policy responses are discussed.

2 Lone parent families

The number of lone parents in the UK has grown rapidly in recent years to over one million, representing 15 per cent of all families with children (see Halsley 1986 and 1989 for estimates of the number of lone parents). This group faces some potential disincentives similar to those of the wives of unemployed men in the structure of the Income Support and Housing Benefit, and the likelihood of low earnings. The problem of finding child-care, which may exist even for women with unemployed husbands, is clearly likely to be even more severe for lone parents (see Walker 1990; Millar 1989; and Bradshaw and Millar 1991, for more detailed discussion).

Figures 7.4 and 7.5, drawn from the 1983 Labour Force Survey, illustrate the hours of work decision of lone mothers and married mothers, with children of different ages. For both groups, participation is strongly and negatively correlated with the presence of pre-school age children, with almost 80 per cent of lone mothers with a pre-school child and 60 per cent of married mothers with a pre-school child not working at all. The figures fall to less than 40 per cent for both groups where the youngest child is of secondary school age.

As for the wives of unemployed men, we would expect to see relatively few lone parents working part-time, since to escape from the supplementary benefit 'trap' will typically require either high hourly wages or long hours. We do indeed see relatively few lone parents working part-time, and many full-time. The contrast with the behaviour of married mothers, amongst whom part-time work is far more common, is plain.

This evidence is again only illustrative, but Walker (1990) presents the results of econometric work using six years of FES data that find robust and significant effects from the benefit system on the participation decision of lone mothers. The presence and age of children, housing tenure, potential wage, level of maintenance payments received and level of Supplementary Benefit entitlement if a non-worker are all found to be significant determinants of participation. Table 7.2 illustrates the predicted probability of participation for a 'reference' individual; a single parent with a child aged 11–16, living as a householder in rented accommodation in Greater London, receiving no maintenance, and the effect of changes in these characteristics.

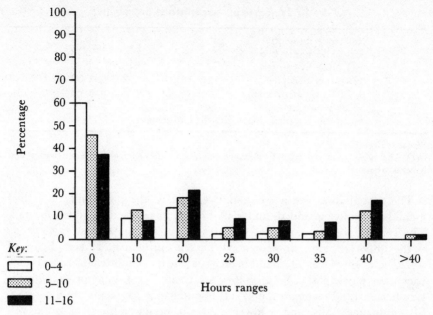

Figure 7.4 Participation rates for married mothers by age of child

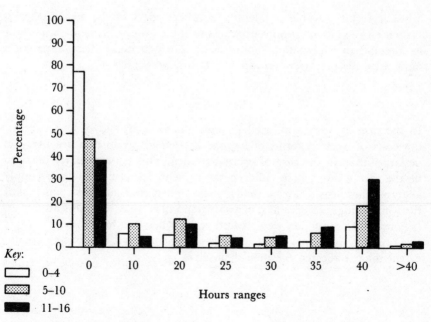

Figure 7.5 Participation rates of lone parents by age of children

Table 7.2 Lone parents participation probability

Reference individual	0.58
+ 1 child under five	0.18
+ 1 child five to ten	0.39
but owner occupier	0.58
+ £10 p.w. maintenance	0.64
+ 10% on wage	0.62
+ £10 on Supplementary Benefit entitlement	0.49

Source: Walker 1990
Note: The table gives the partial effects of changes in characteristics holding wages and benefits constant.

The probabilities are not cumulative, that is, the probability is 0.18 if a child under five is added, and 0.39 if a child aged 5–10 is added instead. The very significant impact of the presence of young children is clear, as is the importance of supplementary benefit entitlement at zero hours of work, and the level of maintenance payments. Maintenance payments encourage participation because they are treated as income for supplementary benefit (and income support). If maintenance payments are increased, SB entitlement falls, and a lower paid job, or fewer hours of work, will exhaust SB entitlement, and thus begin to provide some financial gain.

Distinguishing features

Since it seems possible to identify a robust effect of the social security system on the labour supply decisions of these groups, it seems important to attempt an explanation of the features which make them apparently more sensitive than those groups more usually focused on.

Costs of work

In the case of women married to unemployed men, and of lone parents, the costs of work in terms of forgone household production are likely to be larger than in the case of prime age men. This is particularly likely to be the case where young children are present. In terms of labour supply analysis, these costs can be thought of as fixed costs of work, which shift the whole budget constraint downwards and thus make work less attractive. If household production were shared equally between husbands and wives this problem would not affect the wives of unemployed men to any greater extent than it affected the men themselves.

Attachment to the labour market

It may be the case that women in general, and mothers in particular, are less firmly attached to the labour market than men. Whereas the social pressures on prime age men to work are strong, the social pressures on mothers may be not to work. This difference in expectations would be reflected in the utility function of men and women, such that prime age men might work even where working left them financially worse off, because of the utility they gained from being at work, while women and mothers in particular might need some greater financial reward to persuade them to work.

Low pay

It continues to be the case that women's pay lags behind men's in the UK. It is therefore less likely that a woman will be offered jobs which pay enough to enable her to jump beyond the poverty/unemployment trap. This is particularly true since household responsibilities may make part-time work the only feasible form of work, and part-time work is particularly likely to be low-paid.

Comprehensibility

In the case of both lone parents and the wives of unemployed men, an increase in income, perhaps from taking a part-time job, will lead in principle to an immediate reduction in benefit entitlement, in many cases of a very similar amount to the increase in earnings. If the pattern of re-entry to the labour market for this group is likely to be via part-time work, it will be very clear to them what the impact of the tax and benefit system is, and therefore easy to frame the appropriate response.

GOVERNMENT POLICY: ON THE RIGHT TRACK?

Assessing the extent to which government policy on the relationship between social security and unemployment is on the right track is quite difficult, since it is by no means clear what the overall intent of policy is. However, there are a number of areas where action has been taken or is proposed, which is intended to address this problem.

Perhaps the most obvious element of government social security aimed at improving incentives to work for those who might gain little financially from work, has been increased generosity of benefits available only to those in work. In the years prior to 1988 Family Income Supplement (FIS), and since 1988 Family Credit (FC), which replaced FIS, have become significantly more generous. The explicit aim of FC was to ensure that families with children would be better off in work than unemployed. This is a worthy aim, and the increased generosity of in work benefits must be welcomed. Unfortunately, this initiative suffers from an enormous draw-back; less than one half of those entitled to FC appear to be receiving it. To base a large part of labour market policy on a social security benefit which is so unreliable seems a mistake. (See McLaughlin, Millar and Cooke 1989 and Walker 1990 for a discussion of the role of FIS in labour market behaviour.) The Social Security Green Paper (Cmnd 9691, 1985) originally suggested that FC should be paid in the wage packet and although there are potential problems with such a change, this might have led to a more truly integrated system with a consequently higher take-up (as outlined in Dilnot *et al.* 1984). The payment of means-tested benefits to those in full-time work is the obvious starting point for merging the administration of tax, which is collected very effectively, and social security. Even if further use of tax-based administration is deemed impossible, it seems clear that the current performance of FC is inadequate, and thus that this element of the government's market labour strategy needs rethinking.

Concern about the failure of Family Credit leads naturally to a discussion of the provision of child-care. It is clear from all studies of labour supply that the presence of young children is a major obstacle to work. In the case of benefit recipients the problem of finding and paying for child-care, which is a problem for all parents, is supplemented by the higher level of benefit entitlement, which necessitates a higher paid job before any net financial gain accrues. Recent years have seen much campaigning, and in the 1990 Budget some action, in the form of removing employer provided childcare from the tax base. This change has been widely welcomed, but as a response to the problems of benefit recipients is worth very little, and seems anyway to move in the wrong direction. (See Chapter 9 for further discussion.) By taking employer-provided child-care out of the tax base, the government at present helps an extremely small group, since such provision is very rare. It may well be the case that provision will now grow, but the bulk of the tax reduction will go to the relatively well off; the benefit of tax relief rises with the value of the care and with the marginal income tax rate of the recipient.

There is all too little evidence in this area of serious thought or research. If the state should be aiming to make it easier for parents to work, there are many alternatives to tax relief for employer-provided child-care. One option which seems to have been little considered would be to increase provision of free nursery care, another to encourage schools to provide care after school hours and during holidays. If such direct public spending is unacceptable, the government might consider providing vouchers of a fixed amount which could be used at state child-care facilities, private child-care facilities, or employer provided facilities. If the government is particu-larly keen on employer based provision, a flat rate subsidy to the employer for each place provided might have been possible, although it is hard to see why employer based provision should be so desirable. And if the government was determined to use the income tax system, setting some limit on the amount of care per child which could be tax relieved, and restricting relief to the basic rate of income tax would both have been improvements on what actually happened. The appropriate role of government in the provision of child-care is an important question, it is a shame that so little thought appears to have been given before the 1990 Budget changes.

One last area of policy interest is the payment of maintenance payments to lone parents (that is, lone mothers since most lone parents are lone mothers). As noted earlier, the presence of maintenance payments encourages labour force participation by lone parents. At present, many lone parents receive no maintenance payments at all. Information from the six years of FES data 1979—84 shows that lone parents in receipt of SB receive maintenance in only 20 per cent of cases, compared with 48 per cent for non-recipients,[2] and that maintenance payments received are 25 per cent lower, on average, for SB recipients (Walker 1990; and see Bradshaw and Millar 1991). Policies which might enforce maintenance payments more effectively, such as the use of the tax system to withhold at source, as in Australia, are obviously important. The publication of the White Paper *Children Come First* (Cm. 1264, 1990) with its proposals for more effective and higher maintenance payments is clearly a significant change.

Government policy on the relationship between unemployment and social security benefits is not as yet very clear. In some cases, such as Family Credit, policy seems to be based more on hope than experience; in others, such as assistance with childcare, policy seems to be based on political pressure. This is not an easy area for governments to tackle; as yet this government's ideas for improvement still seem vague.

CONCLUSION

A great deal of research has been done on the impact of social security on unemployment. To the extent that a consensus has been reached, it suggests that cutting (increasing) levels of benefits for the unemployed would lead to a statistically discernible, but rather small, fall (rise) in the duration of unemployment for men. I have argued that in many cases, too simple a view of the benefit system, too simple a view of the labour market, and a concentration on men, may have blinkered research. There are groups whose behaviour is affected by the social security system, two of which were discussed in a little detail, others, such as those approaching or just past retirement, and the young were not. Government policy does not seem very clear, and in some areas seems to be based on hope, rather than reality.

NOTES AND REFERENCES

Notes

1 Thanks are due to the ESRC for financial support, to Jane Millar and other participants at the York Conference, and to the editor for comments on an earlier draft. Remaining errors are my own.
2 DSS administrative statistics suggest that 33 per cent of lone mothers on SB received maintenance in December 1984 – the discrepancy may arise because some lone mothers had their maintenance paid direct to the DSS, which may not be picked up by the FES.

References

Atkinson, A. B., Gomulka, J., Micklewright, J. and Rau, N.R. (1984) 'Unemployment Benefit and Incentives in Britain: How robust is the Evidence?', *Journal of Public Economics*, 23: 3–26.

Atkinson, A.B. and Micklewright, J. (1985) *Unemployment Benefits and Unemployment Duration*, ST/ICERD, London: London School of Economics.

—— (1989) *Unemployment Compensation and Labour Market Transition: A Critical Review*, ST/ICERD Discussion Paper, TIDI 1143, London: London School of Economics.

Barton, M., Pissarides, C. and Zabalza, A. (1980) 'Social Security and the Choice between Full-Time, Part-Time, and Retirement', *Journal of Public Economics*, 14, 2: 245–76.

Blundell, R.W., Fry, V.C. and Walker, I. (1988) 'Modelling the take-up of means-tested benefit: the case of housing benefits in the United Kingdom', *Economic Journal*, 96: 58–74.

Blundell, R.W., Ham, J. and Meghir, C. (1988) 'Female Labour Supply and Unemployment', *Economic Journal*, 97: 44–64.

Bradshaw, J. and Millar, J. (1991) *Lone Parent Families in the UK*, London: HMSO.

Cmnd 9691 (1985) *Reform of Social Security: Programme for Action*, London: HMSO.

Cmnd 1264 (1990) *Children Come First*, London: HMSO.

Dilnot, A.W., Kay, J.A. and Morris, C.N. (1984) *Reform of Social Security*, Oxford: Oxford University Press.

Dilnot, A.W. and Kell, M. (1987) 'Male Unemployment and Women's Work', *Fiscal Studies*, August: 1–16.

Dilnot, A.W. and Morris, C.N. (1983) 'Private Costs and Benefits of Unemployment: Measuring Replacement Rates', *Oxford Economic Papers*, 35: 321–40.

Disney, R. and Webb, S.J. (1990) 'Why Social Security Expenditure has risen faster than expected: A wider cost of unemployment?' *Fiscal Studies*, February: 1–20.

Fry, V.C. and Stark, G.K. (1987) 'The Take-up of Supplementary Benefit: Gaps in the Safety Net', *Fiscal Studies*, November: 1–14.

Garcia, J. (1989) 'Incentives and Welfare Effects of Reforming the British Benefit System: A Simulation Study for the Wives of the Unemployed', in S. Nickell, W. Narendranathan, J. Stern and J. Garcia, *The Nature of Unemployment in Britain*, Oxford: Oxford University Press.

Garman, A. and Redmond, G. (1990) 'The changing characteristics of unemployed men', *Employment Gazette*, September: 470–4.

Halsley, J. (1986) 'One Parent Families in Great Britain', *Population Trends*, 45: 5–13.

—— (1989) 'One Parent Families and their Children in Great Britain: Numbers and Characteristics', *Population Trends*, 55: 27–33.

Jenkins, S. and Millar, J. (1989) 'Income Risk and Income Maintenance: Implications for Incentives to Work', in A. Dilnot and I. Walker (eds), *The Economics of Social Security*, Oxford: Oxford University Press.

Kell, M. and Wright, J. (1990) 'Benefits and the labour supply of women married to unemployed men', *Economic Journal*, 100: 119–26.

Killingsworth, M. and MacCurdy, T. (1986) 'Female Labour Supply', in O. Ashenfelter and R. Layard (eds) *Handbook of Labour Economics*, North Holland.

Lancaster, T. and Nickell, S.J. (1980) 'The Analysis of Re-employment Probabilities', *Journal of the Royal Statistical Society*, Series A, 143: 141–65.

Layard, R. and Nickell, S. (1986) 'Unemployment in Britain', *Economica*, 53: S121–S170.

McLaughlin, E., Millar, J. and Cooke, K. (1989) *Work and Welfare Benefits*, Aldershot: Avebury.

Maki, D.R. and Spindler, Z.A. (1975) 'The Effect of Unemployment Compensation on the Rate of Unemployment in Great Britain', *Oxford Economic Papers*, 27: 440–54.

Micklewright, J. (1985) 'On Earnings related unemployment benefits and their relation to earnings', *Economic Journal*, 95: 133–45.

Millar, J. (1989) *Poverty and the lone parent family*, Aldershot: Avebury.

—— (1990) 'Notes on Social Security and Labour Market Policy', presented to the ES-SPRU Understanding Unemployment Conference, May 1990, York, mimeo.

Minford, P. (1983) *Unemployment: Cause and Cure*, Oxford: Martin Robertson.

Moylan, S., Millar, J. and Davies, R. (1984) *For Richer, For Poorer? DHSS Cohort Study of the Unemployed*, London: DHSS/HMSO.

Narendranathan, W., Nickell, S.J. and Stern, J. (1985) 'Unemployment Benefits Revisited', *Economic Journal*, 95: 307–29.

Walker, I. (1990) 'The Effects of Income Support Measures on the Labour Market Behaviour of Lone Mothers', *Fiscal Studies*, May: 55–75.

8

UNEMPLOYMENT, MARGINAL WORK AND THE BLACK ECONOMY

Catherine Hakim

INTRODUCTION

The 1980s saw unemployment shoot up to unprecedentedly high levels and remain above 2 million for a complete decade. There was also an upsurge of interest in the black economy among policy makers, in the press and, eventually, among social science researchers (O'Higgins 1985; Smith 1986; Smith and Wied-Nebbeling 1986). Towards the end of the 1980s there was enough concern about the black economy, not just in Britain but throughout the European Community, for the European Commission to undertake a major review of the issues along with twelve national reports, culminating in an international conference in 1989 (European Commission 1989). The OECD and the International Labour Office also addressed the policy issues raised by the various types of hidden, clandestine or concealed employment (De Grazia 1980, 1984; OECD 1986).

Concern about the black economy is a direct result of high and rising levels of unemployment. Two key assumptions are commonly made. First, that most of the people active in the black economy are formally unemployed and second, that the earnings of most participants would be taxable. A typical article in a major daily would read as follows:

> Britain's thriving black economy is reckoned to amount to more than 10% of GDP, making it worth about £45 billion in output this year and thus cheating the Treasury of an estimated £7.5 billion. [This article] looks at the ways the Inland Revenue is trying to curb what has become one of the world's growth industries . . . The East London minicab driver – officially listed as one of Britain's 2.3 million unemployed – flourished the £350 he had made in a week and offered no apologies for being part of the black economy. 'You can't support a wife and three kids on £60 a week from the Social', he said, 'it's either cabbing or thieving'.

The unemployed are perceived to have both the time and the motive to work in the black economy. And they make better newspaper copy because they are guilty *both* of benefit fraud and of cheating the Inland Revenue of income tax. The implication is that the economy is more buoyant than appears from continuously high levels of unemployment, and that the unemployed are not in fact financially dependent on unemployment benefits alone. Linking unemployment and the black economy provides the justification for policies which invest substantial resources in investigating possible benefit fraud as well as Inland Revenue investigations of possible underpayment of income tax. Through the implication that there is a more buoyant economy than is at first apparent, it justifies the introduction of stringent job-seeking regulations for the unemployed, the restriction of benefit levels, and creates a climate of opinion in which unemployment is to be explained primarily by the attitudes and behaviour of the unemployed rather than by a downturn in the economy depressing the demand for labour. Measures to deal with the problem seem to have run ahead of the available evidence, which has so far been very thin, and often anecdotal in character. Recent research shows that both of the key assumptions are wrong – at least for Britain.

PROBLEMS OF DEFINITION AND MEASUREMENT

Most reports acknowledge that the black economy is a complicated and multifaceted phenomenon which shades into a variety of innocent activities such as allotment gardening and leisure-time hobbies. The multiplicity of terms is partly a reflection of ambiguity as to what is being discussed as well as a search for precision about the different elements and overlaps between the parts (OECD 1986: 66–79; Harding and Jenkins 1989). Reports sometimes eschew the term 'black' economy in favour of illicit, hidden, informal, parallel, underground, phantom, immersed, submerged, subterranean, shadow or clandestine economy. Whatever term is used, the primary concern for policy-makers is work for profit or pay which lies outside the tax system and employment regulations – gainful work in the market economy, and hence concealed income rather than concealed employment *per se*. In contrast, academic social scientists have often been interested in the wider informal economy and all forms of non-market work, including work in the household and self-provisioning which are of little concern to labour market policy-makers and government statisticians (Pahl 1984; Harding and Jenkins 1989; see also OECD 1986: 66–7). The assumption that all earnings are taxable is thus built into the very definition of the black economy. Commentators often assume that official statistics must necessarily exclude activities in the black economy. In reality this depends very much on the particular statistics being used and their origins – household interview surveys being a very different source of information from national accounts compiled from administrative data supplied by various government agencies.

145

In practice, estimates of the size and rise of the black economy are largely based on gaps and anomalies in national accounts or the statistics they are based on, and on guesswork as much as on facts. As Thomas puts it, researchers look for the 'statistical fingerprints of the black economy' (Thomas 1988). The estimates and guesstimates are suggestive, but never compelling, and some regard them as worthless. Estimates of the size of the black economy range from 2 to 22 per cent of GDP in Britain, although Smith's (1986) estimate of 3–5 per cent is regarded as the most likely. Smith (1986) and Thomas (1988) provide detailed critiques of macro-economic measures of the black economy, concluding that they provide a flimsy basis for policy initiatives.

The other main approach is to look at survey microdata for individual workers and their households. This technique lies somewhat closer to reality, and might allow one to make statements about who is working in the black economy, and whether the unemployed dominate the picture, as so often assumed. Unfortunately it still does not offer reliable answers. For example, one technique is based on detailed analyses of the national Family Expenditure Survey (FES), either seeking to identify the types of worker or household who overspend relative to their reported income, or else identifying discrepancies between consumer expenditure as shown by the aggregate annual FES results and as shown in other national statistical sources (such as Customs and Excise statistics on liquor sales). This sort of analysis routinely shows that the self-employed spend more than their stated current income. But closer knowledge of the FES data invalidates any easy conclusions about undeclared income. The FES does not cover all sources of income, and it does not cover all types of expenditure. The FES *Handbook* warns, time and again, that the survey cannot be used to measure saving and dis-saving; in other words, that no interpretation can be placed on apparent discrepancies between income and expenditure as recorded in the survey. The FES income data relates to the present for most employees, but it often relates to a period twelve–twenty-four months earlier for the self-employed, depending on when their accounts are made up. In contrast expenditure data concerns the two week period after the interview. Thus there is scope for large discrepancies between income and expenditure as recorded in the survey, especially for the self-employed, and especially in inflationary periods, quite apart from any systematic saving and dis-saving patterns that cannot be detected by the survey. There are also problems in drawing conclusions about individuals who are self-employed (with, it is assumed, opportunities for black economy work and under-reporting of income) from data on household expenditure which covers all members of the household. This example is set out at length to illustrate how many concealed obstacles there are to obtaining valid, as distinct from plausible, measures of the black economy, even when good quality and appropriate data have been found.

NEW DEVELOPMENTS IN THE 1980s

Changing patterns of labour market participation and financial behaviour during the 1980s tend to invalidate some conventional interpretations of social and economic data and national indicators. For example, patterns of financial behaviour changed markedly in the 1980s, undermining many of the assumptions that are built into economic estimates of the black economy. There was an unprecedented growth in borrowing, in the use of credit and mortgages for house purchase, so that the ratio of household debt to disposable income doubled over the decade. In parallel there was an unprecedented fall of nearly two-thirds in the national savings ratio, from nearly 14 per cent to 5 per cent by 1988. The average amount owed per household rose over the decade from £600 to £2,300 excluding mortgages, and from £3,000 to £13,000 including mortgages for house purchase. Despite an 8 per cent increase in disposable incomes, consumers are borrowing more and saving less (National Consumer Council 1990). Clearly individuals and households engaged in massive dis-saving and new credit purchases over the 1980s, a development which cannot be separated out of the Family Expenditure Survey results.

Recent research has also shown that low-paid work has not disappeared from the labour market – notwithstanding government complaints that wages are still too high. Homeworking is routinely assumed to be located in the black economy, but a national survey of homeworkers showed that most had earnings well below the tax and National Insurance thresholds. In some groups – such as childminders and people doing manufacturing homework – virtually all workers had earnings so low that they remained outside the tax and National Insurance system, a factor which contributed, in turn, to homeworkers' uncertainty about their employment status (Hakim 1987, 1988). The numbers involved are not trivial. The survey indicated that over one quarter of a million home-based workers had earnings low enough to leave them outside the tax and social insurance net. Homeworkers are almost invariably women, who are usually supplementing their husband's earnings with non-taxable earnings; although homeworkers themselves suspect that others do the work to supplement meagre welfare benefits, actual examples of this seem to be rare (Cragg and Dawson 1981: 29–33).

Workforce restructuring in the 1980s has significantly expanded the number of part-time, temporary, casual and self-employment jobs – all of them types of work most typical of the black economy and all of them typically producing low earnings. This development has been most pronounced in Britain, due to the relatively unregulated labour market, but is repeated across the European Community (Hakim 1990a and 1990b). The Labour Force Survey shows that between spring 1981 and spring 1988 part-time, temporary and self-employment jobs rose from under 7 million to over 9 million, or from 30 per cent to 36 per cent of the labour force (Table 8.1), and the trend continued into 1989. In Britain, all these 'non-standard' forms of work are legal. Continental labour law defines many of them as non-legal, and new legislation has been needed in the 1980s to legalise them – in effect to bring them out of the underground or black economy into the formal economy. For this reason, Britain is believed to have a smaller black economy than some other EC countries.

Table 8.1 Workforce restructuring in Britain 1981–8

| | | 000s and % | |
	All	*Males*	*Females*
1981			
Economically active	26,089	15,653	10,435
In employment	23,606	14,093	9,512
Unemployed	2,483	1,560	923
Full-time regular employees	16,639	11,581	5,058
As % of in employment	70	82	53
All other workers	6,967	2,512	4,454
As % of in employment	30	18	47
1983			
Economically active	25,797	15,379	10,418
In employment	22,943	13,565	9,379
Unemployed	2,853	1,815	1,039
Full-time permanent employees	15,655	10,896	4,759
As % of in employment	68	80	51
All other workers	7,288	2,668	4,620
As % of in employment	32	20	49
1987			
Economically active	27,046	15,660	11,386
In employment	24,257	13,958	10,299
Unemployed	2,789	1,519	938
Full-time permanent employees	15,560	10,616	4,944
As % of in employment	64	76	48
All other workers	8,697	3,342	5,355
As % of in employment	36	24	52
1988			
Economically active	27,440	15,824	11,616
In employment	25,114	14,433	10,681
Unemployed	2,326	1,391	935
Full-time permanent employees	16,053	10,882	5,171
As % of in employment	64	75	48
All other workers	9,061	3,551	5,510
As % of in employment	36	25	52

Source: Hakim 1990b

THE MARGINAL WORKFORCE: PEOPLE BELOW THE TAX AND SOCIAL INSURANCE THRESHOLDS

The complete legality of part-time, temporary and self-employment jobs in Britain does not automatically mean they come within the compass of employment legislation and regulations. For example, millions of these workers have such low earnings as to remain outside the tax and National Insurance nets. Homeworkers are not the only group to be legitimately excluded from the NI system, and legitimately not paying income tax. About half a million self-employed, one-fifth of the national total, have earnings that leave them outside the tax and NI nets. Almost 2 million part-time workers, one-third of the total, have earnings too low to attract NI contributions and tax deductions. Somewhat more surprisingly, there are also thousands of full-time employees who fall into this category, most of them young people. Overall, about 10 per cent of the workforce have earnings low enough to leave them under the tax and social insurance thresholds (Hakim 1989).

In an analysis drawing on several government surveys, I estimated that there are some 3 million people in employment who do not pay income tax – perfectly legitimately. An even higher number, about 4 million, have earnings low enough to leave them outside the National Insurance safety net of contributory benefits. Altogether there are some 5 million people who might be misconstrued as working in what is commonly called the black economy, as shown in Table 8.2. Of this 5 million, I estimate about 2 million to be non-working people, the vast majority of them women out of the labour force rather than the unemployed. It may seem odd to refer to the earnings, albeit low earnings, of the non-working and the unemployed. But surveys in the 1980s repeatedly identify what I shall term marginal workers, or people on the margins of the labour force. They have very low earnings, due to working very few hours or irregularly, and may well not regard themselves as 'having a job' at all. Whether they are classified as working, unemployed or economically inactive in surveys such as the Labour Force Survey or General Household Survey will depend entirely on the precise definitions and classifications adopted in the survey (such as the time reference period), as illustrated by the following examples.

The 1980 Women and Employment Survey (WES) went to great lengths to identify all types of paid work done by women, including casual and occasional work such as childminding, mail order agent, outwork and seasonal work. The 1980 survey found that 13 per cent of *non-working* women between the ages of 16 and 59 years said they did such work – that is, about one woman in eight who would not be classified as being in work on the conventional definition was doing occasional paid work (Martin and Roberts 1984: 9–10). Applying the figure of 13 per cent to

149

Table 8.2 Working and non-working groups liable to be counted in
the black economy in Great Britain

Estimate of size	*Characteristics of group*
Working population	
2 million	People aged 16 and over with earnings below the threshold for National Insurance contributions, and hence also below the income tax threshold – that is, people paying *neither* NI nor tax.
	In 1986 this meant earnings below £38 per week (NI threshold) and hence also below £45 per week (tax threshold).
1 million	People aged 16 and over with earnings above the National Insurance threshold, but below the basic income tax allowance(s) – that is, paying NI but not tax.
	In 1986 this meant earnings in the range £38–45 per week.
0.25 million	People aged 16 and over with earnings above the basic income tax allowance(s) but with sufficient other tax reliefs (e.g. mortgage) to make them non-taxpayers, although National Insurance contributions are paid.
	In 1986 this meant earnings over £45 per week, but the upper limit is variable between persons, being determined by their tax reliefs, but could be over £100 per week.
Non-working population	
1.5 million	Non-working women aged 16–59 years who do occasional and irregular work involving too few hours and yielding earnings too trivial to be described as 'a job' by the women themselves, for inclusion in the job count, or for social welfare benefit purposes.
0.5 million (?)	Non-working men doing occasional work involving too few hours and earnings too trivial to be counted as a job within official statistics or for social welfare benefit purposes.
	In 1986 this generally meant earnings below £5 per week, both for women and men.
3 million (?)	Total number of non-taxpayers within the work-force.
4 million (?)	Total number of people with small (even trivial) earnings below National Insurance threshold.
5 million (?)	Total number of people who might be misconstrued as working in black economy.

Source: Hakim 1989

the total of 11.3 million economically inactive women aged 16 and over shows that around 1.5 million women who would conventionally be classified as out of the labour force earn small sums from subsidiary jobs. On average, these jobs involved only five hours' work a week, and earnings of £4.10 a week or just over £200 a year in 1980 (Martin and Roberts 1984:

32), placing them far below the thresholds at which National Insurance and income tax become payable.

Roughly the same type of work used to be identified in the Family Expenditure Survey as paid employment, but was reclassified as not being 'a job' from 1982 onwards. In 1982 and 1983 the cut off point was earnings from part-time work of less than £3.50 a week (raised to £5.00 a week in the 1985 and 1986 FES), a figure not too dissimilar from the 1980 WES average earnings of £4.10 a week for casual work. The reclassification of such tiny earnings as not 'a job' was also in line with the rules for Supplementary Benefit and Supplementary Allowance (now replaced by Income Support) which disregarded earnings below a trivial amount: £4.00 per week per person net of work expenses (or £8.00 per week for a married couple) being the standard earnings disregard for the unemployed until November 1988. From November 1988, the earnings disregard has been £5.00 per week per person (not net of work expenses), or £10.00 per couple in the first two years of unemployment, and £15 per couple thereafter. Certain groups of unemployed claimants (such as lone parents) also qualify for the higher earnings disregard.

The complexities of the income maintenance system mean that few people know all the rules applying to state benefits. The widespread assumption that people in receipt of state benefits cannot legitimately work at all is not quite accurate, as the above discussion of disregards has shown. And the complexities of the system have made it possible to earn more than trivial amounts legitimately. Traditionally, unemployment insurance benefits were paid to replace earnings from full-time employment Monday to Saturday inclusive, so that the unemployed could earn any amount at all on a Sunday without affecting their benefit entitlement. However the same convention has not been applied to social assistance benefits (Supplementary Benefit, now replaced by Income Support), where benefits are treated as covering the full seven-day week. These oddities are reflected in national interview surveys, and can readily be misinterpreted by labour economists and others as the 'statistical fingerprints' of the black economy. The 1986 Labour Force Survey identified some 210,000 people (120,000 men and 90,000 women) who said they were claiming unemployment benefits and also had some paid work during the reference week. Some respondents may have misunderstood the questions. But the Department of Employment reported the result and pointed out that this situation can arise legitimately and is not necessarily an indication of working in the black economy (Department of Employment 1988: 31).

All the indications are that marginal work among the non-working population is dominated by women. At all ages over 30, part-time work is important among women but exceptionally rare for men. Only over retirement age does part-time work attract both men and women, supplementing pension incomes. Admittedly the very detailed 1980 Women and Employment Survey information is available only for women, but the pattern of behaviour is confirmed by the 1987 British Social Attitudes Survey. This showed 15 per cent of non-working women to have a marginal job involving less than 10 hours a week; when women working in a family business are included the proportion rises to one-fifth (19 per cent) of all non-working women. There was no equivalent pattern of marginal work among men. It is important to note that marginal work (or subsidiary economic activity as the 1980 WES report describes it) is more common among women who are out of the labour force than among unemployed women: 14 per cent compared to 9 per cent (Martin and Roberts 1984: 9). Although both unemployment benefit and income support regulations allow claimants to do a small amount of paid work, the rules permitting it are complex and not well known, whereas the activities of benefit fraud investigators are well publicized and claimants' availability for work is constantly scrutinized. In practice the general drift of the benefit system is to discourage and eliminate any paid work, enforcing full-time unemployment and inactivity on anyone seeking benefit (see also McLaughlin 1991).

Just as there is a much higher proportion of part-time, temporary and self-employment jobs in the non-agricultural British workforce than in other countries of the European Community, Britain has the largest marginal workforce. Minimal employment not subject to social security contributions is said to account for less than 1.5 per cent of the Belgian workforce, between 1.3 and 1.4 per cent of the German (FDR) workforce, and only 1.3 per cent of the workforce in Ireland. (Figures for other countries were not available.) The equivalent figure for Britain is given as between 6.2 per cent and 9 per cent in a 1981 European Commission report (De Gijsel 1981), and rose to just over 10 per cent at the end of the 1980s due to workforce restructuring (Hakim 1989). In all countries the marginal workforce is dominated by women, for the most part married women who may only have access to social security rights through husbands or other indirect routes.

PAYMENT 'CASH IN HAND'

The final type of evidence linking unemployment and the black economy comes from opinion polls treated by economists as providing factual information. By asking a sample of people (sometimes not even a nationally representative sample of people) about the characteristics of those they 'know' to be working 'cash in hand', researchers pretend to create statistical information on the characteristics of people in the black economy (see for example Opinion Research and Communication 1986, 1987; Matthews and Stoney 1987).

One possibility is that respondents to such surveys are quite literally and correctly reporting the characteristics of people they know to be paid 'cash in hand' rather than with cashless pay. The wholesale change from cash pay to cashless pay that has taken place over the last twenty years, particularly among white-collar workers (who include the journalists and researchers who structure our perceptions of reality), leads to the ready assumption that hardly anyone receives their wages in cash any more. Yet even in 1987, almost one-third (29 per cent) of the employee workforce was paid in cash, usually on a weekly basis, as shown in Table 8.3. That is, some 6 million people (4 million of them manual workers) were still being paid in cash by their employers, legitimately, in the late 1980s. (This figure has probably declined rapidly since then, due to legislation making it easier for employers to insist on cashless pay.) There is almost certainly some over-lap between the group of people whose wages are paid in cash and the millions of people identified above as having earnings too low for tax and/or National Insurance contributions to be payable – but the combination could be misread by some as proving the non-legal nature of the work.

Table 8.3 From cash in hand to money in the bank

	1969			1979			1987		
	All	Manual	Non-manual	All	Manual	Non-manual	All	Manual	Non-manual
Percentage of employees paid in cash	75	89	53	54	78	35	29	*	*

Source: Hakim 1989
Note: *Information not available.

Pahl's study of the Isle of Sheppey in 1981 demonstrated just how difficult it is to disentangle the various types of work done outside the formal or market economy:

1 self-provisioning and Do-It-Yourself;
2 informal work done by or for friends, neighbours or relatives, whether paid or unpaid; and
3 black economy work.

Yet Pahl had the advantage of information drawn from lengthy personal interviews where the focus was on the respondents' *own* activities. It is obviously hazardous to attempt to collect such information by proxy, especially when it involves making assumptions about behaviour invisible to the person attempting to report on their neighbour's or acquaintance's activities (such as whether specific income has been, or will be, declared to the tax authorities). Pahl estimated that 5 per cent of the adult house-holders covered by his survey did occasional work in what he classified as the black economy. That is, they acknowledged doing work 'on your own account to get extra money', and Pahl assumed they were paid in cash and might not declare the money to Inland Revenue (Pahl 1984: 247). The finding has been widely used in government as independent evidence of the incidence of black economy work, and because the information comes from personal interviews it allows us to get a handle on the characteristics of black economy workers. One-third of those who did work on their own account to get extra money were housewives with no paid employment. It seems very likely they would fall into the category of non-working people with trivial earnings that would automatically be tax exempt. The remainder were working, rather than unemployed – but here too it cannot automatically be assumed that their aggregate earnings were high enough to attract tax and other deductions.

More importantly, Pahl's study showed that all forms of activity and work were concentrated among those in employment rather than the unemployed. Marginal work, voluntary work, self-provisioning and so on were all in a sense parasitic on having a job in the market economy. The unemployed might have the time and the motive, but Pahl demonstrated that they do not have the other necessary resources – social contacts in the world of work, and spare cash for equipment and so on, being essential to supplementary work and activity of any kind. Similar conclusions have been drawn for other European countries (OECD 1986: 75–7; European Commission 1989).

CONCLUSIONS

In sum, the unemployed do not constitute the most important source of recruits to the black economy; the unemployed represent the smallest source, with the lowest incidence of such activity. This is not to deny that benefit fraud does sometimes occur, with occasional spectacular examples, but such cases are clearly not representative. Social scientists and policy-makers are at cross purposes on the significance of this finding. For academic social scientists the key finding is that the employed workforce is the most important source of concealed income and tax evasion. For labour market policy-makers, the existence of any black economy work among the unemployed is significant, almost irrespective of size and numbers. It is widely assumed by policy-makers that the black economy provides a social and economic lubricant, or safety valve, which thus explains why continuing high levels of unemployment for over a decade in Britain have not produced riots and widespread breakdown of the social and political order, as expected from the early 1980s (Hakim 1982: 434). The main issue then becomes whether a combination of welfare benefits and occasional black economy work becomes a permanent substitute for paid employment (OECD 1986: 76). Public opinion also displays highly ambivalent attitudes towards and perceptions of the unemployed. Benefits for the unemployed are seen as both too high and too low; the great majority of people believe both that many people fail to claim all the benefits they are entitled to, and that large numbers of people falsely claim benefits (Hakim 1982: 457–8; Bosanquet 1986: 131).

The ready assumption that all paid work is taxable overlooks the vast size of the marginal workforce, which is currently ignored by policy-makers. It is interesting to note that neither the Department of Social Security nor the Inland Revenue ever bothered to produce estimates of the numbers of workers below the tax and social insurance thresholds. The estimates of three to five million marginal workers who might be misconstrued as being in the black economy are an overestimate of the relative importance of the hidden, or less visible, part of the economy in that they offer counts of the number of people involved rather than the number of work hours involved; given the intermittent and part-time nature of marginal work, the marginal workforce is a good deal smaller when measured in workhours. Given the weak evidence so far available on the size and rise of the black economy, policies addressing the issue must rest on an act of faith rather than solid fact.

It is tempting to conclude that labour force statistics must be weaned away from their long dependence on the concepts and concerns of labour economics, pulling in a more broadly based sociological definition of work to achieve a fuller, more comprehensive picture of work and employment (see Pahl 1988, 1989). The increasing importance of intermittent and part-time jobs and of work done on a self-employed basis (full-time and part-time) also suggests that some revamping of definitions and classifications is required to ensure that new trends are fully captured by national surveys. For example, people on annual hours contracts, or with very flexible shift systems may find conventional survey definitions inappropriate to their situation. And we need to look harder at new trends, such as students in full-time education who have Saturday jobs (Hutson and Cheung 1991), who constitute a very different type of marginal worker from adults in the labour force. To fully capture changing patterns of work, self-employment and unemployment, and the social and economic implications of change, will require a specially designed national survey along the lines of the 1980 Women and Employment Survey (Martin and Roberts 1984), but covering men as well as women, and possibly very young people and pensioners who are found to be working.

As Pahl (1988) has pointed out there are ultimately some very fine lines to be drawn between employment, voluntary and other work, hobbies and leisure activities, and it is unlikely that these fine distinctions will ever be sufficiently well teased out to offer clear distinctions between 'white' and 'black' economy work – even if people were willing to provide the information. To take one example, childminding may be carried out on a neighbourly 'gift' basis; by using a system of tokens to keep a balance in

155

babysitting clubs; on a barter system exchanging childminding for other goods and services; by paying schoolchildren or pensioners to do it on an occasional basis (that is, people who are outside the labour force and the tax net); or by paying a professional childminder for the service. Almost any dividing line will be arbitrary, and thus also the definitions of 'informal' or 'black' economy.

On a more practical level we must decide whether to encourage or discourage the black economy, whatever its size. For the purposes of unemployment policy and procedures affecting unemployed benefit claimants, it is irrelevant that the employed workforce accounts for the majority of black economy work or, to be more precise, tax evasion. Current policy towards the unemployed is arguably inconsistent: encouraging work in the black economy while purporting to eliminate it. It seems clear that unemployment benefit fraud investigations scare off many perfectly innocent claimants as well as revealing some cases of fraud. People forced off the register may well resort to black economy work for financial survival, even if they were not so inclined until pushed.

Paradoxically, suspicions can become self-fulfilling. On the other hand the Enterprise Allowance Scheme (EAS) is designed primarily to bring budding entrepreneurs among the unemployed out of the black economy and into the formal market economy. The case for EAS rests only in part on the growth potential of what may well start out as hobbies or marginal work. Its key purpose is to remove the stigma and illegality from attempts to create alternative forms of employment, and it has as a result led to demands for similar schemes from employees and (re-)entrants to the labour force – which in itself is indicative of where black economy interest and initiative lie.

I would argue that an equivalent helping hand should also be offered to those taking up temporary or part-time work, to ease the transition out of unemployment for the great majority who seek to return to employee jobs rather than to become self-employed. The idea of part-time unemployment benefit is repeatedly raised, and dropped, but the need for such a scheme, and for a more flexible and sophisticated earnings disregards policy seems to be growing (see also McLaughlin, Millar and Cooke 1989; Millar 1989; McLaughlin 1991). Policy towards the unemployed has failed to address the fact that it is counter-productive to insist on complete inactivity as the price for continued receipt of unemployment benefits. The unemployed need to 'keep their hand in' in their trade or profession, to keep in touch with the realities of paid employment, to keep in touch with the social network of colleagues who can inform them of new job opportunities, in order to maintain the interest, motivation and ability to regain paid employment. Restricting social contacts to other unemployed people is far more conducive to creating a culture of welfare dependency than policies which prevent the social isolation of the unemployed. The policy of rigorously enforced inactivity is counter-productive and should be reconsidered.

Ultimately, the across the board solution is some form of guaranteed minimum income for all. The key advantage of guaranteed minimum income (or social dividend) schemes in this context is that they offer everyone a basic minimum income regardless of work status. Such schemes thus constitute a complete break from policies based on rigid demarcations between employment, economic inactivity, or unemployment, so that these cease to be mutually incompatible situations, thus easing transitions between them and facilitating flexible combinations (Standing 1986, 1989). Many variants have been proposed and considered by all political parties, but the relatively high costs of a universal incomes floor indicate that this sort of solution is likely to be a long time coming.

A more feasible policy option in the short term would be to declare tax-free zones of work as an alternative to regional tax incentives or a national minimum wage. All work known to have narrow profit margins, and very low paid work which is none the less socially beneficial, could be declared to be tax-free. For example childminding, or all work producing an income of less than a specified amount (say £1.00 or £2.00 an hour), could be declared to be non-taxable no matter who did it. Inland Revenue is slowly incorporating some recognition of compliance costs into its procedures, with simplified tax returns for very small businesses being introduced from 1990 onwards. Additional exemptions could be introduced for work that does not warrant the label of 'business' or 'job' – as illustrated by homework. Developments along these lines could have as great an impact as the EAS has had in assisting the unemployed legitimately to set up new businesses. But there must also be some official recognition of the huge scale of marginal work measured in terms of numbers of people involved as well as work hours.

To return to our initial example, homework is attractive to some women precisely because it is invisible to the outside world. The hidden nature of homework led many to think it must be illegitimate as well. In reality few homeworkers earn enough to come within the tax-NI net, but many do not know this and worry unnecessarily about their non-payment of income tax. This example, and others, show that rules and procedures that are simple, transparent, easy to understand and to apply might well eliminate the bulk of the 'black' economy at a stroke.

REFERENCES

Bosanquet, N. (1986) 'Interim report: public spending and the welfare state', in R. Jowell, S. Witherspoon and L. Brook (eds), *British Social Attitudes – the 1986 Report*, Aldershot: Gower.

Cragg, A. and Dawson, T. (1981) *Qualitative Research Among Homeworkers*, Research Paper No. 21, London: Department of Employment.

De Gijsel, P. (1981) *The Concealed Labour Market in a Number of Community Countries – A Summary Report*, research report to the European Commission, mimeo.

De Grazia, R. (1980) 'Clandestine employment: a problem of our times', *International Labour Review*, 119, 5: 549–63.

—— (1984) *Clandestine Employment*, Geneva: International Labour Office.

Department of Employment (1988) 'Measures of unemployment and characteristics of the unemployed', *Employment Gazette*, 96, 1: 28–39.

European Commission, Directorate-General for Employment, Industrial Relations and Social Affairs (1989) *Black Economy, Employment in Europe 1989*, Luxembourg: Office for Official Publications of the European Communities.

Hakim, C. (1982) 'The social consequences of high unemployment', *Journal of Social Policy*, 11, 4: 433–67.

—— (1987) *Home-based Work in Britain*, Research Paper No. 60, London: Department of Employment.

—— (1988) 'Homeworking in Britain', in R. Pahl (ed.), *On Work*, Oxford: Basil Blackwell.

—— (1989) 'Workforce restructuring, social insurance coverage and the black economy', *Journal of Social Policy*, 18, 3: 471–503.

—— (1990a) 'Workforce restructuring in Europe in the 1980s', *International Journal of Comparative Labour Law and Industrial Relations*, 5, 4: 167–203.

—— (1990b) 'Core and periphery in employers' workforce strategies: evidence from the 1987 ELUS survey', *Work, Employment and Society*, 4, 2: 157–88.

Harding, P. and Jenkins, R. (1989) *The Myth of the Hidden Economy*, Milton Keynes: Open University Press.

Hutson, S. and Cheung, W-Y. (1991) 'Saturday jobs: sixth-formers in the labour market and the family', in S. Arber and C. Marsh (eds), *Household and Family: Divisions and Change*, London: Macmillan.

McLaughlin, E. (1991) 'Work and welfare benefits: social security, employment and unemployment in the 1990s', *Journal of Social Policy*, 20, 4: 485–508.

McLaughlin, E., Millar, J. and Cooke, K. (1989) *Work and Welfare Benefits*, Aldershot: Avebury.

Martin, J. and Roberts, C. (1984) *Women and Employment: A Lifetime Perspective*, London: HMSO.

Mathews, K. and Stoney, P. (1987) 'The black economy: the evidence from Merseyside', *Liverpool Quarterly Economic Bulletin*, 30 June 1987.

Millar, J. (1989) 'Social security, equality and women in the UK', *Policy and Politics*, 17, 4: 295–300.

National Consumer Council (1990) *Credit and Debt: The Consumer Interest*, London: National Consumer Council.

OECD (1986) 'Concealed employment', in *OECD Employment Outlook*, Paris: Organisation for Economic Co-operation and Development.

O'Higgins, M. (1985) 'The relationship between the formal and hidden economies', in W. Gaertner and A. Wenig (eds) *The Economics of the Shadow Economy*, Berlin and Heidelberg: Springer-Verlag.

Opinion Research and Communication (1986, 1987) *The Unemployed and the Black Economy*, London: ORC.

Pahl, R. (1984) *Divisions of Labour*, Oxford: Basil Blackwell.

—— (ed) (1988) *On Work*, Oxford: Basil Blackwell.

—— (1989) 'From black economy to forms of work' in R. Scase (ed.) *Industrial*

Societies: Crisis and Divisions in Western Capitalism and State Socialism, London: Unwin Hyman.

Smith, S. (1986) *Britain's Shadow Economy*, Oxford: Clarendon Press.

Smith, S. and Wied-Nebbeling, S. (1986) *The Shadow Economy in Britain and Germany*, London: Anglo-German Foundation for the Study of Industrial Society.

Standing, G. (1986) *Unemployment and Labour Market Flexibility: the United Kingdom*, Geneva: International Labour Office.

—— (1989) *European Unemployment, Insecurity and Flexibility: A Social Dividend Solution*, World Employment Programme Working Paper, Geneva: International Labour Office.

Thomas, J.J. (1988) 'The politics of the black economy', *Work, Employment and Society*, 3, 2: 169–90.

9

HIDDEN UNEMPLOYMENT AND THE LABOUR MARKET

Hilary Metcalf[1]

INTRODUCTION

It is widely recognized that many policies to reduce unemployment have the side effect of bringing more people into the labour force. This is usually seen as a problem: it prevents the unemployed from taking all newly created jobs; and it means that greater measures are required to achieve a given fall in unemployment. In effect, people who did not really want jobs are seen as taking jobs from the unemployed. However, bringing 'non-participants' into employment is as important to the economy (although not to the standing of the government) as placing the recognized unemployed in jobs. Both allow the economy to benefit from a better use of its human resources and utilize the investment made in education, training and work experience. Therefore does it matter that 'non-participants' gain some of the jobs instead of the unemployed?

This chapter will argue that this question only arises because of a misconceptualization about unemployment and non-participation. Various definitions of unemployment exist, the most usual being either based on registration or seeking work. However, this chapter proposes that within those classed as 'non-participants' there is a group who are neither registered unemployed nor are seeking work, who, nevertheless, wish to work but face barriers to employment. It is argued that it is this group who 'take the jobs of the unemployed' and that these 'non-participants' should also be regarded as unemployed – the 'hidden unemployed'.

Before proceeding to the substantive parts of the chapter, it is important to consider whether the purported misconceptualisation of unemployment and non-participation matters. The author would argue that it does for three reasons. Firstly, policy formation is dependent on theoretical analysis of the labour market: if the definitions of unemployment and non-participation are flawed, analysis and policy may also be flawed. Secondly, it is important to address 'hidden unemployment' to enable the economy to maximize individuals' contribution and investment in education, training and work experience. Thirdly, it is argued below that the incidence of

160

hidden and of acknowledged unemployment varies amongst different groups (by gender, race, disability, age) and that the definition of unemployment, omitting the hidden unemployed, is inherently discriminatory and leads to discriminatory employment policy.

The next section discusses the difference between unemployment and non-participation and shows that, theoretically, many so-called non-participants are in fact unemployed – or hidden unemployed. The following section briefly describes the characteristics of the non-employed population, drawing distinctions between the acknowledged unemployed, the hidden unemployed and true non-participants. The chapter then focuses on one group with extensive hidden unemployment – women – discussing, firstly, the causes of, and, secondly, the remedies for, hidden unemployment in this group.

UNEMPLOYMENT AND NON-PARTICIPATION

It is recognized that individuals lie on a continuum between definitely not wanting to work and wanting to work very much. A cut-off along this line is made between the unemployed and non-participants, at the point where people do or do not want a job at the prevailing wage rate. The unemployed are those who want a job but cannot find one, at the prevailing wage rate, and non-participants are those who do not wish to work, at the prevailing wage rate.

The 'prevailing wage rate' is short-hand for the conditions in, and affecting, the labour market, including pay. This is where the problem lies. The definition skates over the many institutional and sociological reasons why a person may be unable to take a job or become discouraged from wanting a job. For example, is a woman who wants to work, but cannot find (or afford) essential childcare for her children, unemployed? Is a 70-year-old who wants to work, but believes no one will consider her for a job, unemployed? These people are often not considered to be unemployed. However, we would contend that both are unemployed: that the barriers they face are constraints to employment.

Figure 9.1 helps to clarify the argument. The degree to which an individual wants a job, at a prevailing wage rate, is shown along the horizontal axis and the barriers to employment (for example, lack of childcare, prejudice, disability) up the vertical axis. For a given individual the lower the barriers and higher their desire for a job, the more likely they are to be either employed or recognized as unemployed. Whether barriers are high or low, those with little desire for a job may be considered as being non-participants; as barriers rise individuals are more likely to be one of the hidden unemployed. Although the diagram has been premised on a prevailing wage rate, wages themselves may be considered as a barrier, when, for example, wages are discriminatory.

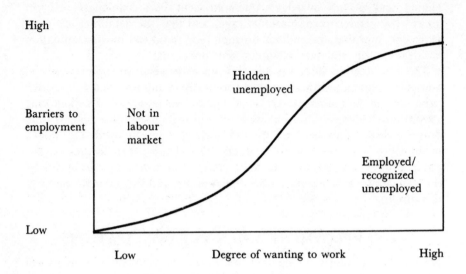

Figure 9.1 The hidden unemployed

The picture is further complicated: it is not just the strength of barriers that may lead to a person's being regarded as a non-participant or not, it is also the nature of those barriers. Certain barriers to employment result in people being classified, by both the population at large and by the state, as unemployed whilst others lead to them being regarded as non-participants. Let the former be described as 'legitimate' barriers and the latter 'non-legitimate'. Legitimate barriers to taking a job include: the job requires moving house; and the job requires excessive travel, where excessive is over, say, one hour each way. Other reasons often also regarded as legitimate (but perhaps decreasingly so by the state) include: the job is outside the person's normal occupation; and wages are below the going rate.

Non-legitimate barriers, that is, those that result in the person being considered as a non-participant, include:

1 failure to find childcare or other dependent care;
2 childcare or other family commitments which shorten acceptable travelling time or hours substantially;
3 discouragement from job search;
4 low pay (except as above).

The non-legitimate barriers tend to impede the employment of women, older workers, people with disabilities and ethnic minorities more than prime age, able-bodied, white males, whilst the legitimate barriers apply to all groups of people.

162

Whilst legitimate barriers tend to be treated by employers and the Government as barriers to employment, non-legitimate barriers are seen as barriers to participation. It is only in times of exceptional labour shortage that measures to increase what is seen as participation will be taken, whereas measures which are seen as reducing unemployment (that is, increasing efficiency among participants by breaking down legitimate barriers) are taken under less pressure. For example, it is well accepted that assistance with relocation given to take up a job or with training when a person does not possess the occupational skills which are in demand, are legitimate labour market interventions. However, action to break down non-legitimate barriers is exceptional. For example, the media and policy attention paid to childcare provision in the late 1980s (culminating in the small change in the treatment of employer-provided childcare in the 1990 Budget) resulted from labour market pressure, reflected in low registered unemployment, particularly in the South, together with recognition that the supply of young people in the labour market would decrease substantially.

What does this have to say about increasing our understanding of unemployment and employment policy? Firstly, that the distinction between the unemployed and non-participants is seriously flawed, treating some people who wish to work as non-participants. Secondly, 'illegitimate' barriers are not seen as affecting the efficient working of the labour market: they are taken as given and the resulting inefficiency is not tackled. Thirdly, the classification of people as unemployed or non-participants is partially determined by ageist, sexist and racist criteria. The lack of recognition of this results in practices (by Government and employers) which depress the employment of certain groups of workers. To address unemployment and to increase economic efficiency, public policy needs to include policies to reduce hidden unemployment.

WHO ARE THE NON-EMPLOYED?

This section briefly describes the labour market status of the main groups which contain the hidden unemployed. As data are unavailable on the hidden unemployed, it compares groups who face different barriers to employment, thereby suggesting the extent of hidden unemployment. It is intended to give an idea of the potential extent of hidden unemployment. Obviously, not all the people in these groups will want to work and many may be unable to work through sickness and disability, but the figures show how many people with characteristics which are recognized to affect employment possibilities are not employed. Other groups also will contain disproportionate numbers of unemployed, for example, people with disabilities who may encounter barriers discouraging them from recognized participation. These are not described owing to lack of data.

Men and women

In 1988 there were 44 million people in Britain aged 16 and over (see Figure 9.2). Of these, 27 million were employed. Twelve million women and 6 million men were not employed, including 6 million women and 3 million men below normal retirement age, equivalent to one third of those who were employed. Approximately 29 per cent of women of normal working age were not in employment and 17 per cent of men, that is, nearly twice the proportion of women were not in employment compared with men. Whilst we would not suggest that the difference is due to hidden unemployment alone, evidence suggests that many of the 6 million women below retirement age would work if they could overcome barriers specific to women (see for example, Dex 1987; Martin and Roberts 1984). This is discussed in detail in the following section.

Older workers

Of the 44 million people aged 16 and above, 8 million women and 6 million men are aged 55 or over, including one million women and 3 million men below normal retirement age (see Figure 9.3). 'Non-participation' for those above retirement age is 93 per cent, whilst for the over-55s (and under normal retirement age) it is 47 per cent for women and 32 per cent for men, compared with 29 per cent and 9 per cent for the below-55s. Although there may be many older people who do not want to work and others may be unable to through incapacity, there is evidence of widespread discrimination in employment of the over-50s (see Chapter 5). The difference in participation rate with age, combined with age discrimination, makes it reasonable to assume that this age group contains hidden unemployed.

Ethnic minorities

It is well known that unemployment rates for ethnic minorities are about double that of whites (see Chapter 4). The Labour Force Surveys for 1984 to 1986 show that there were one and a half million people from ethnic minorities of normal working age compared with 31 million whites (see Figure 9.4). Of these, 34 per cent of ethnic minorities and 23 per cent of whites were classified as non-participants. The difference can be partially explained by the younger age profile of ethnic minority groups, resulting in more people from ethnic minorities being in full-time education. However, the high reported unemployment levels experienced by ethnic minorities and other evidence of discrimination suggests the presence of hidden unemployment.

164

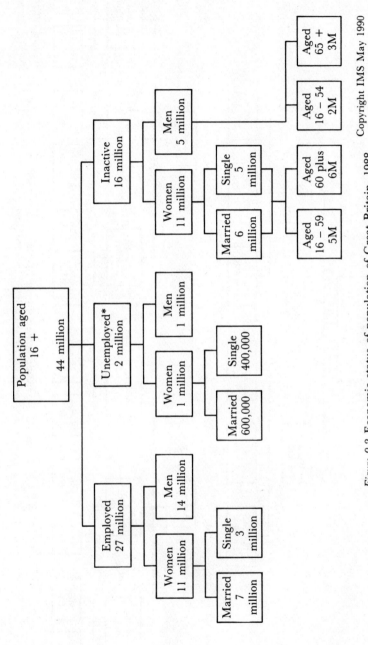

Figure 9.2 Economic status of population of Great Britain, 1988
Source: Employment Gazette, April 1989. Based on LFS 1987 and 1988
Note: * ILO/OECD definition

Copyright IMS May 1990

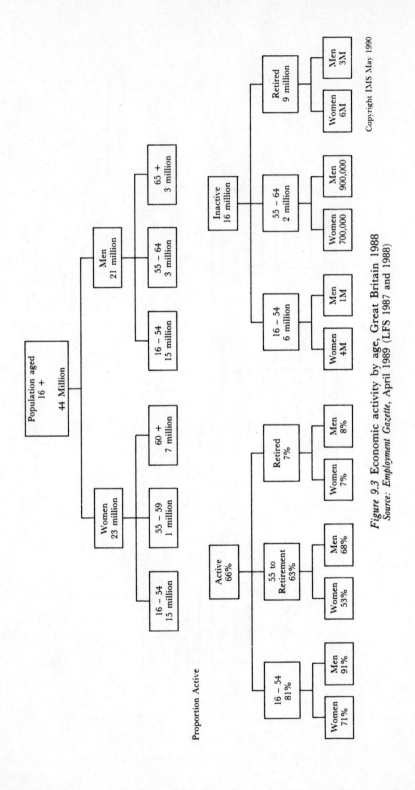

Figure 9.3 Economic activity by age, Great Britain 1988
Source: *Employment Gazette*, April 1989 (LFS 1987 and 1988)

Copyright IMS May 1990

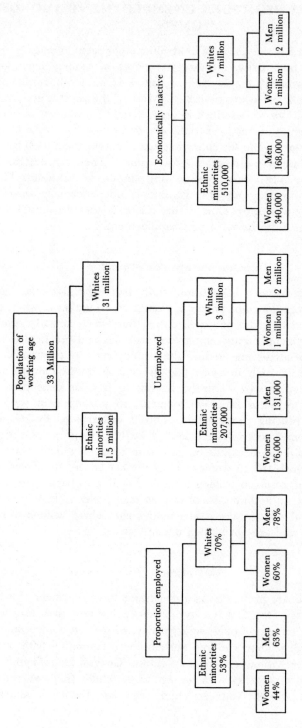

Figure 9.4 Economic activity by ethnic background, population of working age, Great Britain average 1984–6
Source: Employment Gazette, March 1988, © IMS May 1990

THE CAUSES OF HIDDEN UNEMPLOYMENT AMONGST WOMEN

This section describes the causes of hidden unemployment amongst women, the group with, potentially, the largest number of hidden unemployed. The barriers to women's employment, resulting in hidden unemployment, and the numbers affected are described. Most of the constraints are well known and so will not be described in great detail. The sources of barriers are varied, frequently having long traditions, and range from fiscal policies, employment legislation and the characteristics of employment itself through to explicit or implicit prejudice against women. They are described in three groups: dependent care; income; and employers' attitudes. This is not to suggest that each group of constraints is independent. However, the grouping does help identify some of the major factors discouraging and preventing women from being in paid employment.

Dependent care constraints

The responsibility women have traditionally had for children and other dependents reduces the employment of women in a number of ways, most of which are seen as reducing participation but which actually result in hidden unemployment. Firstly, employers' attitudes and practices towards women with dependents may reduce the attractiveness of paid work. Secondly, women who wish to work may be unable to find or to afford acceptable alternative care. Thirdly, having to pay for dependent care reduces the net earnings from employment, so making paid work less attractive and reducing participation. This is exacerbated by the lower average wage women receive (see below). Fourthly, the presence of dependants places additional demands on carers, in terms of unpaid household work, most of which fall on women. Thus the net benefit from paid work is lower. This will result in women being less willing to participate and to offer fewer hours. In addition, some women may prefer to look after their own children and not to take paid employment. These women are true non-participants and are not hidden unemployed.

Children

The lack of childcare provision, as a constraint to employment, is strong. Brown (1988) suggested that it may be more important than taxation in determining the amount of paid work by married women. Only about half of women with dependent children are employed compared with over 70 per cent of women without dependent children (General Household Survey 1986). The constraint varies with the age of the child. Employment rates grow with the age of the youngest child, with only about one quarter of women with a child under three employed, compared with 70 per cent of those with dependant children over nine.

With school-aged children an additional constraint comes in because of the low availability of childcare after school and during school holidays. The former starts to restrict the hours during the day that women may work. The latter prevents some women from being in permanent employment, either moving them into casual and temporary work or out of employment altogether.

Dex (1987) calculated the total demand for paid childcare to enable women to work or work longer hours. She estimated that, if the childcare demand for pre-school aged children were satisfied, a further 8 per cent of women would join the labour force, that is, due to childcare 467,000 women were constrained from employment.[2] This is over one-fifth of women with pre-school age children currently not in paid work.

The barrier to women's employment is not solely about access to childcare: it is also about the possibility of working hours to suit childcare responsibilities. Employers' demand is extremely low for workers in many occupations at less than standard hours. This results in part-time work commonly being offered in a limited number of occupations and being restricted to lower grade (and lower paid) occupations. This is likely to depress the participation of married women, who are most likely to be seeking part-time work, both through restricting their job choice and because their supply is particularly sensitive to wage rates.

Other dependents

Caring for the elderly and infirm is usually taken on by women. From the Women and Employment Survey, Hunt (1988) reported that 23 per cent of women carers not in paid work were prevented from taking a job due to their care responsibilities. Translated into national terms this equals 222,000 women. In addition, 12 per cent of those who were working said that their employment (either hours or occupation) was affected by their responsibilities. In national terms this would affect a further 146,000 women. The survey found that the hours worked of carers was significantly lower than of those without other dependents, with 30 per cent of carers – compared with 39 per cent of others – employed for 35 hours or more a week. These figures suggest a substantial curtailment of the labour supply of this group of women, a problem which is likely to increase both due to current policies to increase community care of the elderly and infirm and due to the ageing of the population.

Income constraints

A major factor governing the supply of labour is the marginal income gained from working. This depends on wages, taxation and social security benefits and the income of other family members, if any. Lower wages for women result in lower participation (that is, higher hidden unemployment) compared with men, whilst social security rules create barriers to participation for married women and family income leads to differences in labour supply behaviour between single and married (or cohabiting) women. The effect of pay on participation is discussed below, before outlining the implications of social security for women with unemployed husbands and the income constraints for lone mothers, both of which are dealt with in more detail by Dilnot (Chapter 7).

Pay

In April 1988, women's average full-time gross earnings were £164.20 per week, or 67 per cent of men's (New Earnings Survey 1988). If overtime payments, shift premiums and longer male hours are allowed for, women's pay still remains at 75 per cent of men's. In addition, part-timers have substantially lower hourly earnings than full-timers. It might be expected that lower female pay might reduce women's participation in the labour force, by reducing the incentive to take paid employment, that is, be a barrier to employment. However, evidence suggests that this may only significantly affect certain groups of women, notably married women.

It has been shown that married women's participation is more responsive to their wage rates than that of single women: that married women's participation increases as their own wage increases, whereas single women, like men, are fairly unresponsive to marginal wage rates, tending to participate, irrespective of wage levels (Joshi 1986). Married women also decrease participation as other family income increases and thus the higher wages of men reinforce women's withdrawal from the labour force (ibid).

Therefore, it seems likely that lower female wages create hidden unemployment in a number of ways:

1 for married women, it reduces the incentive to enter the labour market and to supply a given number of hours;
2 it makes it less worthwhile to take up a job if it results in expenditure on childcare;
3 it makes it difficult to escape from dependency on benefits and the disincentives to work encompassed in the benefit system.

The number of women discouraged from working or working longer hours is not known. However, it seems plausible that a very high proportion of married women are affected in some degree, since lower wages for women, standardizing for education, hours worked and work experience (that is, length of time in employment and occupation) are prevalent (Joshi 1989).

Social security and married women

A second major income constraint on participation is the social security and national insurance system. Two main problems are apparent. Firstly, that the high marginal tax rate claimants face will be a greater disincentive to married women, who are more responsive to marginal rates than other people. Secondly, that discouragement is particularly strong for means-tested benefits because entitlement is assessed on a family rather than individual basis.

Most research on the effects of social security on labour supply has concentrated on the male labour supply and suggests that the disincentive effect of social security benefits on employment are not substantial. However, the little research on the female supply of labour suggests that married women are much more responsive to tax and benefit incentives and disincentives than are men (Dilnot and Kell 1988; Chapter 7). Over half a million women may be living with an unemployed man in receipt of benefits. In addition 150,000 couples received Family Credit last year. Many of these are likely to have been discouraged from working (Metcalf and Leighton 1989).

Lone mothers

Employment rates are much lower for lone mothers than for married women with similar-aged children (ibid). This is likely to be due to lone mothers facing different income constraints to working than married mothers. Firstly, lone mothers may encounter greater demands in the home than married mothers, thus reducing the net benefit from paid employment. Secondly, the participation decisions are individual, not joint – that is, based on other family members' labour market behaviour. Thirdly, lone mothers receive somewhat different social security payments (including one parent benefit) and may receive maintenance payments, affecting the net benefit from employment. There are no estimates of how many women are constrained in this way, but the maximum number would be that of lone mothers receiving income support: 588,000 (Department of Health and Social Security 1988).

Constraints through employers' attitudes and practices

The third set of barriers, creating hidden unemployment, are those resulting from employers' attitudes and practices. A wide spectrum of behaviour based on employers' attitudes and practices directly or indirectly discriminates against women and reduces the numbers employed, through lowering the demand for female workers and discouraging supply. Two aspects are discussed below: employers' reluctance to make most jobs available on a less-than-full-time basis and discrimination in recruitment, training and promotion.

Working time

Most dependent care and care of the home falls on women. Whilst this is the case, many women will prefer to work less than full-time in order to fulfil the non-employment demands on their labour. However, the nature of part-time employment is limited. Although many jobs are available part-time, they tend to be in less skilled areas and hours are often inflexible. Few professional or managerial posts are available part-time and promotion often requires reverting to full-time employment. Thus, for women who wish to work part-time the incentive to take paid employment is low and the nature of jobs available may be a positive discouragement. This will particularly affect higher qualified women, those who have previously held higher level posts and women in the many occupations which are rarely offered part-time.

Selection, recruitment and training

Although sex bias is illegal in recruitment, promotion and training, there is substantial evidence of its existence, contributing to the segregation of women into a few occupations, junior positions and low-paid jobs (see, for example, Joshi 1989; Curran 1985; Collinson 1988). This is compounded by bias against married women on the grounds of their family circumstances, against part-time employees and job-sharers and against women from ethnic minorities on grounds of race.

The extent of these biases is illustrated by research by Curran (1985) into clerical and retail jobs, which, given the prevalence of female employees in these occupations, might be expected to be less biased than employment as a whole. In selection, Curran found that 54 per cent of employers in her sample felt that family circumstances were a legitimate indicator of suitability. One-third of these indicated that present or anticipated family commitments would disbar certain types of job applicant, Curran states that:

> In almost all cases, respondents made the classic connection between family and women, and interpreted the question solely in relation to prospective female applicants.

In selection and promotion, Curran found that twice as many jobs considered as 'male' by the employer, than those considered 'female', offered promotion as an expected progression. Similarly, for 40 per cent of the jobs to which men were appointed promotion was an expected progression, compared with 21 per cent of the jobs to which women were appointed. In training, Curran found that the men's clerical jobs were more likely than women's to offer day release training, 33 per cent and 15 per cent respectively.

Not only is recruitment of women into jobs offering promotion and training biased, but also the achievement of promotion and training. This can be attributed both to sex bias, to unwillingness to promote part-timers or have more senior jobs conducted on a part-time or job-share basis, to the frequent provision of training on a full-time basis and lower availability of day release for women. (Fewer women than men attend part-time courses in Further Education establishments, 400,000 and 517,000 respectively in 1986–7 (*Education Statistics for the United Kingdom* 1988), suggesting that employers make day release less available to women than men). Consequently, fewer women achieve senior posts.

The combination of employers' attitudes and practices, in the provision of part-time employment and in recruitment, selection and training affect the employment of women, and married women in particular, by:

1 limiting the occupations and occupational levels open to women;
2 limiting the possibilities of combining childcare and work;
3 reducing achievable earnings.

These result in women achieving lower earnings, less senior positions and reduce intrinsic job interest. Each of these factors acts as a disincentive to 'participation' and increase hidden unemployment. In particular, the lack of availability of part-time work in all occupations, the underutilization of skills, through pushing women into a narrow band of jobs and the attitude that part-timers are less ambitious, less promotable and less worth training impacts on the majority of women. It has the short-term effect of discouraging participation and a long-term effect through lowering achievement throughout many women's working lives.

MEASURES TO REDUCE HIDDEN UNEMPLOYMENT AMONGST WOMEN

There are many measures that could be taken to reduce the hidden unemployment of women, some of which may be taken by employers, others by the state. For both employers and the state, measures boil down, firstly, to making it easier to combine dependent care and employment, and, secondly, to ensuring that women, equally with men, achieve the appropriate occupational and wage level, that is, they are not discriminated against. Obviously, any of the measures that employers may take could also be encouraged or imposed by the state.

Employers' actions to reduce hidden unemployment amongst women

To reduce hidden unemployment, employers need to change their practices to take on board the family commitments which crucially affect women's employment: pregnancy and childbirth, care of pre-school children, care of school-aged children and care of dependent adults. They also need to recognize that the more attractive work is the more likely women are to remain in employment. Therefore improved career prospects and reduced frustration at work would reduce hidden unemployment. The following practices tackle these areas (see Figure 9.5). It should be noted that, whilst employers may be unconcerned about decreasing hidden unemployment, these same practices are beneficial to employers by enhancing recruitment and retention.

Employers actions
assistance with childcare

part-time work and job-sharing
term-time contracts
flexi-hours
optional working from home

extended maternity leave
extended right to return after maternity
career breaks

reducing discrimination
compensatory training
measures against sexual harassment
perks tailored to women

State actions
pre-school childcare
after school childcare
dependent adult care

improvements to maternity rights

maintenance to lone mothers
subsidies to employed lone mothers

individual assessment for social security

changes to the Sex Discrimination Act

Figure 9.5 Practices to reduce barriers to women's employment © IMS May 1990

Childcare assistance

An obvious measure which would reduce the hidden unemployment of women is assistance with childcare, both for pre-school children and those of school age. Employers may provide the former through the establishment of creches, through supplying information on childcare facilities and through assistance with childcare costs. The latter may be provided through holiday play schemes.

Flexible working arrangements

Equally important with childcare assistance in reducing hidden unemployment are changes in working time to allow childcare and paid work to be combined. The option to work part-time and to jobshare could be extended. It has been suggested that there are relatively few posts which cannot be performed on a part-time or job-share basis, given proper support and effective management (see, for example, New Ways to Work 1984; Equal Opportunities Commission 1981) and the cost implications of introducing part-time and job-share opportunities more widely and in more senior posts are not significant.

Other working arrangements which have been developed to accommodate childcare demands also reduce hidden unemployment. Amongst these are term-time contracts, feasible where work can be programmed accordingly or cover provided by, for example, students. Such arrangements have relatively few direct-cost implications, though do require careful planning and management. Flexitime may also reduce barriers to women working. It is well developed and has been successful in retaining women staff in areas of employment such as the Inland Revenue.

Other options for allowing work to be performed on a more flexible basis involve working at or from home, at least for part of the week. Networking arrangements are thought to be increasing, although they may be more effective on a partial basis.

Extended breaks from employment

An associated issue of organizing working time to reduce barriers to women's employment concerns breaks from work, especially those connected with very young children or the care of the sick or elderly. Extended maternity leave and career break schemes, usually allowing a period of up to five years away from employment, permit women to preserve continuity of employment and hence stimulate re-entry. Under some schemes employers maintain contact throughout to inform career break women of new developments, thus reducing re-entry problems. Such schemes may be expected to reduce hidden unemployment by helping women over the barriers to re-entry. At the same time they will reduce the loss of human capital to the economy and the employer and reduce occupational downgrading.

Reducing discrimination

Reducing discrimination will help reduce hidden unemployment, whilst, at the same time, improve the use of women's skills and encourage retention through assisting women to develop their potential. This entails both reducing discrimination on the part of recruiters and managers, thus enabling women to progress in the job, and compensating for past discrimination, for example through providing training in areas women particularly lack. Other ways of making work more attractive to women are ensuring that sexual harassment does not occur and ensuring that staff benefits include those that women see as important.

The current extent of employers' practices to reduce hidden unemployment

Increased opportunities for part-time work, job-sharing, working from home, and working on a more flexible basis, would enable and encourage women with children or adult dependants into employment. Permitting senior posts to be conducted on these bases would further stimulate participation. In both cases, the loss of human capital and consequent underutilisation of female employees would also be decreased. However, a recent survey of employers' practices which assist women to work suggested that these practices were rare and so barriers remained substantial (Metcalf 1990). The key results of the survey, covering over 2,000 organizations, employing over 1.1 million women, in six industries (chemicals, rubber and plastic, metal goods, retailing, hotel and catering and local authorities), are presented below.

Allowing parents time off, for example when a child was ill, was the main assistance with dependent care, given by 23 per cent of employers. Other assistance was unusual: 3 per cent provided a creche, 2 per cent a school-holiday playscheme and less than 1 per cent a childcare allowance. The number of women receiving these benefits was tiny: in the whole sample, 198 women were reported to have children in an employer-provided creche, 54 women received a childcare allowance and 99 used a holiday playscheme.

Flexible working-time practices were operated by 52 per cent of survey respondents, the most common practices being optional part-time working (26 per cent), flexitime (24 per cent) and jobsharing (18 per cent). Working from home (8 per cent) and school term-time working (6 per cent) were uncommon, whilst other practices such as school-hours shifts and regular seasonal or temporary work very rare. The practices were usually only available in a limited number and narrow range of occupations, concentrated on clerical, administrative and sales jobs. Participation in such schemes was usually at management's discretion and often granted to particularly valued employees only. Apart from flexitime (for which no figures were available) the proportion of women employees working under these systems was small, with, at most, 7 per cent of women employees having chosen to work part-time (when the same job was available full-time), and 0.2 per cent or less working under any other flexible system.

Maternity provision above the statutory minimum was made by 23 per cent of survey respondents. However, most of these were Local Authorities, for whom a national agreement provided for maternity benefits above the statutory minimum. In other industries the proportion fell to 6 per cent. The main improvements were reduced qualifying periods for maternity rights, increased payments received whilst on maternity leave and longer periods of maternity leave. Outside of Local Authorities, which had reduced qualifying periods and enhanced pay, none of these improvements was made by more than 2 per cent of respondents.

Career breaks were offered by 4 per cent of survey respondents. The breaks were more often open to managers, than to other staff, and least often available to manual workers. The number of women reported to be currently having a break was very small, seventy-seven women in the whole sample covering more than one million women. In the majority of organizations, taking a career break was at management's discretion.

The most common other practice, which might affect female retention, was Equal Opportunities training for managers and Personnel specialists (13 per cent) or for others (9 per cent). Personal effectiveness and assertiveness training, women-only courses and special procedures to deal with sexual harassment had each been introduced in four per cent of organizations.

In total this indicates that not much has been done by employers to overcome female-specific barriers to employment and reduce hidden unemployment.

State actions to reduce hidden unemployment amongst women

If, as it seems, employers are not doing much to reduce barriers to women's employment, what may the state do? The state has a number of options open to it (see Figure 9.5) and these are outlined below.

Dependent care assistance

Firstly, and probably most importantly, increased provision or assistance with childcare would decrease the number of women amongst the hidden unemployed. This may be done either through childcare provision, or through subsidies or tax allowances for childcare payments. Non-employer provision of childcare has certain advantages: commuting difficulties may make employer creches undesirable; the child does not have to change creches with job changes; the functioning of the labour market is not inhibited by distortions; and employer resources do not have to be expended learning how to establish and organize a creche. Secondly, the state may help through the provision of care for school-aged children out of school hours. Some Local Authorities already make this provision after school or in school holidays, but it is rare. Thirdly, with the ageing population and the move to community care, an increasing number of women will need assistance with care of adult dependents, if they are to be employed.

Maternity rights

Improvements in statutory maternity provisions may reduce hidden unemployment. Reducing the qualification period for the right to return and extending the period of maternity leave, may result in more women staying in employment and not having to leave their jobs due to pregnancy.

Assistance to lone mothers

The ability of lone mothers to take up employment may be enhanced in two ways: by ensuring that maintenance payments are made (this would raise the income level of those in employment) and through additional payments to working single parents. Ermish (1991) has estimated that a payment amounting to an additional 45p per hour to lone mothers would increase participation by almost 150,000.

Individual assessment for social security

More fundamental changes in Social Security, switching from assessment based on the family unit to individual assessment, would reduce a major barrier to employment for married women with unemployed husbands.

Other legislative changes

Lastly, changes in the Sex Discrimination Act and employment protection legislation could reduce hidden unemployment amongst women. Firstly, changes to the Sex Discrimination Act to make it more powerful and to increase recognition of the reasons why women end up in low-paid, lower level jobs would help to ensure that more women worked. Reform should include making it discriminatory, where there is no overriding reason, not

178

to make jobs available on a less than full-time basis. Such a change could have its roots in the current indirect discrimination provision of the Sex Discrimination Act, as requiring a job to be done full-time (when part-time is feasible) means that a smaller proportion of women than men may take the job. Secondly, the extension of employment protection to employees irrespective of hours worked might reduce opposition to the introduction of more family friendly hours and encourage their greater uptake by employees.

SUMMARY AND CONCLUSIONS

This chapter has suggested that the current distinction between non-participation and unemployment is flawed and that it is based on recognition of only a few of the barriers to employment. The barriers that are recognized (and recognized as legitimate) are those that potentially affect all people, irrespective of age, gender, race and disability; those that are unrecognized (non-legitimate) predominantly affect women, ethnic minorities, older people and people with disabilities. Legitimate barriers are seen as contributing to unemployment and are treated as imperfections in the labour market; non-legitimate barriers are not seen to affect unemployment but rather to affect participation. This results in people who wish to work but either cannot or are discouraged due to 'non-legitimate' barriers being seen as non-participants, rather than unemployed: they are the hidden unemployed. Furthermore, unemployment policies overlook this group and fail to address the barriers which result in their unemployment.

The failure to recognize the hidden unemployed as unemployed has a number of serious consequences. Firstly, in terms of unemployment:

1 the problem of unemployment is underestimated, particularly amongst women, ethnic minorities, older people and people with disabilities;
2 the incidence of unemployment is not only underestimated, but is also higher amongst women, racial minorities, older people and people with disabilities, than amongst prime-aged, white, able-bodied men;
3 unemployment policy is concentrated on increasing demand and overcoming legitimate barriers and tends to ignore non-legitimate barriers, resulting in policies which are sexist, racist, ageist and biased against people with disabilities.

Secondly, for the economy, tackling barriers selectively, influenced by ageist, racist and sexist presumptions rather than an assessment of the potential net benefit to the economy, is likely to result in a misallocation of human resources. In particular, investment in education and training and benefits of experience are wasted. Consequently, national output is likely to be reduced.

NOTES AND REFERENCES

Notes

1 This chapter has benefited from revision in the light of comments from Eithne McLaughlin at the ES-SPRU Understanding Unemployment Conference, May 1990, York.
2 These calculations are based on women who want to work, given the pattern of wages and jobs available, i.e. demand might change if other factors changed. In addition, estimates are based on 1980 data and it is possible that the numbers constrained has grown, if only due to the cohort effect.

References

Brown, C.V. (1988) 'Supply Effects and Work', Summary Prepared for Equal Opportunities Commission, unpublished.

Collinson, D.L. (1988) *Barriers to Fair Selection, A Multi-Sector Study of Recruitment Practices*, EOC Research Series, London: HMSO.

Curran, M.M. (1985) *Stereotypes and Selection, Gender and Family in the Recruitment Process*, EOC Research Series, London: HMSO.

Department of Employment (1988) *New Earnings Survey 1988*, London: HMSO.

Department of Health and Social Security (1988) *Social Security Statistics*, London: HMSO.

Dex, S. (1987) *Women's Labour Supply and the Demand for Childcare Provision in the Women and Employment Survey*, Report to the EOC, Manchester: EOC.

Dilnot, A. and Kell, M. (1988) 'Male Unemployment and Women's Work', *Fiscal Studies*, 8, 3: 1–16.

Education Statistics for the United Kingdom (1988) London: HMSO.

Equal Opportunities Commission (1981) *Job-sharing: Improving the Quality and Availability of Part-time Work*, London: HMSO.

Ermisch, J. (1991) *Lone Parenthood and Economic Analysis*, Cambridge: CUP.

Hunt, A. (1988) 'The Effects of Caring for the Elderly and Infirm on Women's Employment', in A. Hunt (ed.), *Women and Paid Work – Issues of Equality*, London: Macmillan.

Joshi, H. (1986) 'Female Participation in Paid Work', in R. Blundell and I. Walker (eds), *Unemployment, Search and Labour Supply*, London: OUP.

—— (1989) *The Changing Population of Britain*, London: Blackwell.

Martin, J. and Roberts, C. (1984) *Women and Employment: A Lifetime Perspective*, London: HMSO.

Metcalf, H. (1990) *Retaining Women Employees: Measures to Counteract Labour Shortage*, IMS Report No. 190, Brighton: Institute of Manpower Studies.

Metcalf, H. and Leighton, P. (1989) *The Under-Utilisation of Women in the Labour Market*, IMS Report No. 172, Brighton: Institute of Manpower Studies.

New Ways to Work (1984) *Job-sharing: Employment Rights and Conditions*, London: New Ways to Work.

Office of Population Census and Surveys (1989) *General Household Survey 1986*, London: HMSO.

10

REGIONAL AND LOCAL DIFFERENTIALS IN LABOUR DEMAND

Alan Townsend[1]

INTRODUCTION

In considering national prospects for labour supply and demand in the 1990s, the reader is always liable to react that 'my area is different'. This is to anticipate the main theme of this chapter, that relative conditions of different geographical areas are in fact easier to predict than are the average conditions around which that variation will occur. Despite increased mobility for car-owning members of the workforce, and longer distances of daily and weekly commuting, many differences between geographical labour market areas, and internal differences within them, can be expected to continue.

This represents one form of segmentation of the labour force, which was first recognized in the pages of the inter-war Ministry of Labour Gazette in the publication of unemployment data for Principal Towns. In the last fifteen years, academic analyses have increasingly recognized other forms of segmentation, for instance by sex and ethnic status, which interplay at a more local level with geographical forms of segmentation. Much local variation in unemployment is attributable to factors of social geography and housing, and the author agrees in general with the official practice of not quoting percentage rates of unemployment below the travel-to-work area level.

The regional level, however, occupied an important role in a political consensus extending up to 1979 (but often forgotten by London opinion-formers of today), whereby the movement of jobs to the workers was a significant national government activity (Armstrong and Taylor 1985; Townsend 1987). In some cycles it was also given a prominent economic role. For instance, a revival of regional policy in 1963 was partly justified on the basis of relieving inflationary labour shortages in the West Midlands, with the result that government controls and incentives were employed to remove large expansions of the motor industry to Merseyside and Scotland.

Labour shortage in the 1990s will be regional rather than national.

181

There is less industrial and political scope for a strong regional policy of intervention than there was in the 1960s. One question, however, is whether labour shortage in the South East was not already being alleviated in the later 1980s through spontaneous overspill of industry to adjoining regions, and whether this might not, after the 1990–2 recession, be extended in volume and distance to the benefit of a greater number of under-employed regions.

In assessing this question, it will be necessary firstly to assess the regionally differentiated effects of the 'demographic time-bomb' of the 1990s, considering here the distribution of the level of supply of adult labour. These are then compared with one of the few available projections of labour demand to the year 2000 (Cambridge Econometrics and NIERC 1991). This implies continuing regional differences in unemployment. The scale of these differences must in reality remain a subject of speculation. However, the general pattern is well-rooted in trends established since the early 1980s. There has in fact been relatively limited attention paid to trends in the level and nature of labour demand prior to the 1990–2 recession. In what follows, the main geographical trends of that period in different sectors of the labour market, as evidenced in government data on the 'National Online Manpower Information System', are focused on, before concluding with a discussion of the possible place for inter-depart-mental forward policy thinking in the 1990s.

THE 'DEMOGRAPHIC TIME-BOMB'

A remarkable feature to begin with is the extent to which standard projec-tions already posit substantial inter-regional variations in labour supply trends. Recent national projections of population and the labour force demonstrate a 2 per cent increase of the Great Britain labour supply for 1990–2000 (*Employment Gazette*, May 1991). This is the net result of a 19 per cent reduction in the under-25s and a 7 per cent increase among those aged 25 and over, almost entirely among females. Unfortunately, these projections have not been broken down by region, but we can refer to the last such analysis (*Employment Gazette*, January 1990), based on an increase in the workforce for Great Britain of 3.7 per cent for the longer period 1988–2000. The principal results are presented at Table 10.1. In four regions of the South, that is, the South East, East Anglia, East Midlands and the South West, large increases in the adult labour force outweigh the loss of young workers to produce substantial increases in the all-age labour force. In the rest of Great Britain the total labour force remains within 3 per cent of its 1988 level.

There are several important points about the geographical content of the projections. Firstly, statisticians assume that the relationship between an individual region's activity rates and those of Great Britain as a whole

Table 10.1 Regional projections of the labour force (%)

Region	Total	Popula-tion effect	Activity rate effect	Male	Female	Under 25	25 and over
			Civilian labour force 1988–2000				
South East	5.9	3.1	2.8	3.9	8.7	−17	13
East Anglia	13.0	10.7	2.3	10.7	15.9	−20	23
South West	14.2	8.8	5.4	9.1	20.6	−15	22
East Midlands	7.0	4.8	2.2	3.9	11.1	−21	15
West Midlands	0.3	−0.6	0.9	−3.1	5.2	−27	8
Yorkshire and Humberside	1.3	−0.8	2.1	−2.9	7.0	−23	8
North West	−2.6	−2.9	0.2	−5.9	1.7	−26	4
Northern	−3.2	−4.4	1.3	−6.2	1.0	−27	4
Wales	1.9	2.8	−1.0	−4.3	10.5	−19	8
Scotland	−1.9	−2.7	0.7	−4.1	0.9	−29	6
Northern Ireland	7.6	5.9	1.7	4.2	12.6	−9	13
UK	3.7	1.8	2.0	0.6	7.9	−22	11

Source: *Employment Gazette*, January 1990

will continue to change as in the past. Secondly, however, the greatest element of regional variation arises from existing differences in age struc-tures. These build in response to past inter-regional economic variation in the shape of selective migration in fertile age groups, and thus already reflect some past inter-regional differences in employment trends. Reverting then to Table 10.1, we see that *both* 'population effects' and 'activity rate effects' are at their strongest in four regions which we normally identify as the 'South' in the 'North–South Divide'. However, when we take one of the few independent projections which details the supply of jobs to the year 2000, we find continued divergence above and below the same dividing line, a division which is complete for 1993–2000 and would be for 1990–3 but for the East Midlands and Scotland sharing the same expected growth of 4 per cent (see Table 10.2, abridged from Cambridge Econometrics and Northern Ireland Economic Research Centre, 1991). The details of the projections must be regarded as speculative. They emphasize, however, a continuing North–South Divide, and new contrasts within the 'North', particularly between Wales and Scotland.

There are several reasons for supporting the geographical results of these projections, as they reflect two major underlying features. The first of these is the North–South Divide (Lewis and Townsend 1989), in which a cumulative process of change produces relative decline, evidenced in stable or declining levels of employment, a result in the projections of continuing increases in manufacturing productivity. The second, however, may be less familiar, and is known as the 'Urban–Rural Drift', and could be expressed

Table 10.2 Regional projections of employment, 1990–2000 (%)

	1990–3	1993–2000
South East	−3.0	+10.5
East Anglia	−2.0	+15.6
South West	−3.1	+13.0
East Midlands	−4.0	+10.8
West Midlands	−8.0	+7.4
Yorkshire and Humberside	−7.2	+7.7
North West	−6.9	+6.7
Northern	−5.6	+6.7
Wales	−4.9	+8.3
Scotland	−4.0	+2.8
Northern Ireland	−7.3	+4.0
United Kingdom	−4.6	+9.0

Source: Cambridge Econometrics, 1991

in terms of the contrast, for instance, between an expected 5 per cent decline in employment in the (very urban) Greater London area, 1990–2000, and a small increase in (more rural) Wales. These trends both vary between cycles, but are both compatible and deep-seated, and it is intended to underline their credibility from evidence to date.

NORTH–SOUTH DISTINCTIONS

As mentioned above, the UK is notable for its past level of state intervention to even out the regional balance of labour demand and supply. The origins of regional policy lay in regional unemployment of the 1930s; 'assisted areas' have been designated since 1934, principally on the basis of rates of unemployment and beginning with the coalfield areas of Clydeside, West Cumberland, the North-East Coast and South Wales. Figure 10.1 is an unusual map in reckoning up the number of years over the half-century, 1934–84, in which individual areas in Great Britain were designated for assistance, allowing weightings in the years when there was a threefold hierarchy of assisted areas.

What is remarkable is that most of the early Development Areas continued uninterruptedly as assisted areas, suggesting either that the status was of little value, or that problems of employment structure were extremely deep-seated. Assisted area status was extended at a variety of dates to northern rural areas and, variously, to coastal areas of seasonal unemployment. However, the principal changes of the 1960s and 1970s lay in extensions to include more of the northern conurbations, mainly as the national reduction of manufacturing employment began to affect North West England and Yorkshire. The major recession of 1979–82 comprised

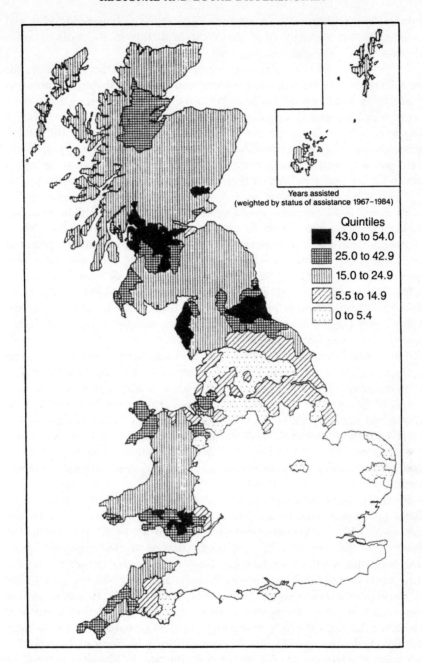

Years assisted
(weighted by status of assistance 1967–1984)

Quintiles
43.0 to 54.0
25.0 to 42.9
15.0 to 24.9
5.5 to 14.9
0 to 5.4

Figure 10.1 Regional policy, assisted areas 1934–84
Source: Figure 14.1, p. 225, Lever, W. (ed.) (1987) *Industrial Change in the United Kingdom*,
Longman

principally a withdrawal of manufacturing capacity (Townsend 1983) and resulted in the recognition of the West Midlands in the assisted areas designated in 1984 and retained since.

In terms then of understanding unemployment, and the possibilities for its alleviation, the recognized problem areas show a spread of problems from the original coastal coalfield industrial areas to embrace today most areas which depended significantly on manufacturing. Until the 1980s it was assumed that it was proper for government to intervene in the market to encourage transfer of manufacturing expansions to these areas, but a new political, and to some extent academic, consensus has since arisen which argues that this intervention was of little success and inappropriate.

There is a large literature on the measurement of regional policy intervention, but most estimates would agree that about half a million manufacturing jobs were transferred to assisted areas by the start of the 1980–1 recession. Conventional wisdom of the 1980s would discredit the potential role of regional policy. The branch factories which it created were proportionately at least as susceptible to closure as was manufacturing at large. There were relatively few new investments in the 1980s to lure away from the 'South', which in any case was itself suffering unemployment. What developments have occurred from the continuing policy in the North have had a lower 'jobs content' than before.

The 1980s literature, however, has at least partly understated some periods of success for active regional policy and some significant transfers of manufacturing work have occurred. Firstly, authoritative work in four areas of Britain by the Northern Ireland Economic Research Centre (Fothergill and Guy 1991) indicates that the branch factory closures of the early 1980s had little to do with the areas they were in; it was simply that the factories, 20 to 40 years old, had become obsolescent in their products and methods within their respective national and multinational organizations.

Secondly, there have been periods when the North–South gap in manufacturing employment trends has been closed, or even reversed. In the long period 1971–8, manufacturing employment fell by 9.5 per cent in the South and 9.8 per cent in the North; that is, regional policy almost overcame the North's disadvantage from its industrial structure. In the peak years of recession, dependence on manufacturing was the main cause of the more adverse employment trends of the North. However, results from the Census of Employment show that by 1984–7 the North was actually achieving relatively better manufacturing employment trends than the South. In that period, the North's factory jobs declined by only 2.6 per cent, compared with 5.8 per cent in the South, almost a reversal of the trends to be expected from industrial structure (Champion and Townsend 1990: 76). The 1989 Census of Employment (published in 1991) covered the 'boom years' 1987–9 and showed these patterns continuing in the shape of an increase of manufacturing employment in certain regions of the North, compared with an overall decrease in the South East (Table 10.3). Parts of this contrast are a continuing marked reduction in factory jobs in Greater London, and a small crop of gains in various kinds of government priority areas such as Telford New Town or steel closure areas. The point is that government intervention can still make a contribution to areas of high unemployment. The net growth of manufacturing employment failed overall to withstand the onset of renewed recession in 1990–1, but data up to 1991 shows how two Regions, one of them in the South, had till then escaped renewed decline of more than 6 per cent (Table 10.3).

Table 10.3 Regional change (%) in employees in employment since 1987

| | 1987 (Census, Sept.) to 1989 (Census, Sept.) | | 1989 (Census, Sept.) to 1991 (Estimate, Sept.) | |
	Manufacturing	Total	Manufacturing	Total
South East	−3.8	+2.7	−9.0	−4.3
East Anglia	+4.3	+8.4	−7.1	−1.7
South West	+2.2	+7.7	−5.8	−2.5
East Midlands	+1.2	+4.4	−7.0	−3.4
West Midlands	+4.1	+5.7	−11.2	−4.4
Yorkshire and Humberside	+4.5	+6.8	−6.7	−2.7
North West	+0.3	+3.7	−8.7	−3.8
Northern	+2.6	+3.9	−7.6	−3.3
Wales	+7.9	+6.7	−7.7	−2.6
Scotland	−1.0	+4.6	−4.8	−0.5
Great Britain	+0.7	+4.5	−8.1	−3.4

Source: NOMIS, University of Durham

Policy effects may be enhanced by the individual decisions of government departments to quit London themselves. There have even been suggestions that the private office sector has been moving north to provincial capitals such as Manchester (Thrift and Leyshon 1989). Detailed study of the Census of Employment shows only one or two possible cases that are growing faster than London. Indeed, the great bulk of the service economy was showing labour demands which were proportionately stronger in the South. When we combine all sectors in data for total employees in the two years ending September 1989 (Table 10.3), we find that, while its manufacturing performance gave Wales the greatest percentage increase in that sector, the area was surpassed in overall trends by two regions of the South, East Anglia and the South West. The worst employment performances were in the South East, North West and the Northern Region.

The North–South dimension dominates the map of unemployment, increasing as a feature in the recovery to 1989 but then weakening. There is regular debate over the most appropriate method for comparing reductions in unemployment between different areas. If one took the difference in percentage rates between date 1 and date 2, then northern regions have not infrequently been seen to be 'gaining' most. However, if one looks at proportionate reductions, the percentage drop in numbers unemployed between dates 1 and 2, then the five years to mid-1991 as a whole have been characterized by North–South divergence; the problem areas show lower rates of reduction. We must, however, recognize that much of the year 1990–1 has been different. If (as in Figures 10.2 and 10.3) we divide the five-year period into the first three years and the last two, we find a fairly precise reversal in the last two years, with areas such as Oxfordshire showing some of the greatest proportionate increases of unemployment, and some of the areas of delayed deterioration lying in the North.

The current period is of great interest in applying a 'corrective' effect to the inflationary service economy of the South, and with it to some of the regional imbalance in labour market conditions. However, it is seen here as cyclical, affecting relatively little the basic map of relative unemployment rates, which is compared here for travel-to-work areas at June 1991 (Figure 10.4).

URBAN–RURAL VARIATION

Many urban statistical areas, notably the ex-metropolitan counties, show worse unemployment rates than surrounding areas, and there are copious grounds for arguing that standard regions are of reduced importance for the study of labour market trends. Urban–rural differences in unemployment, though they do not relate precisely to relative employment trends, are now a well-established feature. In Table 10.4, a comparative ordering of county unemployment rates is shown for 1979 and 1991. For instance, three counties appear among the five worst for unemployment rates at each date, irrespective of changes in the statistical definition of unemployment and massive intervening changes over the twelve-year period. On a first viewing two maps for these dates would appear basically the same. High unemployment in Scotland, the North and Wales is interrupted by areas of low unemployment at both dates in the Grampian Region, the Borders, North Yorkshire and Powys. Conurbation counties occupy worse positions in 1991 than 1979, while the large area of low unemployment around Greater London has expanded to the north and west.

Geographers are clear that, over this period as a whole, urban–rural differences have increased, above all through the expansion of service employment in areas of the South outside London, leaving a starker contrast between them and the city and inner-city populations particularly of

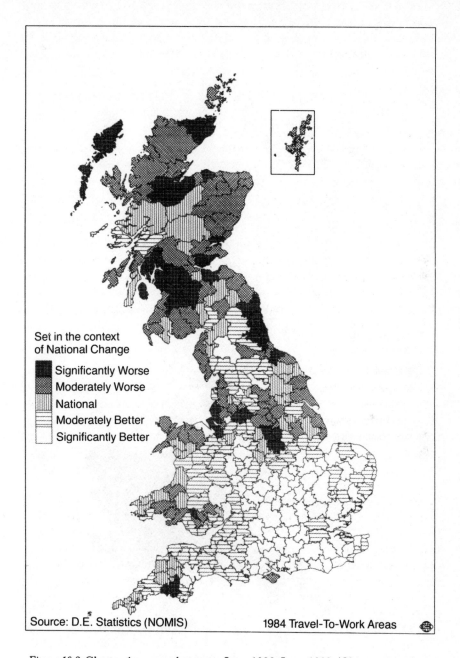

Set in the context
of National Change

■ Significantly Worse
▨ Moderately Worse
▤ National
≡ Moderately Better
☐ Significantly Better

Source: D.E. Statistics (NOMIS)   1984 Travel-To-Work Areas

Figure 10.2 Change in unemployment, June 1986–June 1989 (Chi-square values,
benchmark United Kingdom)
Source: DE statistics (NOMIS)

189

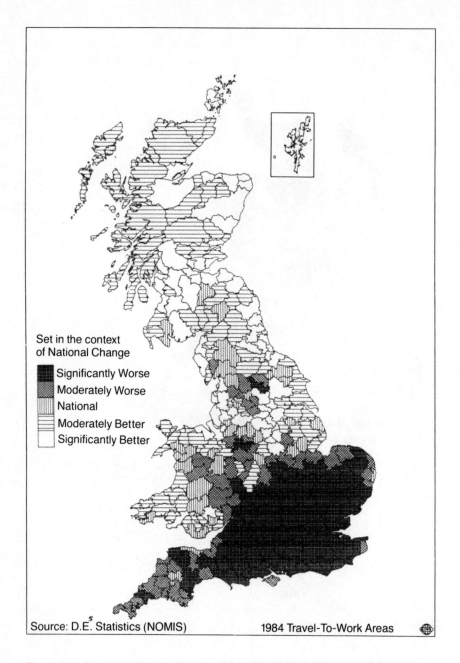

Figure 10.3 Change in unemployment, June 1989–June 1991 (Chi-square values, benchmark United Kingdom)
Source: DE statistics (NOMIS)

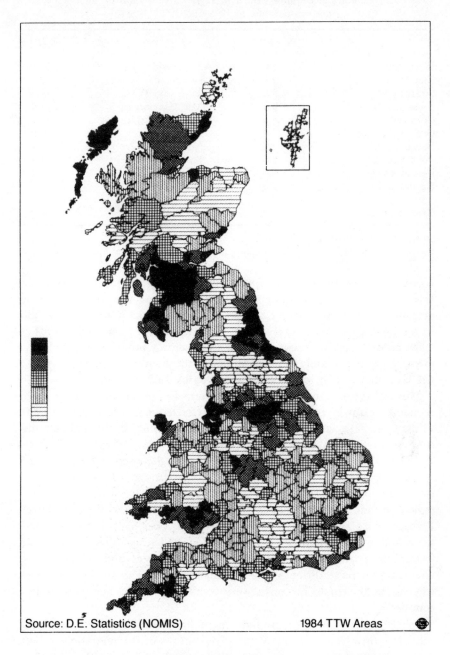

Figure 10.4 Unemployment rate, June 1991 (workforce base)
Source: DE statistics (NOMIS)

Table 10.4 Ranking of counties with highest and lowest rates of unemployment, not comparable, in 1979 and 1991 (June)

	% (1979)		% (1991)
Merseyside	11.8	Merseyside	13.9
Cleveland	9.9	Cleveland	12.1
Strathclyde	9.8	Tyne and Wear	11.6
Tyne and Wear	9.5	Mid Glamorgan	11.4
Cornwall	8.6	South Yorkshire	11.2
Greater London	3.3	Berkshire	4.5
Buckinghamshire	2.9	North Yorkshire	4.4
West Sussex	2.6	Powys	4.4
Berkshire	2.4	West Sussex	4.3
Hertfordshire	2.4	Grampian	3.5
Great Britain	5.4	Great Britain	7.9

Source: NOMIS, University of Durham
Note: Surrey omitted from both years because it does not have a quoted figure in the second.

northern conurbations. Little of the change was due to industrial structure. It was due, rather, to pronounced and systematic var`ations in labour demand, both in manufacturing and the economy as a whole, especially in the immediate wake of recession, 1981 to 1984. In the period 1984 to 1989, however, employment fell by one per cent in Inner London, whereas in more remote, mainly rural, districts of the South it expanded by 14.3 per cent, and in districts with New Towns by 14.5 per cent.

Much of the explanation for these patterns lies in labour demand in the economy's growth sectors, normally characterized in forecasts for the 1990s as the financial sector (broadly defined) and retailing, hotels and catering. Analysis of the Census of Employment for the years 1981 to 1989 shows a well-established sub-regional pattern of growth based mainly on these sectors (see Figure 10.5). For instance, the growth of jobs in finance (including business services) is concentrated in a 'western arc' of sub-regions around London, from Cambridgeshire to Warwickshire and Dorset. Perhaps more surprisingly, we find the same kind of distribution under the standard definition of 'tourism-related industries' (Townsend 1992, forthcoming). Analysis of the same period for males and females shows any heavy increase in male labour demand confined to the 'western arc', whereas large female increases were common to most non-metropolitan counties.

Space does not allow a more fundamental exploration of the urban–rural shift. It is involved with many complex features of the migration of both the occupied and the retired population (see also Chapter 11). Suffice to note that up-to-date migration data show extremely regular direction in net migration balances, among age groups over 24 years, from more urban

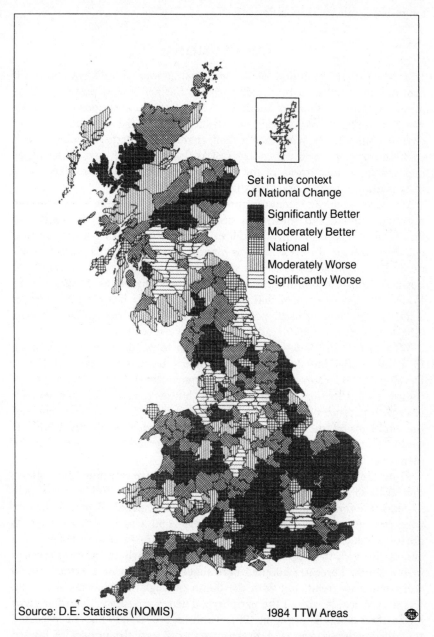

Source: D.E. Statistics (NOMIS)   1984 TTW Areas

Figure 10.5 Change in total employment (farming excluded), September 1981–September 1989 (Chi-square values, benchmark United Kingdom)
Source: DE statistics (NOMIS)

to less urban counties. One may reliably state that more urban counties will continue to suffer selective out-migration, with consequential effects for residual inner-city populations.

CONCLUSIONS

It is clear that resolution of the national labour supply equation will continue to be affected by the dispersal of businesses and people to areas in and around the Greater South East. In effect whole regions such as the North and North West may be left behind because of a large set of characteristics to do with their urban character. Whether employers will spontaneously move to urban areas of Wales, the North and Scotland, as opposed to smaller towns of the Greater South East, will be a key point in mediating labour market conditions in the 1990s.

We have seen that manufacturing industry has again been strongly rejecting London and showing a small drift northwards. It is possible to find some evidence that private offices have been relocating a little further out from London, in areas such as Cardiff and Coventry. It was certainly necessary for projections to the year 2000 to assume some 'overspill' of business from the South East to adjoining regions of the Midlands and Wales. We have also seen that government planning has been involved in some of the major growth points of the 1980s, whether as New Towns inherited from previous decades or as steel closure areas.

What is not clear is whether there is much scope for integrated planning to arrest spatial imbalances in the economy beyond the work of Urban Development Corporations and inter-departmental inner city teams. A return toward 'regional planning' could, however, arise from the severity of growth pressures in the South East and a greater political awareness of the problems of the Liverpool's and Middlesbrough's of this world. It could certainly form part of a strategy for mediating the effects of the 'demographic time-bomb'.

From the international academic point of view, we continued throughout the 1980s to lecture that, without government intervention, the free play of market forces frequently leads to increased regional disparities within countries. Recovery from the 1980–1 recession clearly started later in northern manufacturing and was dominated more than ever before by a cumulative growth of service employment, particularly in business services in the South. Forecasts adopted here suggest that private services growth will resume its trend, but with the South of England achieving a rate no less than twice the size of the periphery. There were some favourable signs for northern manufacturing in 1987–9 and, in the later 1990s, it is expected that the modernization of UK manufacturing and the impact of inward investment will help to sustain GDP growth in Wales and the north of England. However, productivity gains will further limit the growth of employment, and the regions of Scotland and Northern Ireland may be left out entirely. The need for government intervention in the labour market first recognized in the 1930s clearly remains. On its own, the (labour) market does not clear regional or urban/rural differences in employment and unemployment rates. Together with the evidence that active regional policies can work, there is a strong case for a renewed regional policy focus in UK employment policy.

NOTE AND REFERENCES

Note

1 Thanks to the staff of the National Online Manpower Information System, in particular Peter Dodds, for the preparation of figures.

References

Armstrong, A. and Taylor, J. (1985) *Regional Economics and Policy*, Oxford: OUP.

Cambridge Econometrics and Northern Ireland Economic Research Centre (1991) *Regional Economic Prospects, Analysis and Forecasts to the Year 2000*, Cambridge: Cambridge Econometrics and NIERC.

Champion, A. and Townsend, A. (1990) *Contemporary Britain*, London: Arnold.

Fothergill, S. and Guy, S. (1991) *Retreat from the Regions*, London: Jessica Kingsley.

Lewis, J. and Townsend, A. (eds) (1989) *The North–South Divide*, London: Paul Chapman.

Thrift, N. and Leyshon, A. (1989) 'South goes north? The rise of the British financial centre', in J. Lewis and A. Townsend (eds) *The North–South Divide*, London: Paul Chapman.

Townsend, A. (1983) *The Impact of Recession*, Beckenham: Croom Helm.

—— (1987) 'Regional Policy', in W.F. Lever (ed.) *Industrial Change in the United Kingdom*, Harlow: Longman.

—— 1992 'New directions in the growth of tourism employment?; propositions of the 1980s', *Environment and Planning* A, 24.

11

EUROPEAN INTEGRATION: THE IMPLICATIONS FOR UK POLICIES ON LABOUR SUPPLY AND DEMAND

Simon Deakin and Frank Wilkinson

INTRODUCTION

The development of a single market in goods and services within the European Community during the 1990s has potentially far-reaching implications for the conduct of economic and social policy in Britain. The 'social dimension' to economic integration is particularly important in this respect. The role of social policy is yet to be properly defined in relation to the other elements in the Community's programme of legal and institutional reform, namely the liberalisation of trading rules and the harmonization of regulations in capital and product markets. There is no immediate prospect of agreement on an equivalent programme of harmonization in the area of the labour market. At the same time, policy-making in Britain can no longer be carried out in isolation from the growing influence of Community standards and the experience of other European systems.

Despite its limited achievements to date, one effect of the debate on the social dimension is to have placed on the agenda alternatives to labour-market deregulation of the type carried out in Britain in the 1980s. The commitment to deregulation has made it impossible for the United Kingdom government to endorse the principles of the Social Charter, which the other member states accepted without great difficulty. There is a close relationship between the contents of the Charter and the types of labour and social regulation found in many of the mainland European systems. In this regard it is especially noteworthy that other European countries have pursued policies of enhancing labour market flexibility and re-integrating the unemployed into paid employment without seeking to do so by dismantling the framework of social and employment protection (Deakin 1990b, 1991).

UNEMPLOYMENT, DEREGULATION AND LABOUR MARKET POLICY IN BRITAIN IN THE 1980s

The influence of economic theory on labour and social security law

Economic theory was highly influential in the 1980s in providing a rationale for government policies of labour market deregulation. The adoption of monetarist policies of controlling the money supply involved the formal abandonment of government attempts to regulate the level of demand in the economy, and a new emphasis on supply-side measures designed to restore competitiveness. The high levels of unemployment of the late 1970s and early 1980s were put down to the uncompetitive state of the labour market; the recession had 'forced into the open' the 'disguised unemployment of earlier years' (Department of Employment 1985:4). Several sources of labour market rigidities and 'barriers to growth' were identified; these included trade union power in the workplace, centralised forms of collective bargaining and pay determination, social security benefits providing relatively generous levels of income to the unemployed, and employment protection legislation imposing hiring costs upon firms (Department of Employment 1985, 1986, 1988, 1989a, 1991).

Deregulation strategies led to far-reaching changes in labour and social security law during this period (Deakin and Wilkinson 1991). In the area of social security there was a concerted effort to reduce levels of public expenditure at the same time as sharpening incentives for the unemployed. Accordingly there were cuts in the value of contribution-based unemployment benefits in relation to wages, most notably through the abolition of the earnings-related component in 1980 and child dependants' payments in 1982 and 1984. The link between social security and wages was also eroded by the failure to uprate unemployment benefits with increases in earnings, which outpaced prices throughout the 1980s. Further changes to unemployment benefit included the lengthening of the effective qualifying period, the increase in the period of disqualification for 'voluntary' unemployment, the widening of the range of job offers which recipients could be required to accept and the introduction of a condition that recipients should be 'actively seeking work' as a condition of retaining benefit. With the replacement from 1988 of supplementary benefit by income support and the introduction of the social fund in place of special needs payments, the floor of benefits below social insurance was also eroded in value.

Changes to the tax-benefit system were more actively used to promote low-paid work. Rebates on national insurance contributions for the low paid and direct subsidies for the employment of the young unemployed were used to cut employers' hiring costs. More generally, means-tested benefits were targeted away from the unemployed on to the low-paid in work, in particular through the extended housing benefit and the new system of family credit after 1988.

Deregulation of the contract of employment had a parallel effect, aiming to cut indirect labour costs by withdrawing employment protection from part-time and temporary workers and excluding large numbers of young workers from unfair dismissal and redundancy rights. Protection for the low-paid generally was reduced by the abolition of fair wages legislation, the prohibition upon local authorities operating policies of contract compliance and by the curtailment of the powers of the wages councils. Widespread changes to collective labour law were also made, cutting back the scope of the statutory immunities protecting strike action and making enforcement of the closed shop effectively unlawful (Wedderburn 1986; Hendy 1991).

The effects of deregulation

With deregulation, employers became free to compete on the basis of low pay and minimal labour standards, with only social security setting an effective floor to income in the non-unionized sectors of the labour market. These were also the sectors where the substitution of tax rebates and social security benefits for wages were most likely to take effect. Deregulation policies appear to have succeeded in the aim of widening the dispersion of pay and incomes. Between 1979 and 1988 full-time earnings at the lower end of the distribution fell while those at the upper end rose relative to the median. The inter-decile range (that is, the difference between earnings 10 per cent below the highest and those 10 per cent above the lowest) increased from 128 to 182 per cent for women and 138 to 194 per cent for men (Table 11.1). This change can be explained partly by the slow growth in the earnings of the lower paid and partly by the disappearance of many industrial and service jobs in the middle range and their replacement by large numbers of both low-paid and high-paid jobs in services (Adams 1989).

The effect of this trend of relative earnings on living standards was exacerbated by government tax policy (Hills 1988). Cuts in income tax were offset by increases in indirect taxation (most notably VAT), by the reduction in the value of child benefit, and by increases in national insurance contributions which fell most heavily on low-income earners because of the upper threshold on contributions (Deakin and Wilkinson 1991). The effect of these changes is shown in Table 11.2. For married earners with dependants the burden of direct taxation increased on low earnings but it fell for high earners, especially the very highest.

Table 11.3 shows the combined effects of differential rates of growth of earnings and the discriminatory impact of tax policy. Gross earnings at the highest decile level rose by some 70 per cent more than those at the

Table 11.1 The distribution of weekly earnings 1979 and 1989: earnings at different points in the distribution as percentages of median earnings

Percentage of median earnings at:	Women		Men	
	1979	1989	1979	1989
Lowest decile	69.5	62.8	65.9	59.8
Lower quartile	82.0	76.7	80.3	75.6
Median	100	100	100	100
Upper quartile	124.7	137.9	125.1	133.6
Highest decile	158.6	182.2	156.9	179.1
Median weekly earnings (£)	58.4	159.0	93.9	239.0

Source: New Earnings Survey 1989; Deakin and Wilkinson 1991

Table 11.2 Average tax rates at various earnings levels, 1978–9 and 1989–90

	Multiples of average earnings			
	Half average earnings	Average[a] earnings	Twice average earnings	Five times average earnings
Single person				
1978–9	21.8	29.2	30.7	41.5
1989–90	24.2	29.1	30.5	36.2
Married[b] (2 children)				
1978–9	−1.4[c]	17.6	24.9	38.5
1989–90	8.1	21.0	25.7	34.2

Source: Deakin and Wilkinson 1991
Notes:
[a] Average earnings for all male earnings not affected by absence as reported in the New Earnings Survey 1989.
[b] Average tax rate includes child benefits.
[c] In this year child benefits were higher than the total of income tax and national insurance at this level of income – therefore the rate of tax was negative.

Table 11.3 Increase in weekly earnings from employment at different points in the distribution of income 1978–89 for male employees, percentage change

	Lowest decile	Lowest quartile	Median	Upper quartile	Highest decile
Gross earnings	160.9	174.4	191.5	211.1	230.6
After tax real income:*					
Single person	14.7	20.8	28.9	35.8	47.6
Married with 2 children	12.0	17.4	24.7	31.6	43.1

Source: New Earnings Survey 1989; Deakin and Wilkinson 1991
Note:
* After adjusting for income tax, national insurance, child benefit and the rate of increase in retail prices from April 1978 to April 1989.

199

lowest decile between 1978 and 1989, while, when account is taken of tax and price changes, the increase at the higher end was more than four times that at the lower end.

These figures only apply to those on full-time earnings. Part-time work is associated with even lower pay than full-time work (Brosnan and Wilkinson 1988; Rubery 1989). This predominately affects married women workers who make up the bulk of the part-time workforce. Part-time work continued to grow in the 1980s in relation to full-time work, to reach around 23 per cent of the employed labour force. Within this group, there was an increasingly large proportion employed for sixteen hours or less, suggesting that the various hours thresholds in labour law and social security may have had an impact not so much in creating new jobs as in encouraging a deterioration in terms and conditions as employers reduced weekly hours and pay below the various levels (Schoer 1987; Deakin and Wilkinson 1991). Self-employment also grew in the 1980s to around 11 per cent of the labour force; this form of employment consists predominately of male workers and is again associated with lower than average pay in most sectors (Labour Research Department 1986).

The gap between the unemployed and those in full-time work also widened in the 1980s in terms of both income and status. The abolition of the earnings-related component and child dependency additions meant that the extent to which unemployment benefit compensated for loss of earned income fell by around 30 per cent for single men on average earnings and rather more than that for married men with children. The failure to up-rate the short-term income replacement benefits with earnings as opposed to prices also accounted for a significant reduction in the relative value of unemployment benefit (Deakin and Wilkinson 1991: 127). Just as far reaching were the changes in the position of the unemployed which the restriction of benefits brought about. The increased difficulty of qualifying for, and retaining, a social insurance benefit, together with the growing incidence of long-term unemployment, meant that between 1978 and 1988 the number of out-of-work benefit recipients receiving unemployment benefit (in some cases topped up by means-tested benefits) fell from one half to one third. The shift from a social insurance benefit to a means-tested benefit has the effect that the claimant ceases to receive payments in his or her own right, and is liable to have the benefit withdrawn or reduced if other members of the household are in employment. The 'attractiveness' of unemployment to benefit recipients was further reduced by the 'actively seeking work' requirement, which effectively meant an increased responsibility for recipients to account for the use of their time to social security officials. Prior to that the Restart programme had been introduced as a more regular means of monitoring recipients' availability for work.

This erosion of social insurance rights in the 1980s has been achieved at a significant cost in terms of the wider integrity of the social security system. It is an elementary error to regard social insurance in terms of a dependency relationship between the state and the claimant. Insurance entitlements are paid for by claimants and are (or were) claimed as of right on the basis of contributions made. Social insurance has a number of advantages over means-testing: in principle it is cheaper to administer and provides the state with fewer opportunities in coercing claimants. In the 1980s, however, continuous changes in the conditions of the contributory scheme effectively expropriated rights built up on the basis of past contributions, at a time when employees' contributions rose to pay for a fall in Treasury funding of the National Insurance Fund. As a result the value of social security contributions paid by employees in terms of insurance against loss of earnings was greatly reduced.

The tightening of qualifying conditions disadvantaged married women in particular. Following the Social Security Act 1989, they are unlikely to qualify for short-term unemployment benefit, which requires two years' more or less continuous employment in the case of a part-time worker employed just above the national insurance threshold, or for a substantial state pension (given the changes to SERPS made in the legislation of 1986) despite the high and increasing rates of national insurance contributions. As a result, many of them contract out of the national insurance system altogether by adopting self-employed status with their employer's agreement, or by contracting to work for a reduced number of hours, so that their wages do not reach the weekly threshold at which contributions begin. Nor do they qualify for income support if unemployed, as they are regarded as dependent upon their husband's income for this purpose.

The implications for labour supply and demand of the growing inequality of pay and income – both within the employed labour force and between the unemployed and those in work – are far from clear. At one stage the Restart programme was credited with reducing the numbers of the long-term unemployed and helping to bring about the large drop in unemployment between 1986 and 1989 (Layard 1989; Dicks and Hatch 1989). Since then the far more draconian requirements of the 1989 Social Security Act have been brought into effect, without having any visible impact on unemployment levels. As far as the growth in low pay is concerned, as one commentator noted 'the sad conclusion is that even this relative fall was not sufficient to price all the lowest earners into work' (Brittan 1990: 5). How much further relative wages would have to fall for this to happen is not specified.

There are, on the other hand, serious doubts as to the long-term consequences for labour supply of a policy of simultaneously restricting social security benefits while downgrading the conditions of work of those in the lowest paid jobs. The changes to social security law in the 1980s in fact did very little to improve incentives for labour supply. The policy of 'targeting' which lay at the centre of the Fowler reforms succeded in removing marginal tax rates of over 100 per cent for some households only at the expense of bringing many more into the range of marginal rates over 60 and 80 per cent (Low Pay Unit 1988). This was the inevitable result of lengthening the taper by which family credit and housing benefit are gradually phased out as earnings rise up the scale, an effect accepted as 'unavoidable' by the Department of Health and Social Security in 1985 (1985: 32). Nor was any systematic effort made to deal with the long-standing problem of the disincentives created by the penalizing effect of benefit withdrawals, which operate as a punitive form of taxation for the unemployed and low paid.

The combination of benefit withdrawals, high taxation of low incomes and lack of security and continuity of employment makes low-paid work a highly precarious prospect for the unemployed, who risk a loss of income when they re-enter the labour market and will face great difficulty in re-qualifying for benefit (McLaughlin *et al.* 1989). In this regard the existing benefit rules are ill-equipped to deal with the situation of recurrent short spells of employment and unemployment which affect a large proportion of the unemployed (Daniel 1990). Nor can the policy of withdrawing employment protection rights for non-standard jobs be easily justified. As more insecure and low-paid jobs are created, the more difficult it becomes for those who are either partially or wholly unemployed to find a way into full-time work. Many low-paid and non-standard jobs fail to offer effective training, a problem exacerbated by the government policy of linking training subsidies to the payment of lower wages and training allowances which in some cases are simply another form of social security (Keep 1990; Deakin and Wilkinson 1991).

A further problem arises from the long-term burden all this places on the social security system. As employment regulation is progressively withdrawn the pressure on social security to subsidize low incomes is increased, to the point at which social security in the form of family credit and related benefits, and the tax system through rebates and allowances, have to substitute for wages, a situation which is neither efficient for the labour market nor a good use of the resources at the state's disposal. In this sense the state continues to play an important role in structuring the labour market; but the role has shifted from one of seeking to maintain minimum labour standards to one of subsidizing low pay.

On the demand side, the principal effect of deregulation strategies concerns the implicit subsidization of low-paying firms and the wider implications for labour market efficiency. Low pay represents a subsidy to firms, part of which is passed on to consumers in the form of lower prices or, in the case of the public sector, lower taxes. Even during periods of relatively full employment, in sectors where low pay is endemic it serves as a substitute in terms of competitiveness for more effective strategies in marketing and production including the introduction of new technology (Craig *et al.* 1982). The combined result of high unemployment and over a decade of deregulation has been to widen this effect to cover large parts of the economy. As firms become increasingly dependent upon low-paid labour to contain costs, their ability to meet the short-run costs associated with new technology and organizational innovation is correspondingly reduced (see also Chapter 2). The policy of privatizing ancillary services in health and local government, and the undermining of collective bargaining in sectors such as the docks, construction and private services, has not resulted in the more productive use of labour but simply the intensification of work effort and worsening of terms and conditions of employment (Evans 1990; Turnbull 1991; Deakin and Wilkinson 1991). The long-term cost to the national economy will be measured in terms of the growth of an unproductive tail of low-paying firms and industries, continuing decline in international competitiveness and renewed vulnerability to recession and structural unemployment (Nolan 1989).

THE COMPARATIVE EXPERIENCE OF DEREGULATION IN EUROPE

Contrary to what is often stated, or assumed, to be the case, labour market deregulation is far from being a uniform international trend, and experiments with deregulation have been much more limited elsewhere in western Europe than they have been in the UK. In short, 'the major difference with the other Member States, in which "deregulation" has also occurred, is that those States have retained significant workers' participation and have moved towards greater "flexibility" in the employment relationship within a framework of institutional participation and collective bargaining' (Hepple 1991: 14; see also Deakin 1991). Study of the comparative experience of deregulation shows that an alternative approach to the British one, based on the retention and strengthening of labour standards, is both feasible and desirable.

One reason for the different experience of deregulation in the 1980s is that the continental systems started from a higher base of regulation. British labour law was already unusual in the European context prior to the 1980s reforms, in that it provided a comparatively weak floor of legal rights in the employment relationship. Instead, regulation largely took the form of voluntary collective bargaining supplemented by selective legislative intervention for groups of workers left unprotected by the voluntary system, such as those in the wages councils sector. Employment protection legislation, providing rights in relation to dismissal and redundancy, was a relatively late development and suffered from a number of structural weaknesses, most notably its limited coverage of part-time, temporary and casual workers (Deakin 1986).

However, the historical differences between the voluntarist system of labour law in Britain and the more highly regulative continental systems can only provide a partial explanation of their divergent approaches to the issue of labour market flexibility. The retention of a set of comprehensive legal minimum standards below which terms and conditions will not fall is the characteristic feature of systems of labour market regulation in mainland Europe (Deakin 1990b). Britain is practically alone in the European Community, for example, in failing to legislate for a statutory national minimum wage. The minimum wage is directly set by legislation in France, The Netherlands, Luxembourg, Spain and Portugal. The most highly developed system is the French *salaire minimum interprofessionel de croissance*, the basis for which is that the minimum wage must keep pace not just with annual price inflation but with at least half the growth in the purchasing power of the average wage. The official view of the SMIC is that it

> has been a remarkably effective means of combatting low pay while encouraging firms to improve their productivity. As such it is strongly supported by trade unions and it has long been supported by employers.
>
> (French Counsellor for Social Affairs, 1980, cited in MacNeill and
> Pond 1988:16)

In other systems, there are minimum wage substitutes such as national level collective agreements between federations of employers and trade unions (Belgium and Greece) and legally binding sector-level collective agreements (Denmark, Germany and Italy), none of which has any equivalent in the UK. In Germany, for example, sector level agreements are legally binding on all employers in the relevant employers' associations and may be extended by order of the Ministry of Labour to ensure that non-union firms are also bound. Over 90 per cent of employees in the former Federal Republic were covered by such agreements.

In some systems, such as The Netherlands and Denmark, uprating of the minimum wage was frozen for periods in the 1980s, while in others, including Spain and Portugal, the uprating mechanism contains only limited guarantees of a yearly increase to maintain purchasing power. The value of the minimum wage as a proportion of the average wage also differs from country to country. Nevertheless, the general pattern of regulation contrasts with the situation in the UK, where there has never been a statutory minimum wage as such and (just as important) collective agreements do not have automatic legal effect. Following the rescission of the Fair Wages Resolution in 1982 and the repeal of the Schedule 11 extension procedure in the 1980 Employment Act, minimum wage regulation in Britain exists only in the wages councils sector, and even there the effectiveness of wages orders was much reduced by the deregulatory measures of the Wages Act 1986.

A second area where Britain lacks a comprehensive floor of rights is in working time. The hours of male workers have traditionally been regulated by collective bargaining, rather than by direct statutory controls (Wedderburn 1986:408). The hours of women and young people in factories were regulated by legislation, but this was repealed in 1986 and 1989. Following the Employment Act 1989, it is only the working hours of children below the school-leaving age which are regulated by statute (Deakin 1990a); there is no legislation now governing the working-time and holiday rights of adult workers. The decline of sector-level, multi-employer bargaining has also left many workers, both male and female, unprotected. Where working-time is regulated through agreement at either company or sector level, the tendency is to avoid setting an absolute upper limit to overtime hours, with the result that total hours in manufacturing tend to be long by European standards (Marsh 1991).

The continental pattern of regulation of the hours of all workers was, by contrast, established in France and Germany in the inter-war period (Vogel-Polsky 1986). Since then, further legislation and the impact of collective bargaining have seen general reductions in the length of the working week. In France legislation in 1982 set a basic 39-hour week and placed a further limit on weekly overtime hours. In Germany collective agreements set basic weekly hours from 37.5 to 40 hours, and also placed restrictions on overtime. Legislation and collective agreements in mainland European countries also regulate shift-working, nightwork, weekend breaks, holidays and annual leave.

Against this background of basic statutory rights, mainland European systems have sought to introduce flexibility in the form of the contract of employment and in working time through the techniques of controlled derogation. This means that a greater range of exceptions to labour standards is permitted, but only within limits which must be strictly justified by way of a positive job creation effect, and under circumstances where they are monitored and controlled by workers' representatives at plant or company level. In the area of non-standard or atypical work, deregulating legislation in France, Germany, Italy and Spain has consisted mainly of the legalization of various forms of part-time work and temporary work which were previously unlawful (Kravaritou-Manitakis 1988). In Germany, prior to the Employment Promotion Act of 1985, the Federal Labour Court interpreted fixed-term hirings as permanent contracts of employment in any case where the employer could not give a legitimate reason for hiring a worker on a temporary basis. The 1985 Act permitted a greater range of fixed-term hirings in newly created posts, but limited the scope and duration of such contracts in an attempt to avoid their substitution for permanent hirings. The Act's provisions had a strictly limited scope and had to be renewed for a further five years in 1990.

A further feature of legislation of this kind is the attempt to ensure equal treatment between part-time and full-time workers. The French Auroux Laws of 1982 and the German Employment Promotion Act of 1985 both enacted a general requirement of pro-rata treatment for part-timers, in an attempt to make non-standard work more attractive for employees; in France, legislation of 1991 extended this principle to cover fixed-term contract workers. This is the opposite of the British approach of setting out to lower the quality of part-time work in order to cut employers' hiring costs. Although Britain has a higher proportion of part-time employees in employment (around 23 per cent), than either France or Germany (where the figure is closer to 13 per cent), most of the growth in British part-time working took place before the deregulatory measures of the 1980s. In France there was a considerable rate of growth in part-time work in the 1980s when employment rights were being extended rather than reduced; 'progress in the social protection of part-time workers in France after 1981 and 1982 did not discourage the use of part-time work' (Marshall 1989: 26). In both Britain and The Netherlands, where hours thresholds operate to exclude part-time workers below a certain level from most forms of social security and employment protection, there is a larger than average number of part-time workers employed for fewer than ten hours per week (Marshall 1989: 23).

A common form of continental deregulation is the devolution of rule-making power from courts and government agencies to the collective bargaining process (Wedderburn and Sciarra 1988; Wedderburn 1991). In Italy this technique of bargained deregulation covers a range of areas in working time law, the treatment of part-time and fixed-term contract workers and training. In France and Germany it takes the form of greater powers for plant level agreements to depart from statutory working time standards. In France the manner of implementation of the 39-hour week set by statute in 1982 was left up to agreement at plant and company level, with provision for flexibility over basic hours on a week by week basis as long as the 39-hour average was maintained over longer periods. In 1987 legislation was passed to encourage company-level agreements on flexible annual working hours, Sunday working and women's nightwork (Erbes-Séguin 1989). Similar proposals have been considered in Germany, where works councils have already played a significant role in implementing at plant level the agreement for reduced working hours in the engineering industry after the strike of 1985 (Mückenberger and Deakin 1989). In Belgium legislation following the Hansenne working-time experiments of the mid-1980s permitted company agreements to set totally flexible annualized hours as long as the 39-hour average for the basic week was maintained on a yearly basis.

It is significant that this form of deregulation is conditional upon the role of independent trade unions and enterprise works councils validating the resulting standards through collective bargaining. In the absence of a collective agreement on flexibilization, the basic statutory provisions continue to apply. In Britain, where there is no collective agreement, terms and conditions are simply imposed on employees under the guise of 'individual contracting'. Without a duty upon employers to bargain or even to recognize representative trade unions, British labour law lacks procedures for underpinning the role of workers' representatives in the enforcement of labour standards at plant and company level.

Further contrasts emerge in terms of the relationship between social security and the wage system. Despite cuts in all systems in the relative value of unemployment benefits, replacement rates are far lower in the UK than elsewhere in western Europe, mainly as a consequence of the abolition of the earnings-related component. According to the OECD (1991: Table 7.2), the initial gross replacement rate of unemployment benefit for a single worker employed on average manufacturing earnings is 59 per cent in France, 58 per cent in Germany and 70 per cent in The Netherlands; in the UK it is 16 per cent.

The severity of benefit withdrawals for the unemployed has been mitigated in several continental systems by imaginative schemes to permit the unemployed to retain part of their benefit entitlement after they enter into part-time work (Euzeby 1988). Such allowances are paid in France and Ireland, and in Belgium, Denmark and Spain the principle of compensation for 'partial unemployment' operates to top up the individual's wage to a notional minimum full-time wage. Flexible contribution conditions for social insurance benefits, enabling the aggregation of separate periods of service and the crediting of contributions to the unemployed and part-time workers, are also common features of these systems.

In Britain, as we have seen, it is not possible for regular wage income above the national insurance threshold to be combined with short-term contributory benefits, and the earnings disregards for income support are miniscule (see also Chapters 5 and 8). It is important, moreover, to appreciate the difference between the continental systems of wage allowances and the family credit system in the UK. In the continental systems, wage cutting by employers is generally prevented by effective minimum wage policies and by the enforcement of multi-employer collective agreements.

THE SOCIAL DIMENSION TO EUROPEAN ECONOMIC INTEGRATION

The technique of regulating through a basic floor of employment rights, coupled with guarantees of worker representation and participation at enterprise level, is the basis for the European Community Social Charter and Action Programme of 1989. The Social Charter consists of a set of basic rights and principles which are intended to set the minimum form of social and labour standards within the single market. The rights contained in the Charter can be divided into individual and collective rights (Wedderburn 1990). Individual rights provisions refer to the need to establish basic protection in the areas of freedom of movement, health and safety, working conditions, working hours, employment status and security of pay. Certain special protections for children and young workers are envisaged, as well as provisions for securing equality of treatment by reference to sex, age and beliefs (but not race, except in so far as equality of treatment of EC nationals is protected by the principle of freedom of movement). A reference is made to the need to ensure basic and continuing access to training and the establishment of the necessary bodies and institutional means at state level to achieve this. On pay, the Charter states that 'in accordance with the arrangements applying in each country, workers shall be assured of an equitable wage, that is, a wage sufficient to enable them to have a decent standard of living' (Art. 5); each worker shall also enjoy 'a right to adequate social protection and shall, whatever the size of the undertaking in which he [sic] is employed, enjoy an adequate level of social security benefits' (Art. 6).

In the area of collective rights, there are provisions on freedom of association and collective bargaining, information and consultation rights, and the right to take part in industrial action. However, the collective rights outlined in the Charter are much less specific and more conditional than the individual ones. Although the 'right of association' of workers and employers is mentioned, there is no reference to the duty of employers to bargain with representative trade unions, nor to the right of a worker to be covered by a relevant collective agreement. The right to take collective industrial action is apparently limited to strikes over conflicts of interests, that is, matters outside the scope of existing collective agreements. There is, in contrast, a much stronger emphasis on the establishment of machinery for worker consultation and participation at company level, along the lines of works councils and enterprise committees (Art. 17).

The Charter suffers from two main defects, one of form and one of substance. In terms of legal form, the Charter adds nothing of significance to existing international instruments, as it is not intended to be legally binding on Member States: it is just a 'solemn declaration' of rights. For this reason the Charter cannot on its own achieve the aim of incorporating the social dimension into the continuing single market project. Community legislation in the form of directives and regulations, as outlined in the Social Action Programme of November 1989, must still be issued by the Commission and agreed by the Member States in the Council of Ministers. It is at this stage that the question of the veto becomes important. A number of draft directives in the social field were blocked in the 1980s by the sole veto of the UK government; these included proposals for extending the rights of pregnant workers and establishing a right to parity of treatment for part-timers and temporary workers. Under the reforms to the Treaty of Rome made by the Single European Act in 1986, the Council of Ministers now has the power to act by qualified majority in voting on measures to implement the single market, including health and safety at work, but the single veto is specifically preserved for matters concerning taxation, the free movement of persons and the rights of employees. The Commission's attempts to circumvent the requirement of unanimity in the social policy area have met with a hostile response from the Member States. More generally, it seems unlikely that the Council of Ministers will approve in the immediate future the new draft directives put forward by the Commission in the areas of 'atypical' work, working time, the rights of pregnant workers, and the establishment of European works councils.

In terms of substance, not only the Charter and Action Programme but also the new draft directives contain numerous references to the principle of subsidiarity, whereby 'the Community acts when the set objectives can be reached more effectively at its level than at that of the member states'. This means that proposals for legally binding instruments will be limited 'to those areas where Community legislation seems necessary to achieve the social dimension of the internal market and, more generally, to contribute to the economic and social cohesion of the Community' (Social Action Programme paras. 1.5, 1.6; see Wedderburn 1990: 54; Hepple 1991: 10). In due course this may pose a major obstacle to any serious attempts at harmonization in the social field, as it implies that in many areas the Community will not seek to set a general standard but will instead allow Member States a good deal of leeway in choosing the form and content of labour law protections.

A more fundamental problem is the lack, at present, of any agreement among the Member States to raise the profile of the social dimension. The absence of consensus over basic goals is one reason for the highly diluted content of many of the new draft directives, particularly those on atypical work which are weaker in many respects than the failed proposals of the 1980s (Hepple 1990). Yet the more recent proposals also seem unable to gain the necessary consent of the Council of Ministers. It is arguable that substantial progress will only be made if and when the Treaty of Rome itself is amended, to incorporate a specific reference to a floor of social rights in the labour market. Proposals of this kind have been considered as part of the work of the Intergovernmental Conference on Political Union, but with no clear sign as yet that they will eventually be adopted by the Member States.

However, the unpromising short-term political and legal future of the social dimension is no reason to assume that economic integration will not have a longer term impact upon the social and economic policies of the Member States, the UK included. This may come about through a variety of means, of which direct legal harmonization is only one; other factors at play will include the increased mobility of capital and the increasingly transnational character of corporations which the single market programme is meant to encourage, and the development of transnational collective bargaining and of 'social dialogue' at Community level. It is too soon to say how far these forms of integration will both promote and necessitate a degree of convergence in labour market regulation and industrial relations systems, but to the extent that they do they will strengthen the case for some form of legal harmonization based around a programme of minimum rights.

One area where Community law is sure to have a continuing influence on domestic legislation, notwithstanding the lack of clear progress in the wider social dimension, is that of equality of opportunity between the sexes. The right to equal pay is a basic principle of Community law, being incorporated into the Treaty of Rome and numerous directives. Several decisions of the European Court of Justice have necessitated changes in UK law, most recently the Barber judgment requiring equal pensionable ages for men and women in company pensions schemes. It was thought possible that this route could be used to improve the rights of part-time workers, on the grounds that their unequal treatment constitutes a form of indirect discrimination against women. However, there are signs that the European Court will leave it up to national courts to apply the test of indirect discrimination in practice, so diluting the requirements of EC law (Hepple 1990: 16–19).

LABOUR STANDARDS, UNEMPLOYMENT AND ECONOMIC POLICY

If, by one means or another, the economic and legal effects of European integration limit the autonomy of Member States in the area of labour market policy, it is arguable that the impact of convergence will be most strongly felt in the UK, where over a decade of deregulation has left labour law protection extremely weak by the standards of advanced industrial economies. Underlying the Social Charter is the view expressed in its Preamble that

> social consensus contributes to the strengthening of the competitiveness of undertakings and of the economy as a whole and to the creation of employment . . . in this respect it is an essential condition for ensuring sustained economic development.

This directly contradicts the view of the UK government since 1979, namely that cuts in social and employment protection are vital if competitiveness is to be restored and unemployment reduced. According to the Department of Employment:

The real social dimension of the single market is the opportunity it will generate to create jobs and reduce unemployment (identified by the Commission as the greatest social problem facing the Community) to stimulate growth and prosperity and to improve living standards. Far from creating jobs, introduction of future measures as envisaged by the Charter would hamper job creation, hinder competition within the market and the ability to compete in world markets and put at risk the benefits of the single market. Some of the measures proposed in the Charter would put at risk the progress made in the last 10 years in the UK to set the economy on the right track.

(Department of Employment 1989b: paras 8, 9)

Put in such terms, the attitude of the UK government is the strongest argument there could be for widespread harmonization based on a floor of rights, to prevent Member States engaging in the destructive competition of cutting labour and social standards in an attempt to encourage inward capital investment. The experience of the United States since 1945 suggests that this is a real possibility in a federal system where capital is highly mobile and where no attempt is made to impose minimum social standards on all states (Bluestone and Harrison 1982; Tarullo 1989). Given the evident vulnerability of the UK economy at the beginning of the 1990s to cyclical recession and large-scale job loss, it is not surprising that the government's attempt to export deregulation to the rest of western Europe via the Community has met with so little success. If progress on the social dimension is totally stalled, however, there is every danger of 'creeping deregulation' as 'firms are able to escape, or threaten to escape, statutory or collectively agreed social protection by relocating their operations within the increasingly Europeanized economy' (Mosley 1990: 163).

As far as the UK is concerned, one of the benefits of 1992 is to have widened the debate about deregulation and its alternatives. Those who continue to argue that deregulation is necessary and that the UK cannot afford the social rights programme contained in the Charter have yet to face up to the implications of this approach in terms of an increased social security budget, made necessary by the absence of effective wage and employment protection, and the continued growth of an under-competitive industrial structure, kept afloat by low pay and government subsidies. From this point of view, labour market regulation in some form should be seen as an absolute pre-requisite of a productive and competitive economy. The policy of establishing an effective floor of rights through labour law setting minimum labour standards can be seen to have implications not just for wage equity but also for the efficient functioning of the labour market. Within social security, it will be imperative to reverse the trend towards means-testing by reasserting the importance of rights obtained through social insurance and by reconsidering the possible role which could be played by a basic income (Mückenberger and Deakin 1989; Deakin and Wilkinson 1991; Chapter 8). Although there is a range of such alternatives which differ in their emphases and prescriptions, and a variety of concrete policy options to be observed in other systems, there is a growing consensus rejecting the disjunction between economic efficiency and social justice upon which policies of deregulation have proceeded for the past twelve years.

REFERENCES

Adams, M. (1989) *The Distribution of Earnings 1973–1986*, Research Paper No. 64, London: Department of Employment.

Bluestone, B. and Harrison, B. (1982) *The Deindustrialization of America*, New York: Basic Books.

Brittan, S. (1990) 'The case for basic incomes', in S. Brittan and S. Webb, *Beyond the Welfare State. An Examination of Basic Incomes in a Market Economy*, David Hume Institute, Aberdeen: Aberdeen University Press.

Brosnan, P. and Wilkinson, F. (1988) 'A national statutory minimum wage and economic efficiency', *Contributions to Political Economy*, 7: 1–48.

Craig, C., Rubery, J., Tarling, R. and Wilkinson, F. (1982) *Labour Market Structure, Industrial Organisation and Low Pay*, Cambridge: CUP.

Daniel, W. (1990) *The Unemployed Flow*, London: Policy Studies Institute.

Deakin, S. (1986) 'Labour law and the developing employment relationship in the UK', *Cambridge Journal of Economics*, 10: 225–46.

—— (1990a) 'Equality under a market order: the Employment Act 1989', *Industrial Law Journal*, 19: 1–19.

—— (1990b), 'The floor of rights in European labour law', *New Zealand Journal of Industrial Relations*, 15: 219–40.

—— (forthcoming) 'Legal change and labour market restructuring in Western Europe and the US', *New Zealand Journal of Industrial Relations*, 16.

Deakin, S. and Wilkinson, F. (1991) 'Labour law, social security and economic inequality', *Cambridge Journal of Economics*, 15: 125–48.

Department of Employment (1985) *Employment: the Challenge for the Nation*, Cmnd. 9474, London: HMSO.

—— (1986) *Building Businesses . . . Not Barriers*, Cmnd. 9794, London: HMSO.

—— (1988) *Employment for the 1990s*, Cmnd. 540, London: HMSO.

—— (1989a) *Removing Barriers to Employment*, Cmnd. 665, London: HMSO.

—— (1989b) *Explanatory Memorandum on Commission Document concerning a Preliminary Draft Community Charter of Fundamental Social Rights*, 19 June 1989, COM (89) 248 final, Brussels.

—— (1991) *Industrial Relations in the 1990s – proposals for further reform of industrial relations and trade union law*, Cmnd. 1602, London: HMSO.

Department of Health and Social Security (1985) *Reform of Social Security*, Vol. 2, Cmnd. 9691, London: HMSO.

Dicks, M. and Hatch, N. (1989) *The Relationship between Employment and Unemployment*, London: Bank of England.

Erbes-Séguin, S. (1989) 'Flexibility and the relationship between the individual employment contract and collective labour law', *International Journal for the Sociology of Law*, 17: 307–26.

Euzeby, A. (1988) 'Social security and part-time employment', *International Labour Review*, 127: 545–56.

Evans, S. (1990) 'Free labour markets and economic performance', *Work, Employment and Society*, 4: 239–52.

Hendy, J. (1991) *The Conservative Employment Laws* (2nd. edn.), London: Institute of Employment Rights.

Hepple, B. (1990) *Working Time: A New Legal Framework?*, London: Institute for Public Policy Research.

—— (1991) 'Comparative trade union rights in the EC: threats and challenges presented by the single market', in R. Trask (ed.) *Trade Union Rights in the Single Market*, London: International Centre for Trade Union Rights.

Hills, J. (1988) *Changing Tax*, London: Child Poverty Action Group.

Keep, E. (1990) 'Training for the low paid', in A. Bowen and K. Mayhew (eds), *Improving Incentives for the Low-Paid*, London: Macmillan/NEDO.

Kravaritou-Manitakis, Y. (1988) *New Forms of Work: Labour Law and Social Security Aspects in the European Community*, Luxembourg: European Foundation for the Improvement of Living and Working Conditions.

Labour Research Department (1986) 'The growing army of the self-employed', *Labour Research*, February.

Layard, R. (1989) 'European unemployment: cause and cure', Discussion Paper No. 368, London: Centre for Labour Economics, London School of Economics.

Low Pay Unit (1988) 'Escaping the clutches of the poverty trap', *Low Pay Review*, Spring.

McLaughlin, E., Millar, J. and Cooke, K. (1989) *Work and Welfare Benefits*, Aldershot: Avebury.

McNeill, K. and Pond, C. (1988) *Britain Can't Afford Low Pay. A Programme for a National Minimum Wage*, London: Low Pay Unit.

Marsh, C. (1991) *The Hours of Work of Women and Men in Britain*, Equal Opportunities Commission Research Series, London: HMSO.

Marshall, A. (1989) 'The sequel of unemployment: the changing role of part-time and temporary work in Western Europe', in G. and J. Rodgers (eds), *Precarious Jobs in Labour Market Regulation*, Geneva: International Institute for Labour Studies.

Mosley, H. (1990) 'The social dimension of European integration', *International Labour Review*, 129: 147–63.

Mückenberger, U. and Deakin, S. (1989) 'From deregulation to a European floor of rights: labour law, flexibilisation and the European single market', *Zeitschrift für ausländisches und internationales Arbeits- und Sozialrecht*, 3: 153–207.

Nolan, P. (1989) 'Walking on water? performance and industrial relations under Thatcher', *Industrial Relations Journal*, 20: 81–92.

OECD (1991) *Employment Outlook*, Paris: OECD.

Rubery, J. (1989) 'Precarious forms of work in the United Kingdom', in G. and J. Rodgers (eds) *Precarious Jobs in Labour Market Regulation*, Geneva: International Institute for Labour Studies.

Schoer, K. (1987) 'Part-time employment: Britain and West Germany', *Cambridge Journal of Economics*, 11: 83–94.

Tarullo, D. (1989) 'Federalism issues in United States labour market policies and employment law', paper presented to the Annual Conference of the International Working Party on Labour Market Segmentation, University of Nancy, mimeo.

Turnbull, P. (1991) 'Labour market deregulation and economic performance: the case of Britain's docks', *Work, Employment and Society*, 5: 17–35.

Vogel-Polsky, E. (1986) 'The problem of unemployment', in B. Hepple (ed.) *The Making of Labour Law in Europe*, London: Mansell.

Wedderburn, Lord (1986) *The Worker and the Law*, Harmondsworth: Penguin.

Wedderburn, Lord (1990) *The Social Charter, European Company and Employment Rights*, London: Institute of Employment Rights.

Wedderburn, Lord (1991) 'The Social Charter in Britain – labour law and labour courts?', *Modern Law Review*, 54: 1–47.

Wedderburn, Lord and Sciarra, S. (1988) 'Collective bargaining as agreement and as law; neo-contractualist and neo-corporative tendencies of our age', in A. Pizzorusso (ed.) *Law in the Making*, Berlin: Springer-Verlag.

INDEX